Policy Studies Institute

WOMEN IN TOP JOBS
1968–1979

Policy Studies Institute

WOMEN IN TOP JOBS
1968–1979

Michael P. Fogarty, Isobel Allen
and Patricia Walters

 Heinemann Educational Books · London

Heinemann Educational Books Ltd
22 Bedford Square, London WC1B 3HH
LONDON   EDINBURGH   MELBOURNE   AUCKLAND
HONG KONG   SINGAPORE   KUALA LUMPUR
IBADAN   NAIROBI   JOHANNESBURG
EXETER (NH)   KINGSTON   PORT OF SPAIN

ISBN 0 435 83806 7

Printed in Great Britain by
Biddles Ltd, Guildford, Surrey

Contents

Acknowledgements

This book contains the findings of a second round of case studies of women in top jobs in the Civil Service, two large industrial companies, the BBC, and architecture, both private practice and in the public service. They are a follow-up, ten to twelve years later, of studies made by Political and Economic Planning (since 1978 incorporated into the Policy Studies Institute) as part of its wider *Sex Career and Family* series on women's opportunity in higher managerial and professional careers.[1] The original studies were requested and financed by the Leverhulme Trust, and the present series by the Joint Panel of the Equal Opportunities Commission and the Social Science Research Council. The present studies were made by the same three research workers as in the 1960s. Michael Fogarty (Part I and the study of architecture) and Isobel Allen (the two industrial companies and the BBC) are on the staff of PSI, and Patricia Walters (the Civil Service study) is a lecturer at the University of Salford.

The authors wish to express their particular thanks to the organisations studied for their willing collaboration in this second round. So many individuals have contributed information and advice that we thank them collectively rather than attempt to list them all. One special characteristic of a joint work of this kind is that it involves an unusual amount of re-drafting and editing, and a wearisome burden to those who have to type the third, fourth, and fifth versions. We thank especially our colleagues who have tolerated this process to its end.

Isobel Allen, Michael Fogarty, Patricia Walters
December 1980

Reference

(1) The main publications were M. P. Fogarty and R. and R. Rapoport *Sex Career and Family*, George Allen and Unwin, 1971: M. P. Fogarty (ed.), Isobel Allen, A. J. Allen and Patricia Walters, *Women in Top Jobs – Four Studies in Achievement*, George Allen and Unwin, 1971: R. and R. Rapoport, *Dual Career Families*, Penguin, 1971: and M. P. Fogarty, *Women in Top Jobs – The Next Move*, PEP Report 535, 1972.

PART I

Review of the Findings

Review of the Findings

The aim of the four case studies in this book is limited and practical. It is to take advantage of the fact that this group of occupations – the Civil Service, two industrial companies, the BBC, and architecture, both private practice and public service – was studied at the end of the 1960s[1] and to establish what happened in them during the 1970s as regards equal opportunity for women in professional and managerial work, and what more might be done to that end in future. What happened to the women who were already in this type of work in the 1960s – where are they now? What progress was made in bringing in more women and removing career barriers, and did more women actually reach the top? If not, what precisely were the remaining obstacles: and how effective, in terms of actual progress, were the changes in the 1970s in the social climate and the law?

The focus of these studies is on women's progress towards levels in the professions and management which few of either men or women can in any case expect to reach. Progress to the top, however, begins in junior grades, and the studies show that the biggest obstacles to women's progress towards the top arise at ages and levels of promotion far short of those relevant to top appointments themselves. Though, therefore, the case studies start from a question about opportunities for the few, most of their discussion is about issues more widely relevant to women in general, or at least to women at all levels of professional and managerial work.

The answer to the case studies' main question is, in broad terms, that the battle for acceptance of the principle of equal opportunity has been won, but its implementation remained during the 1970s limited and slow, and is likely to remain so unless new and stronger pressures are brought to bear. Four case studies do not, of course, amount to a comprehensive review of women's position in the professions and management. But these studies span a wide range of occupations, and comparisons with national data show that their notably negative findings do in fact have a much wider application.

All the more so since the organisations studied are and have long been regarded as good employers, and in matters of discrimination like to think of themselves, in a phrase from the BBC, as 'on the side of the legislative angels'. It is in them if anywhere that progress would be expected.

The research team's general approach

The theoretical and conceptual framework underlying the case studies was developed in the original *Sex Career and Family* series. The reason why it did not seem necessary to adopt a new framework, however, is itself of interest both for the interpretation of the case studies themselves and for the general theory of social developments. *Sex Career and Family* drew attention to the S-curve of learning which is typical of social developments generally, and to the long time spans required for each stage in a major social change. This is as relevant to the movement for equal opportunity for women as to any other.

The movement for equality in professional and managerial work began towards the end of the nineteenth century. By the 1920s many originally rigid barriers were broken, and a number of women passed through them. But the proportion of actually or potentially qualified women who were able in practice to use these new opportunities remained relatively small, and by the 1950s statistics showed that the original breakthrough had been followed by 'a plateau suggesting stagnation'.[2]

It took till the end of the 1960s for a new climate of opinion to build up in reaction to this situation, but by then it came with a rush and was reflected among other things in the development of the *Sex Career and Family* project itself. The project was originally understood rather narrowly as a study of barriers to women's progress in a limited though important range of jobs, but it widened into a more general discussion of sex roles, and of the complex problems of revising the work and family roles of men as well as women in the light of the new understandings which were crystallising at the time. As the investigators then recorded, they themselves 'would not have shifted so far and so fast if they had not been and felt themselves to be sailing with the tide'.

This change in the social climate was expressed among other things in the equal pay and sex discrimination legislation of the

1970s, and accounts for a number of the positive changes recorded in the present reports. But the research team also noted at the time of the earlier study how much of the change in thinking about the meaning of equality of opportunity in demanding careers was still at the level of ideology. In 1972, three years after the original *Sex Career and Family* reports were drafted, the researchers found that in most fields 'little has actually been done to translate ideology into action' at the down to earth level of the individual organisation and its management. A new accent on practical measures of implementation was called for.[3]

That is not surprising when one looks in detail, as the present case studies do, at what implementation actually requires. Principles have to be worked out into precise indicators of what is to be done. In some areas, especially as regards family and career and men's and women's roles in family and work, there is even now no general consensus about the direction in which to move, and, as the reports show, only limited understanding of the nature and scale of the problems to be solved. On the side of management alone, literally thousands of decision-makers – not only a few at the top – have to be informed and motivated, and similarly with the trade unions. For this purpose procedures and incentives have to be developed both within organisations and outside them: new roles for women's movements, for example, or appropriate strategies for the Equal Opportunities Commission and the use of the law.

All this takes time: the process of social learning has to be worked through. It is predictable that the time span needed for full and effective implementation of the principle of equal opportunity as broadly agreed by the early 1970s will be no shorter than that required for earlier phases of the women's movement. The relevant time-span is still of the order of twenty-five to thirty years. Meantime, these studies have caught the process of implementation in mid-flight. The reason why no new conceptual framework seemed to be called for is that what can be observed today is, not a new phase of development, but the working out of one whose terms of reference could be and were already defined at the start of the 1970s.

How many women reach the top?

Earnings statistics are a first rough guide to who is at the top, and for the country as a whole the Table below is revealing about the progress, or lack of it, made by women between 1968 and 1979. If 'high earners' among employees are defined as the top 2½–3 per cent of all who are employed full-time, women accounted for just over 2 per cent of such earners in 1968 and just under 2 per cent in 1979. At the highest earnings levels in the table they were scarcely represented at all in either year. The proportion of all men in full-time employment who were 'high earners' was 3½–4 per cent, but the proportion of women in full-time employment with earnings at this level was under 0.2 per cent in both years. There is not much sign here of greater success for women in reaching the top.

Men and Women (Full-Time employees, not affected by absence) with earnings at certain levels, 1968 and 1979.

	Number in Sample			Women as %
1968	*Men*	*Women*	*Total*	*of Total*
Total in sample (All Earnings Levels)	42,510	16,926	59,435	28.5
High Earners:—				
£2,600–3,199	755	16	771	2.08
£3,200–3,639	316	11	327	3.36
£3,640–4,159	166	3	169	1.78
£4,160–5,199	175	3	178	1.69
£5,200 and above	130	—	130	—
	1,542	33	1,575	2.1
High Earners as % of number in sample	3.6	0.19	2.65	
1979				
Total in sample (All Earnings Levels)	77,964	34,735	112,699	30.8
High earners:—				
£9,360–10,399	1,235	19	1,254	1.52
£10,400–11,439	654	22	676	3.25
£11,440–12,999	552	11	563	1.95
£13,000–15,599	441	7	448	1.56
£15,600–20,799	244	1	245	0.41
£20,800 and above	61	—	61	—
	3,187	60	3,247	1.85
High Earners as % of number in sample	4.1	0.17	2.88	

Source: *New Earnings Surveys*, 1968 and 1979.

There could be an occupational bias in these figures, in that many women are in occupations such as teaching where the ceiling on earnings is relatively low, and those (whether men or women) who reach the top are unlikely to rank among the highest earners in a comparison which takes all occupations together. If, however, to allow for this one extends the comparison downwards to the next bracket of earners, the results are similar. Just over 20 per cent of all full-time employees fell into these brackets in both years; this is getting a long way from the top. But this included 27½ per cent of men, but only 4.15 per cent of full-time employed women in 1968 and 3.75 per cent in 1979. The proportion of all employees in these income brackets who were women did not actually decline, but was low in both years at 5.7 per cent.

In three of the case studies – architecture is the exception – the 1968/9 data are precise enough to allow a clear comparison with 1978/9. The picture which they present is only marginally more optimistic than that shown by the national figures. There was a fractional increase in the proportion of women in the most senior posts in the two companies, and at the level just below the top at the BBC, but not among its highest managers and department heads. Women Civil Servants achieved genuine equality of promotion chances, and the proportion of women among Deputy and Under Secretaries increased, but only from a very low level to one marginally less low. Essentially the picture in these occupations, and in architecture, does not differ from that shown by the national statistics. In 1978/9 there were still very few women at the top, and, where there had been a measurable increase since 1968/9, it was numerically very small.

The entry gate and first steps

However, though there has been little increase in the number of women actually at the top in the occupations studied, the case studies show – again in line with national statistics[4] – that in all of them there has been a major increase in the intake of women as recruits to career lines which could in principle lead there. The statistics for the Civil Service and the BBC are particularly impressive. In several cases wastage among women, in the sense of entrants leaving during their training period, also now compares much more favourably than in the 1960s with that among men, either because wastage among women has fallen or because that among men has increased.

Nevertheless, the studies do show how much more might still be done both to increase the proportion of women to men recruited – in industry and architecture, for example, it is still low, and in technical posts in the BBC very low indeed – and to ensure that women make a more effective start to their careers. Direct discrimination against women is not a major factor, though it occurs sporadically. In the case of schools of architecture the statistics suggest that women may actually have a better chance of acceptance than men. For industry as a whole a Department of Employment survey comes to a similar finding that, though relatively few women graduates apply for professional and managerial posts, those who do may have as good a chance of acceptance as men, or better.[5]

Two other considerations stand out more sharply. One is the familiar one that more could be done to draw women's attention to new types of career while they are still in full-time education: see, for example, the evidence on the class and regional bias which remains among women recruits to the architectural profession. In the case of industry a MORI poll in 1979 showed that a large majority of final year women undergraduates were either actively interested in a business or industrial career or at least willing to consider it, but also that these women were less likely than men to have been reached and influenced through interviews with company recruiters, meetings with recent graduates or others employed by companies, or familiarisation with company products.[6]

Secondly, while the case studies show that young highly qualified women were more likely at the end of the 1970s to expect and assume equality of opportunity, they remained – in the view of many informants – more likely than men to apply for jobs below their real potential and to drift during the first stages of their career: as one of the reports puts it, to think in terms of 'a job, not a career', or to get effectively launched only 'after the first five years of dithering about'. This was partly due to differences in career motivation. The same MORI poll found that in 1979, as in the 1960s,[7] highly qualified women were less likely than similarly qualified men to attach importance in choosing a career to factors such as a high starting salary, opportunity for rapid promotion, or the chance to reach a level at which their work would be free from supervision. But the case studies also make it clear that much could be done by better career guidance during these women's first working years, and that this is a matter to which employers and professional organisations need to give more attention in the interests, not only of women themselves, but of returns from the heavy investment by employers and taxpayers in their education and initial training. This is not, however, simply a deficiency in employers' and professional organisations' attitude to women. It reflects more general deficiencies in manpower management and induction training which other reports[8] show to apply also to many categories of men.

Family and career

If the inflow of women into the junior levels of professional and managerial careers is accelerating – even though there is reason to think that it could be accelerated further – then the central question, so far as equal access for women to top jobs is concerned, is whether these women will be more successful than their predecessors in working their way up through the middle grades to the levels from which promotions to the top are finally made. The key finding of the case studies is that this is in fact unlikely and by far the most important reason for this is the continued neglect by employers, and by other agencies such as public authorities responsible for community care for children, of the difficulties of reconciling a career with a family.

This issue is central in all the case studies. It is not that women at this level easily abandon their careers when they have children. The statistics on continuation in work by women professionals and managers in the BBC or in architecture show, again in line with national data,[9] that they do not do so. What the case studies document over and over again is the failure of managements, unions, and professional bodies to give to issues about family and career the degree and continuity of attention which might be expected if they were seen as genuinely important and unavoidable. Among them are the issues of flexibility of working time, including part time, flexible time, and family leave; of the return to work after maternity or a career break, including the right to reinstatement and the opportunity to enter new employment; and of the stereotyping of promotion ages: as well, of course, as the wider issue of facilities and finance for child care. Issues like these have not been entirely ignored. They may even have been formally considered and policies laid down, as notably in the Civil Service. But at a practical and down to earth level, the case studies find action on them to be not much further advanced than at the time of the *Sex Career and Family* studies. At the end of the 1970s as of the 1960s, the statistics show that the way to the top is still much clearer for women who, in terms of family responsibilities, travel light.

These comments apply particularly to the 'bureaucracies' – the organisations which are large-scale or, as in local government, have nationally determined codes of employment practice – with which the case studies were chiefly concerned. The one sector of small-scale employment included in the studies is architectural private practice. In line with what national experience would lead one to expect,[10] this shows a relatively high degree of flexibility in career patterns. There are family firms in which architect wives have a comparatively good chance of bringing up a family and yet going on to become high-earning principals. There are also much better opportunities than in the 'bureaucracies' of finding a part-time job or building up a small, and often part-time, independent practice: though often at the price of drifting too easily along with work below a woman architect's actual potential.

At some points, neglect of problems of family and career in the 'bureaucracies' reflects deficiencies which apply to men as well as women. This is notably true in the case of re-entry or recruitment to a new employment after a prolonged career break. At a time of staff cuts and redundancies, as one comment from local government put it, the departure of either men or women for whatever reason is likely to be 'greeted with a sigh of relief', and there is little incentive to follow up leavers for re-recruitment or to seek recruits from new sources. The case studies note some areas of work where it is usual to seek experienced recruits from outside an organisation; this is particularly true of local government. But they also illustrate the widespread tendency to a 'culture of promotion from within', sometimes supported with a markedly rigid pattern of career planning and career expectations, which makes it difficult to fit in either men or women who may, for instance, return after a second-ment, let alone new recruits above normal career entry levels.

One of the paradoxes of British employment practice is that in recent decades there have been tendencies both (as illustrated in the case studies) towards a stronger 'culture of promotion from within' and towards a demand for increased managerial mobility.[11] For the manager currently well established in his job, who can pick his time and make his conditions for a move, the opportunities of this situation may well outweigh its disadvantages. *Sex Career and Family* also reviewed the very successful experience of the Forces with launching into new civilian careers middle-aged officers who cannot pick their time for a move, but who do have long notice in which to prepare for it and to develop a planned strategy with strong institutional support. For those, whether men or women, who do not have these advantages – the woman with a broken career record, the man made redundant at short notice, either men or women in civilian occupations where backing like that of the Forces Resettlement Service is not available – the case studies illustrate how damaging the present situation can be.

Essentially, however, both men and women informants in the case studies saw family and career as primarily a women's problem, though with some gestures – usually by women or women's groups – towards issues such as paternity leave or the availability of nursery facilities to fathers as well as mothers. As such, it did not rank high in managements' scales of priority.

Direct discrimination in mid-career

Direct discrimination against women in the middle and later stages of their careers did not, with one exception, appear to be a primary problem, though there was enough of it to be significant. The exception is private practice in architecture, where a comparison of single and married women's careers and of salary statistics points definitely to discrimination. It is probably once again significant that this is a small-firm sector, for the experience of women architects in private practice contrasts with their experience in the architectural departments of the 'bureaucracies' as well as with the experience of women in the 'bureaucracies' in general.

What is significant for the 'bureaucracies' is the clear and explicit commitment in all cases to equal opportunity at board or equivalent level – as indeed also in the Royal Institute of British

Architects – and yet attention is drawn by informants to the extent to which women's opportunity still depends on the not always supportive attitudes of individual managers and supervisors and the traditions of particular subsidiary companies or departments. In the Civil Service women as well as men agreed that the procedures for enforcing equal opportunity were in general effective, and the record of promotions at higher administrative levels (though not in some other grades) bore this out. In industry and the BBC, by contrast, there were signs of a failure by top management to make its policies uniformly and reliably effective at the levels where many of the key decisions for women's progress in mid-career are made.

Motivation and guidance in mid-career

A common criticism on the part of employers, and a defence against charges of discrimination, is that women tend to be 'not career conscious'.[12] In the case studies there were also many comments of this kind, from women as well as from men, and with reference to later stages of careers as well as to progress just after initial entry. When these comments are analysed, they turn out to be making three points.

First, though there were still traces of diffidence among women at the end of the 1970s, they were much less marked than they had been in the 1960s. Women were more likely to have confidence in their own abilities, to think (though possibly after a shaky start) in terms of a career rather than simply a job, and if necessary to use appeals procedures and protest at being passed over.

Secondly, however, in mid-career as at earlier stages women were still seen as tending to strike a different balance from men between career and other commitments. More women than men appeared to be interested in job content rather than job prospects, and likely, for example, to turn down an unpopular posting even though it was a stepping stone to better prospects later on. Women were more likely than men to be reluctant to come forward for some types of managerial work, either because this meant moving away from more directly 'creative' work or because of the heavy or rigid time commitments which it might involve. They were seen as not anxious to 'say their work is their life', 'have very little private life', or accept the commitments for evening meetings, external contacts, and internal

politicking which a woman Chief Officer in local government illustrated from her own experience.

Thirdly, while a number of younger women who were interviewed
had clear and definite ideas about planning and managing their
careers, older women and men had their doubts about whether this
clarity and precision would survive actual experience in mid-career.
One comment which was made in the 1960s and recurred in the
1970s was that women were less likely than men to be skilful and
single-minded in 'packaging' their claims to promotion where seeking
it depended largely on their own initiative, as it did in all the
occupations studied except the Civil Service. But this was not merely
a comment on women's marketing expertise. It also reflected the
view that women in mid-career were in any case likely to be less
certain than men about where they were trying to go, not least
because of the inter-relation between family and career, which tends
to become salient for women just at the age when for men in
managerial and professional work, careers are acquiring a definite
shape and beginning to take off.[13] For men, as the studies in the 1960s
found, marriage and children tend to sharpen ambitions and increase
determination to reach the top while for women they tend to have
the opposite effect.[14] As the case-studies show, the consequences of
the options available to women at this point in their careers are often
not clearly spelt out or understood.

From the point of view of policy, these comments are a mixed bag.
If a woman, or a man, genuinely prefers to stay close to the cameras
or the drawing board or to choose a job which leaves time for family
and leisure interests – as men, as well as women, increasingly do,
and for good reason[15] – there is nothing more to be said. If, however,
resistance to moving from 'creative' to managerial work rests on
misunderstandings about the nature and prospects of a management
job which would fade away once a woman had actually experienced
it: or if there is a real deficiency in 'marketing expertise'; or if the
implications of choices over family and career and the possibilities of
reconciling them are not well understood: that is altogether a
different matter. What a number of respondents implied, and some
explicitly said, is that the need for positive action by way of career
guidance and encouragement for women continues to apply in the
middle as well as in the earlier stages of their careers. Though men
as well as women may have problems over managing their careers a

convincing case was made for thinking that women in this respect still tended at the end of the 1970s to be 'different', and that this is a matter to which employers and professional bodies need to pay much more consistent attention than they do.

Management: the means and will to act

Given, as has been said, that the principle of equal opportunity is fully accepted at the top level of all the organisations included in the case-studies, how has it happened that action to implement it has been so incomplete: that so little progress has been made over family and career, that in some organisations so many traces of direct discrimination remain, and that the need for special guidance and encouragement for women from recruitment on through the middle stages of careers has been neglected?

(i) *Machinery for monitoring and implementation*

Effective implementation of equal opportunity requires, for one thing, machinery within the management structure for developing, enforcing, and monitoring its application. Many of the key decisions about postings or promotions which affect women's prospects of ultimately reaching the top are made while they are still at relatively junior levels, and by managers well below the top. Action on issues such as part-time employment or the return to work may require policy decisions which are outside the competence of middle or even senior managers, but it will still be for these managers to apply the resulting policies with more or less enthusiasm, and often also to perceive and press the case for them in the first place.

The guidelines on internal procedures published by the Equal Opportunities Commission[16] accordingly begin by emphasising the need for a clear statement at board or equivalent level of an organisation's commitment to the principle of equal opportunity, but then stress the need for specific and detailed procedures to ensure that this principle is translated into action down the line. A senior executive should be assigned responsibility for devising and monitoring appropriate policies and procedures and for reporting to the board on progress. There should be detailed procedures for recording and analysing women's progress in employment and the employment practices underlying it, for action by managers or joint committees, for staff information and consultation, and for evaluating results.

Measured against these standards, the machinery existing in the case-study occupations at the end of the 1970s ranged from excellent to almost non-existent.

The BBC acquired during the 1970s potentially excellent machinery which matches the EOC's standards closely. The Civil Service also has a potentially excellent framework for monitoring and implementation, including a long-established practice of individual career planning and of seeking out potential candidates for promotion and bringing them forward.

The two industrial companies studied had not in 1978/9 reached this stage. A number of large American corporations, under the pressure of equal employment legislation and of changing public attitudes, have in recent years developed managerial procedures very much as proposed in the EOC guidelines. They include the assignment of specific responsibilities to senior managers, educational programmes for managers ('consciousness-raising for senior management', to quote from one IBM report), the establishment of career plans for able women, and regular monitoring in a form which makes it clear to managers at all levels that this is an area in which they are expected to achieve results and will be held accountable for them.

> There must be plans to move women into management. Equal treatment must be adopted by planners as an accepted goal, like market share or debt ratio or return on investment. There must be specific, clear objectives which answer the questions: How many women managers? What kind? Where? The goals established should be realistic – that is capable of being attained. It is essential to reach agreement inside the company, and if possible with compliance authorities, on what constitutes acceptable performance in a given time frame . . . There must be standards of performance for equal treatment, and there must be ways of measuring whether those standards are being met.[17]

Elements of policies of this kind were found in the two British companies. In both, for example, 'considerable emphasis had been placed on informing managers about the legislation'. But in general a systematic managerial approach to the enforcement of equal opportunity policies was lacking. In this respect the two companies are typical of the much larger sample of five hundred studied earlier by the EOC.[18]

In local government there is the difficulty that local authorities are independent employers, promotion often means applying to a new authority, and within most authorities the numbers in any profesional group are small, particularly in the higher ranks. These conditions can make it difficult to monitor and act against discrimination at individual authorities' level. Local government does, however, have well developed national codes of employment practice, one of whose foundations is a clear and generally respected commitment against discrimination in its more obvious forms. But at the time of our study national procedures did not provide for systematic monitoring of women's progress in local government as a whole, nor for setting national standards in less immediately obvious areas of discrimination such as family and career. National staff statistics did not distinguish between men and women, and an official of the Local Authorities Conditions of Service Advisory Board questioned whether monitoring sex discrimination would even be within the Board's terms of reference.

In architecture, the creation of regular machinery for monitoring and enforcing equal opportunity was at the time of the present study still a task for the future. Architects are spread among a wide variety of employers, including the many small independent firms in private practice. The case study nevertheless points to the possibility of setting up systematic procedures for monitoring women's progress and a code of practice on appointments and promotions, which might in due course be given force either by agreement within the profession or by law.

(ii) *Understanding the implications of equal opportunity*
If machinery for enforcement was inadequate or under-used at the time of our enquiry, one reason was that its purposes were in some respects inadequately understood. The case-studies show that direct discrimination as defined in Sections 1 (1)(a) and 3 (1)(a) of the Sex Discrimination Act 1975 was widely understood, but indirect discrimination (Sections 1 (1)(b) and 3 (1)(b)) was not. Indirect discrimination arises where the same formal conditions of employment apply to both sexes and to people of any marital status, but in practice a considerably smaller proportion of people of one sex or marital status than of another can comply with them. When, in particular, problems of family and career were discussed with

respondents in management, it was clear that the idea that the rule against indirect discrimination might apply to their practices under this head had not been understood anywhere near as clearly as that against direct discrimination.

There was also some difference of view among respondents, both men and women, about whether and in what respects positive discrimination in favour of women was desirable. In the case of some company respondents there was clearly a misunderstanding. They took positive discrimination to mean preference for women over better qualified men: 'reverse discrimination', which is in any case illegal under the Sex Discrimination Act. Legal or not, women and men who understood positive discrimination in this sense almost unanimously rejected it as likely to lead to a backlash.

The Sex Discrimination Act permits positive action in the sense of better career guidance – encouraging women to come forward in equal competition for posts where they have been under-represented – and of action by employers and training bodies to give women special facilities for relevant training. Positive discrimination in this sense attracted widespread support from both men and women, but some respondents still sounded a warning note. Several shared the view of a senior company manager who said that 'people who get to the top don't get there through other people'. This argument does not entirely correspond to the facts. The personal support of patrons plays an important part in the careers of successful managers, men as well as women, as recorded in other research as well as in these studies. One of the difficulties which respondents in the case studies saw awaiting women who tried to resume a career after a break was that the patrons who had known and helped them earlier would now have moved on. But whatever the form of special guidance and encouragement for women, whether by individual senior managers or on a more systematic basis, many women as well as men warned against allowing it to be carried to the point of obscuring the need for women, like men, to rely in the first place on their own initiative and effort.

(iii) *The will to act*
In the last resort, however, it is the will to act which matters most. Over and over again, respondents in the case studies saw room for managements or professional bodies to do more about family and

career, or career guidance, or elimination of the remnants of direct discrimination: but it was not done. What has just been said about failure to create or use the machinery needed for implementation, or to consider deeply enough the meaning of discrimination points in the same direction. The case studies record with justification comments about 'benign neglect' (the BBC), a 'low key approach' (Civil Service), or 'resting on their oars' (local government). The key question for the future of action on equal opportunity in management and the professions is how this situation came about, and what might be done to change it.

Pressures to act

(i) *The economic climate of the 1970s*

The British economy was already in difficulties in the late 1960s but a number of organisations still reported 'a shortage of well-qualified staff, not perhaps at the very top, but for senior posts lower down'.[19] The Civil Service would have been willing to take more administrative recruits if men or women of the right standard had been available. One of the case-study companies noted at that time a potential shortage of well qualified scientists. Unilever's company quarterly wrote in the mid-1960s that proposals for new ventures had sometimes to be postponed 'because the necessary management to put the plan into effect could not be deployed'. Even in the face of shortages, however, many managements were reluctant to experiment with re-designing jobs and career patterns to accommodate the differences between the typical life cycles of women and men. As a manager in the same case study company said at that time, 'Let the other chap be the first to start re-designing jobs for married women'.

At the end of the 1970s comments about current shortages of managers and professionals were no longer heard, though some far-sighted managers might wonder what the position would be if and when the economy recovered.[20] Since the mid-1970s growth in the economy has been cut short and managerial and professional like other staffs have been slimmed. The change in attitudes on sex equality which had developed through the previous decades, and was reinforced in the 1970s by legislation, was sufficient even so to produce the positive results recorded in the reports, in particular the greater recruitment of women through the entry gates which might lead to the top, and the diminution of overt discrimination. But the state of the labour market has given employers still less incentive than in the 1960s to go beyond this and to explore the more complex measures needed to complete the elimination of direct discrimination and to reconcile men's and women's careers with their family responsibilities. The case-studies make it clear that, in conditions like these, progress in these directions could have been maintained only if additional pressures from other sources had been brought to bear. They indicate both where pressures of this kind fell short and how they might be strengthened for the future.

(ii) *Trade unions*

Action on equal opportunity by trade unions, as it affects women at the career levels covered in the case studies, has, like that of management, been uneven: on the side of the angels as regards intentions, but not always in practice balanced or systematic, and often lacking in thrust.

In the two companies studied managerial and professional grades became unionised during the 1970s, and there was some limited union discussion in one company about nursery provision and women's pension rights. But no strong or general union pressure for equal opportunity was reported from either company.

In the public services unions were more active. The Association of Broadcasting Staffs helped to develop a systematic approach to implementing equal opportunity in the BBC. The Association of Cinematograph Television and Allied Technicians, which is not recognised in the BBC but is strong in ITV, published its own study of the position of women in films and television. NALGO promoted a similar study of women in local government, and analysed what it found to be the rather unsatisfactory degree of participation of women within the union itself. Unions in all the public services studied, including the Civil Service unions and the GLC Staff Association, have shown positive concern with issues such as nursery provision, maternity and paternity leave, flexible time, and the right to reinstatement after a break in employment.

This interest has, however, tended to be sporadic, and union support on equal opportunity issues has sometimes been weak or hesitant, reflecting the fact that these issues are not a primary concern, and may cut across others of greater interest to the membership as a whole. The report on architecture quotes NALGO's hesitation over supporting a demand to extend mothers' rights to reinstatement up to five years from a birth, since this might interfere with the career opportunities of other members of staff, and over support for nursery provision for local authority staffs, since at a time of strict cash limits and cuts in local authority expenditure anything spent in this direction was likely to be recovered by cuts elsewhere. GLC respondents, similarly, had not seen the GLC Staff Association as an effective or reliable source of support for their crèche campaign.

On one issue central to the problem of family and career, that of part-time, freelance, and contract work, the public service unions have still to develop a policy which meets the needs so often expressed by women respondents. They see in these types of work the risk of unfavourable effects on the work load and opportunities of full-time staff, on union recruitment and participation in union work, and through discrimination against part-time, contract, and freelance workers themselves. The risks to which the unions point are real. What they have not done is to explore systematically the possibility of policies which would reconcile safeguards in these respects with satisfaction of the need and demand by many women for spells of work with a limited time commitment, with or without an extension of the same facilities to men.

In so far as the unions have been active on equal opportunity, much of the impulse for this has come from more or less organised groups of women activists, for example in NALGO or the Civil Service unions. Conversely, one reason for union inactivity on equal opportunity in the two companies has been limited union partici-pation – and sometimes hostility – by women themselves.

(iii) *Women's pressure groups*

The attitudes of most women respondents to women's pressure groups, union-based or otherwise, in their own organisations turned out to range from lack of interest, but no positive objection, to definite opposition, at least in current circumstances.

In the two industrial companies women flatly rejected any suggestion that they might form their own internal pressure groups, nor had they done so. This was partly because of a tendency to 'dislike group involvement of any kind', with a suggestion that women tend to be 'more individualistic than men'. There was also, however, a feeling that the formation of a group to press for women's rights was likely to be interpreted as conduct unbecoming to a manager, and to be counter-productive in terms of improving women's position generally, as well as damaging to the careers of the individual women concerned.

In architecture fewer respondents objected in principle to women's pressure groups, though a number did. Still fewer, however, were impressed with the performance of such groups as there were or had been. The common criticism of one current women's group, the New Architecture Movement, was that it was too abstract and remote from the actual issues of equal opportunity.

Among women in the BBC there was less objection to the principle of pressure groups. One, Women in Media, had campaigned for several years for equal opportunity both in BBC careers and in the presentation of women in broadcasting, and with significant success. More recently there had been a crèche campaign. Two-thirds of BBC respondents knew at least about the existence of some pressure group of this kind. Even in the BBC, however, many women respondents' knowledge was vague, and few showed interest in becoming actively involved themselves. It was said, as in the other occupations studied, that successful women tend to focus on their own work. Some respondents also thought that even in the BBC militancy might backfire on a woman's own career.

The most promising recent development of women's groups has occurred in the Civil Service. Two, Women in the Civil Service and the Civil Service Women's Rights Group, were formed at the end of the 1970s, and have worked to raise women's consciousness generally in the Service and to bring forward practical and down to earth claims through the Civil Service unions. But even these groups' actual achievement was still marginal in 1979.

As individuals, or as participants in specific one-off campaigns, many women were more active. Even in the industrial companies, senior women were more willing to give advice and a helping hand, or to say a word in the right place, than some other respondents gave them credit for. Many individual women Civil Servants contributed their views to the Committee on the Employment of Women in the Civil Service, and more recently a number have taken action under the legislation on equal pay and sex discrimination. In architecture it was individual women who took the lead in the RIBA Council's discussion of the report of the architecture case-study, and particular groups of women who promoted the co-operative Company of Women in Architecture and led the campaign for nursery provision in the GLC.

There is a grey area between continuing group involvement and the action of individuals or *ad hoc* groups. There can be a great deal of informal communication and discussion (the 'women's Mafia') even where continuing pressure groups are absent or ineffective. One cannot, however, avoid the impression that many women respondents under-estimated the case for continuing and systematic action on an organised and professionally expert basis. It is clear that further movement towards equal opportunity in the re-studied occupations needs a degree of continuous study and effort which has been lacking in the unions as well as in management. With rare exceptions, it has also been lacking in the case of the efforts made by women themselves, and as a result too many problems, like those around family and career, have been left half-studied and unresolved, and too many particular initiatives have been allowed to run into the sand.

The report on architecture makes a point of particular relevance to sectors which, like private architectural practice, are made up of many independent small firms. These may or may not be unionised, and, if they are unionised, it is local rather than national officers who will have to be activated on issues of equal opportunity. Though these firms may come into contact with the law on discrimination, they are unlikely to be picked out for direct attention by the Equal Opportunities Commission. If there is to be direct pressure on them, it will often need to originate from some other local source, and the most obvious one is women's movements operating within each professional and industrial sector at local level.

The detailed support and investigative role of women's pressure groups does not, however, have to be confined to small firms and organisations. Given the problems which exist over women's own motivation and need for career guidance, there is a wide potential field of action for women's groups in supporting and encouraging women in large organisations from detailed knowledge of local and individual circumstances. So there is also in cases where legal action is required and, though the EOC or unions may step in when an individual's claim has reached the stage of formal action, there is a role for a women's group in providing advice and support in initiating the claim as well as in carrying it through.

(iv) *Women's movements nationally*

On the effects of the women's movement in its wider national and international sense, women respondents were again ambivalent. Many, particularly in the BBC and among older women in industry, saw it as having value in raising women's consciousness and changing attitudes in society at large. In the particular case of the BBC it ·had helped to change the balance of programmes and to make BBC women themselves read and think. But many also criticised it, at least in its earlier manifestations, as shrill, extremist, liable to cause feelings of guilt among non-employed women, and therefore counter-productive. For some younger women in one of the companies studied it seemed simply to be by-passed by events, as attitudes changed to the point where women under 35 or 40 'expect to do everything men do'. 'Women can only expect to be treated as equal if they behave as equal.'

There seemed to be the same under-estimate of the potential role of women's movements nationally as in respondents' attitudes to pressure groups within their own organisations. The problems of further progress towards equal opportunity which emerge in the case-studies are not confined within the boundaries of these particular occupations. In a number of cases, such as influencing subject and career choices in schools and colleges, extending community care for children, developing national policies on family and career as a joint rather than a women's problem, or making national policies and procedures for implementing the law on discrimination more effective, these problems need study and action on a basis much wider than that of any one employing organisation or profession. Respondents appeared to under-estimate the degree of organised effort still required for the effective implementation of policies for equality, and to have given rather little consideration to the ways in which the women's movement in its wider sense might contribute to this.

The risk foreseen by many respondents that greater activity by women's movements at either national or organisation level could provoke a backlash is of course real enough, and their own comments on past experience illustrate it. Consciousness-raising, as one comment on the first draft of this book said, is a Z-shaped weapon. It was, however, by taking this risk that women's movements contributed what they did to earlier breakthroughs towards equality in pay and opportunity. The reports show little appreciation by many women of the case for taking, with all due caution, a similar risk today.

(v) *The law and the Equal Opportunities Commission*

The Civil Service is the only occupation studied where the reports refer to a direct impact of the Equal Pay and Sex Discrimination Acts in the sense of management being actually taken to a tribunal, though a wider sweep round local government, not confined to architects, would of course have shown cases there. Respondents in all the case-studies recognised, however, the value of this and other legislation, notably the maternity provisions of the Employment Protection Act 1975, in changing attitudes, making management more careful, and setting clear standards in certain areas, such as advertising or maternity provisions.

They tended to be more doubtful about the effectiveness of the law, at least as currently applied, in improving equality of opportunity in higher level careers in their own organisations or professions. Its impact had not been carried through to the point of creating real pressure on line managers to 'look harder' (BBC), or to undertake an 'informed audit' (industry). It was in any case seen as difficult to monitor discrimination in promotion to higher posts, and (as both men and women said in the BBC) compliance with the law as it was currently understood could too easily in practice lead to 'tokenism' and the appointment of the 'statutory woman'. Some industrial and Civil Service informants wondered whether the law might not be inducing a backlash – a feeling that women were over-protected – or a tendency (a suggestion from the Civil Service) to let issues of equal opportunity lie unless the need to attend to them was made compelling by a legal decision.

These doubts about the effective administration of the law were paralleled in comments on the role of the Equal Opportunities Commission. In its reports for 1977 and 1978 the Commission outlined a strategy which, without devaluing legal procedures or the handling of individual complaints, laid stress on a wider programme to educate the public about the problems of equal opportunity not only in employment but in other areas, and about the resources and remedies available not only through courts and tribunals but through voluntary and co-operative action.

That is precisely the 'positive stance' which a number of women in the two industrial companies recommended. There could be danger, one said, in the EOC becoming 'labelled with fighting cases'. Some of the areas where others wanted to see action by the EOC include careers education in schools, advice on job opportunities, campaigns to change attitudes towards working mothers and to help them through better child-care facilities, and issues such as mortgages, tax, and pensions.

It was clear, however, that the EOC's wider and educational policies had not at the date of the case-studies spread far or penetrated deeply enough to be well understood by these informants. They did not know of a number of things which the EOC was actually doing, for example on taxation. For many of them the image was still of 'fighting cases', and a number of them in the companies and the BBC linked this to what they saw as the unfortunate impression of the EOC created in its early days by a 'silly' or 'ludicrous' press.

But respondents' criticism of the EOC was not only a matter of misunderstanding. Whether or not they had any clear idea about the EOC's national strategy, they did know what was happening in their own immediate employment. The view of both men and women respondents right across the board was that, except in the case of EOC support for certain women who took successful legal action in the Civil Service, the Commission was making no significant impact on the problems which they currently perceived in their own situation. If the EOC produced a quotable document, it might be quoted. There might be some more or less organised contact between organisations or unions and the Commission, as in the Civil Service and the BBC. But nothing which the EOC had done was seen as putting effective pressure on management to go on to the next stage of action on equal opportunity: systematic study and action, within the respondents' own organisations, on family and career and the other remaining problems summarised earlier.

Informants themselves tended to be vague about what more

might be done by the EOC. Many were not particularly interested. But the most illuminating comment came from a man in the BBC who thought that the Commission's existence might be counter-productive, not for such reasons as over-protection of women or taking up 'silly' issues, but because the EOC is not an 'achieving organisation'. 'What teeth do they have? They do more harm than good in raising expectations that they can achieve what they can't.'

That raises a major question about the balance in the EOC's strategy between educational work and legal action. Systematic action for the detailed implementation of equal opportunity is clearly the next target in the occupations studied here, but the practical situation is still one of respect for the law in principle but a substantial measure of 'benign neglect' in practice. Progress can still be made in this situation: a good example is the movement in the 1970s towards more effective monitoring and implementation in the BBC. More may be made as the EOC's campaign to inform employers and the public develops, and more, again, if stronger pressures can be developed through trade unions and women's own pressure groups and movements. But the impression from all the case-studies is that, so far as higher careers are concerned, progress is likely to remain slow unless some further factor is brought into the situation, and it looks as if this will need to be a sharper bite from legal action.

Pressure groups need leverage if they are either to work effectively or to seem interesting and worth working for, and on the evidence of the reports they do not have too much of it at present. The economic climate is unhelpful. The change in public attitudes has had only a limited impact on the problems of implementation which are most relevant today, and the case-studies show no reason to think that the EOC's recent educational programme will operate rapidly enough to change this situation. There remains the law.

The obvious international comparison for policies on discrimi-nation is with the United States. It is questionable whether the systematic and increasingly effective policies of American corpora-tions for fair employment would have developed as fast and far as they have without the leverage provided by major demonstration cases in the courts, and the managerial effort and disturbance, the bad publicity, and the financial penalties which they have involved for the corporations concerned. If the problem is that sleeping dogs are let lie, the answer at this stage of the movement towards equal opportunity may be a sharper legal bite to wake them up.

The line which the EOC itself was exploring at the beginning of 1980 was the establishment of a code of practice which would not be directly binding, but of which industrial tribunals would have to take account when considering sex discrimination and equal pay cases: very much on the lines suggested in the report on architecture. It is one thing, as a senior woman manager in one company said, for managers to see general principles of non-discrimination written into the law. It is another to know that, if a case comes to court, its outcome will depend among other things on whether they have observed a clearly specified set of managerial procedures.

(vi) *The three-pronged approach*
Though, however, more active use of the law is likely to have a key part to play in re-launching the movement for equal opportunity, it would be wrong to end with an exclusive emphasis on it. Collective bargaining, lobbying, direct personal approaches to decision-makers, education, and publicity both generally and in individual cases all have their part to play. Neither the trade unions, nor women's movements locally and nationally, nor the Equal Opportunities Commission have contributed all that they might to equal opportunity in professional and managerial work. The size and nature of the effort needed to re-launch the movement for equal opportunity is such as to require a much more dynamic, and mutually reinforcing, contribution from all three agencies, both locally and in detail and in influencing national policies: a new three-pronged drive. The law will provide one main point of leverage for this, but the essential point is that rapid progress is likely to be made only through a new level of effort involving all types of action and all three agencies at once.

The focus of action
Let us, finally, summarise the argument of this Part into a series of pointers to action.

(1) The fact that the number of women actually holding top jobs in the case-study occupations has not increased greatly in recent years

is not necessarily a sign of discrimination in promotions at the highest level, since few women have lasted long enough in their careers or climbed high enough to be in the zone from which these promotions are made.

(2) Nor is the major question today the attraction of women into career lines which might lead to the top, for the number of women entering these career lines did increase substantially through the 1970s. More can, however, still be done to widen the recruitment of women and to ensure that they make an effective start to their careers. In some cases this means combating discrimination at or just after the entry gate. But the chief need here is for more effective career guidance both before entry and by employers and professional bodies during the first years of employment.

(3) The major problem now is over progress in mid-career, and the largest question for the coming years is whether the increasing number of women who have entered career lines which could lead to the top will be any more successful than their predecessors in continuing on towards the top through mid-career barriers.

(4) The most important mid-career barrier remains, in all these occupations, indirect discrimination in respect of family and career: inflexibility of working time, the lack of opportunity and systematic procedures for reinstatement and progression after a career break, the stereotyping of promotion ages, and lack of child-care facilities. The issue of family and career is still in all cases under-estimated, and seen too exclusively as a 'women's problem'.

(5) Other problems in mid-career include remaining elements of direct discrimination, usually sporadic, but in the case of architectural private practice more general: and under-estimation of the need for continued advice and guidance for women themselves in managing their careers and making the necessary choices, both in their careers and in relation to career and family.

(6) There are also still deficiencies in some of the occupations studied in procedures for systematic monitoring of women's careers and for ensuring that action is taken by management at all levels on problems such as those just mentioned. Machinery in the BBC and the Civil Service is potentially excellent, though in the case of the

Civil Service under-used and in that of the BBC relatively new and untried. In local government, the industrial companies, and the architectural profession adequate machinery and procedures have still to be designed.

(7) If action by managements and professional bodies on the preceding points has been ineffective, and the full implications of the principle of equal opportunity for women have not been understood and followed through, the main reason has been lack of pressures and incentives to do so, at a time when labour market pressures and general changes in social attitudes are by themselves too weak to ensure this. A re-launch of the movement towards equal opportunity in professional and managerial careers will require a three-pronged drive through activist groups in the trade unions, a new level of activity by women's pressure groups in individual organisations and professions and nationally, and more systematic pressure, led by the Equal Opportunities Commission, through the law.

References
(1) M. P. Fogarty (ed.), Isobel Allen, A. J. Allen and Patricia Walters, *Women in Top Jobs – Four Studies in Achievement*, George Allen and Unwin, 1971.
(2) M. P. Fogarty and R. and R. Rapoport, *Sex Career and Family*, George Allen and Unwin, 1971, p. 20.
(3) M. P. Fogarty, *Women and Top Jobs – the Next Move*, PEP Report 535, 1972, p. 18.
(4) 'The Market for Highly Qualified Labour', *Employment Gazette*, March 1980: Equal Opportunities Commission, *Annual Report* for 1978, Tables 3.3 and 3.4.
(5) 'Going into Industry', *Department of Employment Gazette*, January 1979.
(6) 'Career Attitudes of Final Year Graduates', *Employment Gazette*, January 1979, Tables 7 and 8.
(7) *Sex Career and Family*, op. cit., pp. 200–213.
(8) R. Berthoud, *Training Adults for Skilled Jobs*, PSI Report 575, 1978 (on the induction problems of Skillcentre trainees): M. P. Fogarty and Eileen Reid, *Differentials for Managers and Skilled Workers in the United Kingdom*, PSI Report 586 (for PSI and British-North American Research Association), 1980 (on the more general 'crisis of the crafts').
(9) Contrast, for example, the proportion of married women architects who work while their children are under five with the national figures shown in the *General Household Survey* for 1977 (HMSO), Table 4.5: and see the national analysis of return to work by occupational level in W. W. Daniel, *Maternity Rights*, PSI Report 588, 1980.
(10) See Daniel, op. cit.

(11) Mobility data from a number of British Institute of Management surveys are summarised in *Pension Rights on Changing Jobs*, Management Information Sheet 59, BIM, 1980. In the 1970s managers aged 35–39 were likely to have changed employers twice as often as their predecessors who were at the same age thirty years before, and in 1978 managers in their thirties had already on the average made more employer changes than those over fifty.

(12) A. McIntosh, 'Women at Work – A Survey of Employers', *Employment Gazette*, November 1980.

(13) R. T. Beattie *et al.*, *The Management Threshold*, BIM, 1974.

(14) *Sex Career and Family*, op. cit., Table VI 3 and 5 and Figures VI 2 and 3.

(15) See e.g. the analysis in M. Young and P. Willmott, *The Symmetrical Family*, Routledge and Kegan Paul, 1973 (notably Tables 18 and 53) of how 'interference' between work, family, and leisure rises on moving up the occupational scale from routine to professional and managerial work and eventually to top jobs: most steeply for married women in full-time work, but also for men.

(16) EOC, *Guidance on Equal Opportunity Policies and Practices in Employment*, especially paras. 5–8.

(17) Comment by the Director of Human Resources and Planning of American Telephone and Telegraph. For a useful summary of practice in this and other corporations see *Women in Management*, report of an international colloquium at the European Institute of Business Administration (INSEAD), Fontainebleau, May 1977.

(18) Equal Opportunities Commission, *Equality Between the Sexes – How Far Have We Come?*, 1978.

(19) *Sex Career and Family*, op. cit., pp. 466–7.

(20) See e.g. Ruth Miller, 'Eternal Dilemma of Working Mothers', *Daily Telegraph*, 24 November 1980.

PART II

Four Case Studies

A. Women in Civil Service
   Administration
B. Women in Two Industrial Companies
C. Women in the BBC
D. Women in the Architectural
   Profession

A. Women in Civil Service Administration

Introduction

This study undertaken in 1978 looks at what changes there have been in the position of women in the higher administrative grades of the Civil Service since the previous study of Women in Top Jobs made in 1968.[1]

Since 1968 the Civil Service has been affected by structural changes that followed the report of the Fulton Committee on the Civil Service. In 1971 the Administrative Class, which was the focus of the 1968 study, disappeared in name. In response to the Committee's criticism of what it considered the rigid class system of the Civil Service, the Administrative Class was split in two. Its top-most posts, the commanding posts of the whole of the Home Civil Service – those at the level of Permanent Secretary, Deputy Secretary and Under Secretary – were formed into a lateral band called the 'Open Structure' incorporating top posts in a number of occupational groups in the Service. The effect of the establishment of this 'Open Structure' has been to supplement the generalist administrator career ladder to the top with a ladder running through professional posts. Thus in the 1970s about a quarter of Permanent Secretaries have had careers in other than general administration. The middle and lower parts of the Administrative Class hierarchy have become part of the Administration Group which also incorporates the old Executive and Clerical Classes: some grades in the Administration Group, particularly that of Principal, are amalgamations of a former Administrative Class grade and grades in other classes. Within the Administration Group there is a hierarchy of entry gates through which young recruits embark on life-time careers: the top-most entry gate, that of Administration Trainee, takes in university graduates. There is, however, a promotion route into the ranks above Administration Trainee.

These structural changes have implications for this re-study. First, one cannot make direct comparisons between 1968 and 1978 of the proportions of women in particular grades. As will be shown, comparisons pre- and post-1971 require a knowledge of the way in which membership of certain constantly named categories has changed. Second, despite the disappearance of the Administrative Class, there is still a special, express route to Open Structure posts commencing at the entry grade of Administration Trainee. It is sometimes informally referred to as the 'crown prince' route. AT entrants to the Civil Service still have a greater chance than do any other kind of entrants of reaching the top posts. The present study concentrates on depicting women's position on this route in the 1970s, comparing, between 1968 and 1978, the numbers of women entering the express route and the degree of success they achieve on it. In the new structure it is the case that whilst the AT route is still the major route to the top, there are enlarged possibilities for professional officer and Executive Officer entrants to attain top posts. What happens to women on these routes is thus part of the overall picture of women's position *vis-à-vis* top jobs. However, it was not possible to enlarge the 1978 study to make a systematic comparison between the careers of women on the AT route with the careers of women on the routes upwards from other entry points. Nevertheless, wherever possible this study refers to the experience of women on other routes, particularly that with the entry grade of Executive Officer.

The 1968 study reviewed the historical experience of women in the Civil Service, tracing the steps whereby the Service moved from being a totally male institution to one where it was accorded accolades for its employment practices relating to women. In the 1970s the Service's concern to be a good employer of women is still apparent: early in the decade it reviewed women's employment opportunities within the Service and implemented various changes. In the 1970s compared with the 1960s, however, the Civil Service is operating in a changed context. There is much more public commitment, expressed by a range of institutions such as the women's movement and the legislation on sex equality, to fostering women's career opportunities; in particular, those of married women with children. This present Women in Top Jobs study is concerned with discovering how the Civil Service has responded to the more radical context of the 1970s.

The study has employed a similar range of techniques to that of the previous one to gain information. Chapter 1 uses aggregate statistical data supplied by the Civil Service to discuss changes in the proportion of women working in and being recruited to the higher grades of the Administration Group. The subsequent three chapters are based on direct enquiries that the present study made of civil servants. A small sample of men and women administrators answered a questionnaire and, in some cases, were interviewed.[2] They gave information on their own careers and furnished their impressions of the factors affecting women's careers in the Civil Service over the last ten years. Chapter 2 uses these data to provide a limited but objective account of men and women administrators' career patterns: it also reports the impressions and interpretations of the situation given by these administrators. In Chapter 3 the same source of information is used to discuss the effect that having children and caring for them has on women administrators' careers. In both of these chapters information from another set of direct enquiries is used: the Civil Service permitted the researcher to contact civil servants in several departments who had responsibility for aspects of employment policy affecting women. A number were interviewed, replied to questions by letter and supplied documentary information. In addition, the researcher contacted union officers and members of recently formed women's groups in the Civil Service. The aim of these enquiries was to establish details of current Civil Service policy towards women and to gain a sense of whether group views, be they of management, unions or women's groups, existed over particular issues. Information from these enquiries appears in Chapter 2 when women's progress through the AT streaming process is discussed and in Chapter 3 in the discussion of part-time working and child-care provision: it is used more extensively in Chapter 4 which seeks to ascertain how policy on direct and indirect discrimination has been implemented in the Civil Service in the 1970s and to assess what, if anything, still has to be achieved.

References
(1) M. P. Fogarty (ed.), Isobel Allen, A. J. Allen and Patricia Walters, *Women in Top Jobs – Four Studies in Achievement*, Allen and Unwin, 1971.
(2) Details on number of informants, and on how they were initially identified, appear on pp. 47–48.

CHAPTER 1

The Number of Women in the Higher Grades

At the time of the previous study in 1968, numbers and proportions of women in the grades of the Administrative Class were as follows:

No	women Permanent Secretaries	0% out of a total of	28
2	women Deputy Secretaries	2.5% out of a total of	80
7	women Under Secretaries	2.4% out of a total of	291
51	women Assistant Secretaries	6.1% out of a total of	837
112	women Principals	9.8% out of a total of	1,140
54	women Assistant Principals	17.0% out of a total of	318½

226 women higher Administrators   8.4% out of a total of 2,694½
Note: Figures dated 1st January and part-time posts count as half.

In 1978 subsequent to the re-structuring of the Administrative, Departmental and other classes to form the Open Structure and the Administration Group, numbers and proportions of women in the equivalent grades[1] were:

Open Structure

No	women Permanent Secretaries	0% out of a total of	39
4	women Deputy Secretaries	2.7% out of a total of	149
22½	women Under Secretaries	4.0% out of a total of	557

Grades in the Administration Group

55	women Assistant Secretaries	4.7% out of a total of	1,172
346½	women Principals	7.8% out of a total of	4,435½
258	women ATs & HEO(A)s	27.2% out of a total of	948

686 women higher Administrators   9.4% out of a total of 7,300½
Note: Figures dated 1st January and part-time posts count as half.

The 1978 figures show that women are still a small minority in the authoritative and prestigious grades of the Civil Service. The only substantial proportion of women is the 27 per cent in the training grades: at the top of the hierarchy there have been no women Permanent Secretaries since Dame Evelyn Sharp retired in 1966.

These two sets of figures do not provide a precise guide to changes in the proportion of women in the various grades between the two years, because the figures for 1978 are much wider in scope than the 1968 figures for the Administrative Class. Interpreting the figures in terms of changes in their coverage leads to the conclusion that in 1978 women's representation in administration grades beyond the training grade is not as low in comparison with 1968 as it at first seems. There are grounds for depicting a small increase in the proportion of women in several grades: clearly in the case of the training grade the increase has been substantial.

At the top, in the grades of Under Secretary and above there is a strong similarity between both years – no women Permanent Secretaries and all but a handful of women appearing in the Under Secretary grade. In 1978 the proportion of women Under Secretaries, whilst still small (4 per cent), is an increase on the 1968 figure. The 1978 total for the grade incorporates professional posts whereas that for 1968 does not, and this almost certainly depresses the proportion of women recorded in 1978 by comparison with 1968. Traditionally, women have been scarcer at the top of the Civil Service professional hierarchies as a whole than they have been in the administrative hierarchy. This is borne out by the fact that the 1978 women Under Secretaries were more likely than men Under Secretaries to have had previous careers in administrative posts as opposed to professional posts. The increase in the proportion of women Under Secretaries between 1968 and 1978 results from the fact that more women were recruited into the Administrative Class in the 1940s than in the 1930s. Women entrants from the 1940s have not, however, repeated the experience of the 1930s women and provided Permanent Secretaries from amongst their ranks. Changes in the posts incorporated in the Assistant Secretary grade probably help only to a limited extent to account for the proportional decline in women at this rank between the two years. Earlier recruitment patterns, however, have probably had a greater influence. In the late 1950s and early 1960s the proportion of women amongst Administrative Class entrants fell, consequently in the 1970s, the Assistant Secretary grade has been recruiting from a promotion field relatively bereft of women compared with that from which Assistant Secretaries were recruited ten years ago.

The Principal grade is one which between 1968 and 1978 has undergone both significant change in coverage and marked expansion of numbers. As a result the number of Principals recorded is four times higher in 1978 than in 1968: women's proportionate place in the grade, however, showed a decrease. This could well be accounted for by the changes just referred to: both changes involved the incorporation into the Principal grade of Executive Civil Servants with twenty years or so work experience, amongst whom men vastly out-numbered women. The 1968 and 1978 figures really refer to two different entities, with the Principal grade in 1968 containing a far higher proportion of 'administrative' Principals.[2] In 1978 just under 15 per cent of Principals could be counted as 'administrative' Principals and amongst them the proportion of women was higher than that amongst Principals generally.

In both 1978 and 1968 women's representation is strongest in the training grade: in 1968 women formed 17 per cent of this grade; by 1978 this was 27 per cent, an increase of just over half. Interpreting these figures involves following up two separate changes, first, change in the nature of the training scheme which has operated since 1971 and which has involved a sizeable increase in the number of recruits into the scheme, and second, the increase in the rate at which women have been entering the administration competitions.

In 1971 Administration Trainee competitions replaced the competitions through which Assistant Principals had been recruited. The major Assistant Principal competition, the 'open' competition, was for young university graduates who competed through a qualifying examination, Civil Service Selection Board competitions and a Final Selection Board interview. A minor competition which produced a much smaller number of Assistant Principals, the 'limited' competition, was restricted to candidates already in the Civil Service. The AT competitions preserved the distinction between two entry routes, i.e. one for young university graduates and one for in-service candidates, and, amongst the latter, they allowed candidates to enter either on their own initiative or through the nomination of their department. During the 1970s between 100 to 200 ATs have been recruited each year. These numbers represented a considerable increase on those recruited annually through both Assistant Principal Competitions. The reason for this was the changed nature of the training scheme in the 1970s: instead of serving solely the function of recruiting future top administrators, it had the enlarged purpose of recruiting to middle management in the Administration Group. Thus built into the scheme has been a streaming process which the Civil Service Department has described as follows:[3]

> For their first two years ATs are on probation. If at the end of that period their performance is judged satisfactory, their status as ATs is confirmed. They are then eligible to be fast-streamed, that is promoted to HEO(A), with the expectation of reaching the Principal grade in a further 2–3 years. Those ATs not thought suitable for the fast stream can be assigned to the main stream at any time after the end of their third year. After a minimum of 3 years ATs are eligible for promotion to HEO and can be put before an HEO board in competition with EOs. No AT can remain in the grade for longer than 4 years: by that time all must be either promoted to HEO(A) or promoted to HEO, or, for those who fail the departmental HEO promotion board, regraded to EO . . . Fast-streamed ATs join the HEO(A) grade: after 2–3 years they may be put before a Principal promotion board and compete with SEOs for promotion to Principal. Most of them are expected to reach at least Assistant Secretary level in the course of their subsequent careers. Main-streamed ATs serve as HEOs and look for promotion through the SEO grade. In due course most of them can expect to reach Principal and the best can expect to go to Assistant Secretary and beyond. There are no obstacles to their outstripping those in the fast-stream whose development has not matched their early promise.

How have women fared in the recruitment process of the 1970s compared with that of the 1960s?

There has been a substantial rise in the proportion of women among external candidates in the competitions. Between 1960 and 1967 women formed nearly 19 per cent of the candidates in the Method I and Method II procedures. Between 1971 and 1978 there were 6,003 women applicants and 9,256 men applicants and women formed 38 per cent of the total external applicants in the years from 1970 to 1978: in 1978 alone they formed 45 per cent. The increasing proportion of women in the number of external applicants in the 1970s is a result both of the increase in the proportion of women amongst graduating students and the increasing propensity of these women to apply for competitions. Thus in the six years between 1960 and 1966 women formed 37 per cent of the annual number of graduates with first and second class honours degrees in arts and social sciences:[4] in the six years between 1971 and 1977 the figure had risen to 45 per cent. In these two six-year periods women applicants to the AT competitions were 4 per cent and 8 per cent respectively of the total of such women graduates.

The recent rapid increase in the recruitment of women to the undergraduate body of Oxford and Cambridge may well subsequently have a marked effect on the number of women entering the AT competitions. Male and female arts and social science students at Oxford and Cambridge have always been both more likely to enter the AT selection process than arts and social science students elsewhere, and more likely to succeed in it.[5] Up to now, however, the number of women arts and social science undergraduates at Oxbridge has been much smaller than that of men undergraduates in these subjects; for example, between 1961 and 1975 women formed 18 per cent of the graduates in arts and social sciences produced by Oxford and Cambridge. This situation is, however, changing rapidly. Thus in October 1979 women formed 36 per cent of the undergraduate admissions to Oxford and 29 per cent of those to Cambridge. In another two or three years this rise might feed through into the AT application process.

One aspect of women's candidature in the direct entrant competitions has not changed between the 1960s and 1970s: women are still less successful than men in the competitions. In the years from 1971 to 1978 there were 543 successful women and 1,284 successful men – respectively 9 per cent and 14 per cent of women and men applicants. In the eight years between 1960 and 1967 women formed 12 per cent of the successes in the open competitions compared with 19 per cent of the candidates and in the eight years between 1970 and 1977 they formed 30 per cent of the successes compared with 39 per cent of the applicants. Furthermore, in the 1960s and 1970s women succeeding in the competition have on average attained lower marks than men.

In 1968 the Women in Top Jobs study found it was easier to show that women did worse than to judge why. Since then the Civil Service Department has analysed the performance of external candidates in the 1973, 1974 and 1975 AT competitions. The approach adopted was a multivariate one that enabled account to be taken of any relationships that existed between the background features themselves rather than simply examining them one at a time. It was found that sex had virtually no independent effect: the same was true of school background. Oxbridge attendance, however, was a variable with a strong independent effect: candidates from Oxford and Cambridge did better than candidates from other universities. The apparent variation in the success rates of men and women in these years, it was concluded, was largely accounted for by the fact that a smaller proportion of the women than of the men applicants had attended Oxford and Cambridge: between 1971 and 1975 for instance 27 per cent of the male external AT candidates, compared with only 12 per cent of the females, had attended Oxford and Cambridge. Again, one would expect the increasing proportion of women amongst Oxbridge undergraduates to work through in the next few years to affect women's success rates in the external AT competitions.

External recruits dominate the AT competitions. Between 1971 and 1978 close to 75 per cent of the applicants and nearly 80 per cent of the successful competitors were external. In the minor in-service competitions the proportion of women applicants is smaller than it is amongst the external competitors (20 per cent between 1971 and 1978 as opposed to 39 per cent). In-service women applicants have a slightly better success rate than in-service men applicants: 7 per cent of the in-service women applicants were successful between 1971 and 1978 as opposed to 6.6 per cent of the in-service men. Women's somewhat better performance is probably connected with the higher proportion of departmental nominees amongst them.

Today, as in 1968, the main route to the top posts of Under Secretary and above in the Civil Service is a ladder stretching from the AT grade through the intervening grades of Principal and Assistant Secretary. Thus the key to considering the proportion of women in top Civil Service posts at any one time lies initially in their numerical representation amongst express route entrants some thirty years earlier, and then, in the factors that act upon the careers of women entrants. At all times in the past the women who arrive at the top have been a much smaller minority than those who set out. An indicator of this can be culled from aggregate grade statistics. In 1978 women formed about 5 per cent of the Assistant Secretary grade. Looking back to the entry grade of Assisant Principal in 1958, a year when 1978 Assistant Secretaries were likely to have been in it, women then formed 14 per cent of the personnel. Obviously no two groups of entrants separated by a number of years have the same experience. But it is very likely that the proportion that women now form of the training grade – 27 per cent – will be reduced by the time these trainees reach the Assistant Secretary grade: the significant questions are by how much and why? The subsequent chapters of this study examine the forces which during the 1970s have affected the careers of women on the express route.

References

(1) In the new structure virtually all the old nomenclature of the Administrative Class has been retained. Only one of the former grades has been renamed: the Assistant Principal grade has been replaced by the two grades of Administration Trainee, (AT) and Higher Executive Officer (Administration), (HEO(A)).

(2) For an elaboration of the distinction between 'administrative' Principals and others see subsequently p. 45.

(3) House of Commons Papers 1975–1976 No. 368–VII, *Developments in the Civil Service since the Fulton Report, Evidence of the Civil Service Department.*

(4) Graduates in arts and social sciences with first and second class honours degrees are the population from which AT applicants are most likely to come.

(5) House of Commons Papers 1975–1976 No. 368–VIII, *Developments in the Civil Service since the Fulton Report, Evidence of Civil Service Commission.*

CHAPTER 2

Careers in Higher Administration

The first hurdle of the administrative career is the streaming process, undertaken by each department, which commences after the two years spent as Administration Trainee. Immediately at the end of the two years or at some time during the subsequent two years ATs are either 'fast streamed' – become Higher Executive Officers (Administration) and two or three years after that are considered for appointment to Principal, or they are 'main streamed' – serve as Higher Executive Officers and look for promotion through the Senior Executive Officer grade. Women AT entrants in the early 1970s left at a somewhat higher rate than men during the first five years of their career. But the proportion of men leaving has been almost one fifth: thus the wastage rate amongst both men and women during the first few years is quite considerable. Amongst those who stay five years beyond entering, a smaller percentage of women than of men is fast streamed. The observation that women are not being fast streamed to the same extent as are the men is important and points to the need for careful scrutiny of women's performance at this particular entry-point to the Principal grade.

Research has been done by the Civil Service Commission which involved analysing the evaluations made, during the first two training years, of ATs who entered in 1971 and 1972. According to the report on the research[1] there was some slight statistical evidence that sex and the evaluations made of ATs were associated. Thus:

> The slight tendency for men to fare better on present performance ratings than women is not strong enough to respond positively to statistical inference tests, except in one instance [out of four].

and

> The relationship between the long-term potential rating and sex is stronger here than is the case for 'present performance'. Although the evidence is not entirely unequivocal, the men are expected to progress further than the women.

One department has closely scrutinised progress through the AT scheme. The numbers of both men and women were very small – 50 and 21 respectively – but the findings cannot be completely discounted on these grounds. Departmental findings were in line with service-wide findings: proportionately less of the women than of the men were fast streamed. The departmental analysis contained information on the distribution of the Final Selection Board marks achieved by the ATs, i.e. as to whether individuals had been graded A, B or C. This enabled a comparison to be made between the performance in the AT streaming process of men and women who had been judged at the FSB to have broadly equivalent levels of ability. Attainment of an A or B grade from the FSB can be considered high achievement: so too can the attainment of fast streaming in the AT scheme. Comparing this set of departmental entrants in terms of their two performances, the following observations can be made. First it appears that overall the department judged them more favourably than had the FSB:[2] it placed a small proportion of them in the main stream (35 per cent) than the FSB had placed in the C category (53 per cent) and a higher proportion of them in the fast stream (65 per cent) than the FSB had placed in the A and B categories (47 per cent). So overall it seems that the evaluations made by these people during the AT scheme were enhanced compared with those made at the entry. It is also clear from the data that the evaluations made of women did not shift upwards to the same degree as did those made of men. In the FSB 44 per cent of all the men gained C marks but in the AT process 13 per cent of all the men were mainstreamed: of the women 63 per cent were C streamed at FSB and 56 per cent were mainstreamed. The department concerned looked closer at the individual men and women who gained a C mark at FSB and who were streamed in the AT process. It was found that 23 per cent of these men were put into mainstream as compared with 90 per cent of the women. According to a senior woman official in the department:

> We fear that women entrants may be being judged by different standards compared with the men, without the streaming boards being conscious that this is happening. There may be truth in the contention that women have to prove clearly that they are successful whereas the men are assumed to be successful until they definitely demonstrate that they are failures.

Fast-streamed ATs generally join the Principal grade in their late twenties. Principals of this age are a minority in the grade. A recent study of the Civil Service[3] comments that

> the level of Principal provides the greatest contrast between the ex-members of the old Executive Class and the administrative élite. An 'executive' Principal is typically in his late forties and fifties and in charge of a staff of 150. An 'administrative' Principal is usually about thirty, with a minimal staff, working at a Department's headquarters on a range of policy-related problems.

Whilst direct-entrant ATs/HEO(A)s are the major source of young administrative Principal appointments there are four other sources from which the young Principals are appointed. These are:

(i)   promotion from the grade of Senior Executive Officer;
(ii) promotion from the HEO(A) grade having been an in-service entrant into the AT scheme;
(iii) appointment from amongst a body of applicants who have held other occupations outside the Civil Service – 'direct-entry Principals';
(iv) appointment from specialist occupations in the Civil Service.

In the two years 1977 and 1978 there were 165 and 164 promotions respectively from all routes into the Principal grade of people under 35 years of age. Averaging the two years out, the proportions amongst them were as follows: direct-entry ATs 48 per cent, SEO promotees 24 per cent, in-service AT or HEO(A) entrants 10 per cent, direct-entry Principals 9 per cent and specialist occupations in the Civil Service 9 per cent.[4] These routes by which young Principals arrive tend to distinguish themselves in terms of whether those on them have either entered the Civil Service with the intention of becoming higher grade generalist administrators (this is so in the case of the HEO(A) direct entrant and the direct-entry Principal routes) or have been spotted and encouraged from within the ranks of the Civil Service (this is so in the case of the remaining three routes). The division of the grades in this way tends to coincide with a division made on the basis of the degree to which women are present on these routes. Thus on average in 1977 and 1978 the proportion of women on the direct-entry route and the direct-entry Principal route was 23 per cent and 20 per cent respectively, whilst on the route from SEO and that from grades outside of the

Administration Group it was 6 per cent and 0 per cent respectively. The major explanation of the difference in the presence of women in these two sets of routes lies in a preceding difference in the proportion that women form of the groups from which young Principals are drawn, e.g. in 1978 women formed 27 per cent of the AT/HEO(A) grades, whereas in 1977 and 1978 combined women formed 8 per cent of the SEOs aged between 30 and 34. These observations emphasise that were there to be future moves to increase the contribution that SEOs and specialists make to membership of the express route at Principal level (this is still urged by those who feel the Civil Service has not done enough to 'open up' the express route), then, without measures to improve the career achievement of women in the executive ranks and specialist grades, the proportion of women in the higher administration grades would suffer as a consequence.

The point of getting people into the Principal grade in their twenties is to give talented individuals time to reveal and form themselves in the grade *and* to leave time for them to function subsequently at the four other levels of the administrative hierarchy. It is from amongst young Principals that high flyers are spotted. High flyers are those who establish a good reputation for themselves and who as a consequence are given a number of job assignments at Principal and Assistant Secretary level that are recognised as being the most demanding of the range of jobs at these levels.

The characteristics of those who become high flyers and the shape of high-flying careers does not seem to have changed very much in the ten years between 1968 and 1978. Whilst in the 1970s the Civil Service has increased the recruitment of young Principals from several routes, it still appears to be the case that Principals recruited through the traditional mechanism of University $\longrightarrow$ Civil Service Selection Board Competitions $\longrightarrow$ Training Grades possess the greatest chance of becoming high flyers. Compared with ten years ago, central management of high-flying careers appears to be somewhat more pronounced. In 1968 the personnel management functions for the Service as a whole were taken from the Treasury and became the province of the newly established Civil Service Department. Currently departments inform the Civil Service Department about the civil servants who appear to have the potential to reach the Open Structure: the Civil Service Department seeks to ensure that those identified have the chance of postings in central departments, i.e. Treasury, Cabinet Office, Civil Service Department. Promotion to and within the Open Structure is a responsibility shared by individual departments and the Civil Service Department.

Amongst the posts at Principal and Assistant Secretary level to which departments appoint flyers in order to test and to develop them are private secretaryships to a Cabinet Minister, politically sensitive posts that can well expect a pretty constant stream of pressure issues and also, increasingly, posts which involve weighty managerial responsibilities in running large-scale government services. High flyers can expect promotions to Assistant Secretary and Under Secretary grades earlier than those who become Principals alongside them: currently high flyers are attaining Assistant Secretary rank at thirty-three to thirty-five years of age and Under Secretary rank during their early forties. The culmination of a high-flying career is appointment to Permanent Secretary rank after some time spent as Deputy Secretary. Not all young Principals become high-flyers and there are late developers: there are amongst top administrators a minority who were not tipped as high-flyers until their late thirties or early forties.

What can one say about women's chances of moving beyond Under Secretary? The most conclusive evidence that one can bring to bear on this question derives from a close examination of the careers of men and women who entered by the gate most favourable for subsequent success (the direct entrant, open competition route) and who have been in the service for similar amounts of time.[5] This present study draws upon its own cohort study in providing evidence on the careers of men and women direct entrants who have served for similar lengths of time.

Cohort study: method and findings

To assure direct comparison and continuity with the 1968 study the Civil Service agreed to the women and men who featured in the 1968 investigation being recontacted. In 1968 these respondents were chosen in the following manner: all the women who entered as Assistant Principals in the years 1947, 1948, 1949, 1953, 1954, 1960, 1961, 1962 and 1963 and were still in the service in 1968 were identified by the Civil Service (total 36). A sample of male entrants matched by department was made to yield a similar number of men (total 41). Response to the questionnaire was voluntary and yielded 26 women and 34 men. By 1978 the number of these respondents identifiable as still in the service was 20 women and 27 men: of these 17 women and 21 men returned the questionnaire sent to them at the end of 1978. Eight of the women respondents were also interviewed. In 1968 all the respondents were in the middle management ranks of the Administrative Class; they were Principals and Assistant Secretaries. By 1978 many of them had made or were close to making the transition to Open Structure posts. From their accounts of this transition the current study extends the 1968 picture of their career achievements.

In addition, administrators who had entered as Assistant Principals in the years 1966, 1967 and 1968 were contacted. Questionnaires were sent to all the women and a sample of men who, having entered in the years mentioned, were still in the service in 1978. From the total of 24 women and 20 men sent questionnaires, 17 women and 14 men returned them. Subsequently 7 women were interviewed. The reason for choosing these new respondents was to study again in 1978 the crucial years of the administrative career identified in 1968. Administration Trainees are appointed Principal in their late twenties and early thirties: important decisions are made about them and their capabilities in the early years in the Principal grade. The age at which this is happening is also the age at which men and women administrators are involved in establishing and caring for young families.

The resources available meant that this survey had to proceed by voluntary questionnaire, that it could only take a sample of men, and that it had to limit itself to a selection of years of entry. All of these factors help to account for findings that are, from a statistical point of view, based on small numbers. For this reason the following account is not expressed in numerical terms.

In the subsequent presentation men and woman administrators are divided into different age groups determined by difference of time of entry. There is basically a two-fold division into entrants between 1947 and 1954 and entrants between 1960 and 1968. These are frequently referred to as the 'older' and 'younger' entrants. Most of the former are in their fifties: most of the latter are in their thirties.

The older entrants featured in the 1968 investigation. As will become clear in the subsequent discussion, there is a further sub-division of both the older and younger entrants – distinguishing amongst the older between those who entered in the 1940s and those who entered in the 1950s and amongst the younger between those who entered in the early 1960s and those who entered in 1966, 1967 and 1968.

The 1968 study came to the conclusion, from a number of sources of information, including its own cohort study, that up to then women had not progressed through the administrative world with the same success and mastery as men. The difference in attainment seemed to narrow as one came closer to 1968. Differences seemed most pronounced in the case of pre-1939 entrants to the class: two-thirds of the women entrants from this period covered by the Survey of Civil Servants were still serving as Principals in 1968, whereas only one-third of the men entrants were. Women subsequently had not done as badly as this: nevertheless, in the post-war period they appeared less likely than the men to provide the high flyers. The women who became Under Secretaries seemed more likely than men to attain this post at the end of their career rather than as a step to higher things.

Ten years on, in 1978, the older respondents in the cohort survey have had careers of twenty-five to thirty years' duration. Amongst the 1940s entrants there appears to be some distinction between the men's and women's experience that is not present amongst the 1951 to 1954 entrants. In the case of the older entrants women respondents lag behind the men, certainly on the age at which they attain Assistant Secretary and Under Secretary appointments and, some-what less clearly, on the extent to which they have been made Under and Deputy Secretaries. By contrast what is noticeable about the 1951 to 1954 entrants is the exact similarity between the sexes in average age at which promotions have been attained and the similarity between them in the degree to which they have gained grades of Under Secretary and higher. Furthermore, when the older entrants were questioned about future promotion, it was from amongst the 1951 to 1954 entrants that one or two senior women administrators emerged who felt sufficiently confident about their remaining career not to limit their hopes to attaining Deputy Secretaryships. As a guide these responses obviously have little reliability but there does seem the possibility that in the next five years one or two senior women civil servants will be in line for Permanent Secretary appointments.

Looking at the careers – between ten and eighteen years in length – of men and women recruited in the 1960s, there are obviously less career indicators by which to distinguish individuals. These entrants are now in the field for Assistant Secretary appointments: a glance at what is happening here does not suggest that the men have the edge in these appointments. Comparing the women and men who entered in the early 1960s, the picture is the same for both: the majority in each case were Assistant Secretaries by 1978 and there was no difference in the average age at which they had attained their promotion. Looking at the later (1966, 1967 and 1968) entrants it appears at first sight that men have the edge: thus a higher proportion of the men entrants than of the women had been appointed Assistant Secretary. But on closer examination the average age of the men exceeded that of the women by a year, thus giving the men at the time of the enquiry a somewhat greater chance of promotion. Certainly there was no discernible difference in the age at which the appointments of men and women Assistant Secretaries had been made.

These men and women were asked about their careers in the future: a highly speculative exercise for people who still have 20 to 30 years of working life. It was, noticeable, however, that between men and women there was a very similar distribution of estimates of the grade in which they expected to end their career.

From the preceding account it can be suggested that the Civil Service made a discernible move towards establishing equality of treatment in promotion between men and women administrators with recruits who came in from the beginning of the 1950s. Practice with those who entered in the 1940s seems to have been somewhat different. The strongest evidence from which one can argue equality of promotion treatment post-1950 concerns the move from Principal to Assistant Secretary: this is the career step for which this study has the longest series of findings. Women have, since the early 1950s, proportionately made this step as early as men. It is certainly the case that early attainment of Assistant Secretaryships is important to further high flying. There is no such serial evidence on the step from Assistant Secretary to Under Secretary but the experience of the 1951 to 1954 cohort does suggest that currently the Civil Service recognises and rewards ability to a fairly similar extent amongst men and women eligible for the career step to Under Secretary.

Administrative careers can be compared not only in terms of the grades attained and the age at which grades are attained: they can also be compared in terms of the postings that they involve. Such a comparison is a much more difficult exercise: there are very large numbers of postings; detailed inside knowledge is required to make assessments of their prestige and importance, and this can, in any case, change over time. Nevertheless as was pointed out earlier, it is a feature of career management in the Civil Service that significant front-line, especially important, posts are identified in the administrative work of departments and care is taken to staff them with high flyers. High-flying careers, ending at Permanent Secretary level, are likely to have had two elements: earlier than average attainment of the grades of Assistant and Under Secretary *and* a series of front-line postings. It follows from this that if there is some evidence that women have less successful careers in terms of postings then they may be less likely than men to be appointed Permanent Secretaries.

It seems possible that in the postings process a 'streaming' effect operates: that the performance of those picked in the first five to ten years of their careers to fill front-line posts becomes enhanced by the expectations held of them, and by the opportunities present in the job. Of course, it is possible for high flyers to disappoint and, of course, it is possible for those assigned to more routine posts to shine: but it is questionable whether such occurrences are frequent enough to cast doubt on the streaming hypothesis. Evidence as to the enhancing effect that good postings have on administrative performance was supplied by the follow-up study that the Civil Service Department conducted of five years of AT entrants. It was found that where AT entrants gaining 'lower grade' FSB marks in the entrance competition were given 'high quality' training posts then they were more likely to be 'fast streamed' at the end of their training process than were those ATs with 'higher grade' FSB marks who had been placed in 'low quality' training posts.[6]

What criteria are used in the early career years in assigning people to front-line posts? The account given by Civil Service management is that what counts is demonstrated ability, initially in the selection process and, beyond that, in the training and early

Principal years. Their explanation of any evidence that women as a group occupy less of the front-line postings than men is that this is a result of different group rates of demonstrated ability from the selection process onwards. The present research, similar to the 1968 research, raised the question of whether there was some element of a 'sex factor' in the postings process.

Evidence that men were preferred for the acknowledged tough and crucial assignments was certainly furnished in interviews in the 1968 study: and there is evidence that the lower career achievements, compared with their male contemporaries, of women entrants in the 1940s had within it an element of discriminatory treatment over postings. The question is, has this continued in the careers of younger entrants? Overall the evidence is ambiguous. Some older women respondents in the 1978 study took the opportunity to emphasise demonstrable improvement. One wrote that compared with 10 or 20 years ago:

> Women are certainly getting better opportunities in administrative work. We have recently had for the first time a woman Principal Private Secretary to the Minister – and she was promoted from that job to one in charge of large numbers of technical training staff which had never previously been held by a woman. There are no inhibitions now about the types of work to which women principals are allocated – they are used for example on industrial relations which was not the case when I was young.

But the 1978 enquiry also yielded evidence that consideration of sex did appear to play a role in some posting decisions. Thus one 1966 entrant recounted a very explicit instance in which she was 'passed over' for a highly responsible post on grounds of sex; another contended that Ministers in her department had discriminated against women in making choices of Assistant Private Secretaries. One male informant recounted:

> I know of only one case where prejudice reared its head: my department thought the best person for a certain foreign post was a woman but hesitated to ask her because of complications about her husband's job. I said 'you must ask her'. They did so and she and her husband sorted things out.

This particular account is double-edged in that it illustrates that assumptions do tend to be made about women's lesser availability compared with men's, about the constraints that will limit their usefulness to the organisation: it also illustrates that there are within the administrative Civil Service mechanisms grounds for challenging the application of these assumptions to particular individuals. The double-edged nature of the evidence is further present in the evidence on postings available to the 1978 cohort study. Certainly it was much less usual for women to be appointed Private Secretary to a Minister during their Principal and Assistant Secretary years. But when it came to another set of 'high-flying' postings – secondments made to the central departments of Cabinet Office, Treasury and Civil Service Department – then women Principals and Assistant Secretaries fared as well as men.

On the basis of the evidence presented here one can argue that currently no very gross stereotyping of men and women takes place with relation to the postings process in the Principal and Assistant Secretary grades. One would not, however, say there were grounds for completely abandoning the judgement made in the 1968 study that there are 'understandings, attitudes and mores which are part of the texture of the informal organisation of higher administration and which operate to steer women more than men away from the scenes of important action and hence lessen the likelihood of their being seen as candidates for top posts'.[7]

The 1968 report noted that the administrative world was one where women have entered a unitary structure; that they have not had the opportunity to carve specialised spheres for themselves but have had to prove to a predominantly male audience that they can do as well as men what formerly men alone used to do. It went on to remark that if one considered the careers of the small number of women who up to the 1960s had broken through to the top ranks of administration then a noticeable feature of the careers of quite a few of them was that they had been given important demanding posts during periods of crisis and manpower shortage. The war years and the reorganisation of economic departments in the 1960s seem to have been occasions when acute shortage of talent loosened up the informal structure and its sex type-casting tendencies. In the 1970s there have been factors which have helped to weaken these tendencies still further. One respondent described them thus:

It has become almost fashionable to support the feminist cause at the upper levels . . . most (but not all) men in the Administrative Class equivalents are sensible and intelligent enough to realise that they have little rational basis for discrimination against women. And they recognise that the increase in the number of women recruited at this level has created career expectations which must be met.

It is also possible that the improvements which many of the older women saw in the postings being given to women in the 1960s and 1970s are a function of improvements in general career opportunities. The past fifteen years, bar the last one or two, have been years of expanding job opportunities in the middle and higher administration ranks: years in which many new posts have been created. In the 1950s different circumstances prevailed: large numbers of post-war recruits faced fairly limited career opportunities and in those circumstances departments seem to have brought men to the fore. How do career opportunities look for people at present Principals and Assistant Secretaries? In the immediate future the Civil Service is looking to bring people on fairly quickly to Under Secretary level to replace the large proportion of that level who are currently retiring. It is this policy which has recently brought down the lower age limit of Assistant Secretary appointments. But after the next few years, relatively young Under Secretaries may well face compara- tively few opportunities for further upward movement. If there is a log jam in the Open Structure in the 1980s it will be interesting to see how relatively well the two sexes negotiate through it.

Certainly this present enquiry into the express administrative career stream cannot support the judgement that a tendency to discount women against men is completely a thing of the past. The discounting that does take place is subtle and not readily identified: it is closely bound up with cultural judgements of appropriate behaviour for men and women and often involves fine distinctions of language. The judgements made about men and women rarely seem questionable in individual cases. It is only when a broad sweep is taken through a large number of reports that the pattern of the language used and the judgements made starts to emerge. Thus the 1968 study reported a Civil Service Commission comparison of men and women administrators in terms of the rating that their work performance received on a special report form.[8] There were no significant differences between the sexes when six highly specific aspects of administrative performance were considered: significant differences between the judgements made of men and women appeared when (a) their ability and (b) their future potential were considered. Women were judged less likely than men to be highly dependable, adapt well to new situations and take most difficulties in their stride, and a significantly lower proportion of them were judged as having the potential to gain Under Secretary ranking. What seemed significant in this data was that when comparing men and women in specific aspects of their work such as 'paper work, figure work, meetings' the evaluators saw little difference between men and women, but when faced with a category that called for an overall evaluation of style and approach to work then the evaluators strongly distinguished between them. In the 1970s the departmental evidence on evaluations of men and women made in the AT scheme[9] points to the possibility that whilst women ATs of high administrative potential recommend themselves to their superiors no less than talented men, amongst ATs who are more run-of-the-mill then the men are preferred and given the benefit of the doubt in the way that the women are not.

This study is concerned with the highest administrative posts and women's chances of attaining them. Consequently it has focused on the Principal grade as a gateway to the top. For the majority of people in it, however, the Principal grade is a terminal career grade, albeit one involving significant responsibility and, in national terms, high salary. The present study collected no direct evidence on promotion up the executive career ladder into the Principal grade. It did, however, encounter two departments where calculations had been made of the rate at which men and women Senior Executive Officers were appointed Principal during recent years. One department looking at three years' figures remarked on the 'nose-dive' which women's rates took at this level of promotion. Figures from the other department, the Department of Health and Social Security, were published and are referred to later in this study. They show that for one of the two years investigated women were clearly less successful than men in the promotion board interviews and that in both years women were definitely less likely than men to be invited to a promotion board. It was noticeable in the interviews conducted for this current Women in Top Jobs study that the strongest statements about discriminatory attitudes in the Civil Service referred to the middle Administration grades. It was here, said one woman Assistant Secretary, that there was 'a real problem'. She continued:

For those who make it to HEO the pyramid above narrows dramatically. In my organisation we have a field staff of 15,000. There are a number of women EO/HEO managers of local offices, a respectable proportion of SEO district managers are female. There is *one woman Principal* in the field organisation, out of some 35–40 posts; all the 18 Senior Principals and three field Assistant Secretaries are male. There are plenty of women SEOs in the field who are capable of progressing. They do not get through promotion panels and I do not believe that potential mobility difficulties explain this. This is where discrimination still operates. I suspect that the position is typical of other departments with a large field staff. The moral is that in the 1970s women get on very largely by merit if they come in near the top – but not otherwise.

References
(1) Civil Service Commission, Research Recruitment Unit, Report No. 3, pp. 23–24.
(2) Officers writing annual reports on ATs do not know FSB marks, though the Board which makes the streaming decision does.
(3) Peter Kellner and Lord Crowther Hunt, *The Civil Servants*, MacDonald and Jane, 1980.
(4) Calculations made from information supplied by Civil Service Department.
(5) There are different ways in which one can obtain this information. If one has a large enough sample of the total population of the Administration Group stratified by age, then one can analyse respondents' careers, controlling for date of entry: the Survey of Civil Servants conducted for the Fulton Commission (Fulton Committee, Vol 3(1), *Surveys and Investigations: the Social Survey of the Civil Service*, HMSO 1969), used this method and the 1968 Women in Top Jobs study drew upon its findings. One can also use a cohort approach selecting years of intake and following up careers. In 1971 the Civil Service College carried out such a study based on personnel records of all Assistant Principals who entered in the years 1946 to 1950 and who were still in the service in 1971. (P. Sherriff, *Career Patterns in the Higher Civil Service*, Civil Service Studies 2, 1976). Unfortunately this study did not distinguish between men and women.
(6) Civil Service Commission, Recruitment Research Unit, Report No 5, March 1979, p. 11. The grading of posts was based on responses to a questionnaire filled in by AT career-managers in departments, at the end of an AT posting.
(7) Fogarty, Allen, Allen and Walters, op. cit., pp. 303–304.
(8) Ibid., pp. 280–281.
(9) See previously p. 44.

CHAPTER 3

Work and Family

This chapter considers how the careers of women administrators are affected by their family responsibilities. It has two broad aspects: it seeks to establish patterns of behaviour amongst the women administrators questioned in 1978 and to compare these patterns with those identified amongst women respondents to the 1968 study;[1] it also examines how the Civil Service has treated married women employees in the 1970s. In 1971 the Civil Service accepted the proposals of a Committee (the Kemp-Jones Committee)[2] that had been established to consider

(a) how far women might be given more part-time employment in positions of responsibility;

(b) how it might be made easier for a married woman to combine looking after a family with a Civil Service career; and

(c) what retraining might be given to make it easier for women to return to Civil Service employment after a lengthy period of absence.

This chapter reviews the implementation of the Committee's proposals affecting married women.

Leaving and re-entering

Some women administrators decide at the birth of a child not to continue working. One can make no annual estimate as to what proportion of women civil servants having a child – first or other – make this decision and how this proportion has varied through the years: to obtain such information would require a special study of maternity amongst civil servants and this has never been seen to have any justification. Compared with the 1968 Women in Top Jobs sample study of administrators, the present study has an omission. It was not possible in 1978 to obtain systematic information on the last known address of leavers. Thus the present study does not make any sustained comparison between earlier and later entrants in

terms of the proportion of women leaving over a ten-year period, or
the point at which they leave, or their reasons for doing so, or their
desires for later re-entry.

Women currently resigning for family and domestic reasons are
told that they may seek reinstatement at a later date. The onus is on
them to keep in contact with their former department and the Civil
Service Department: they are told there is no guarantee of reinstatement. Gaining it at the grade at which they left the service depends
on a department's assessment of a candidate's capabilities and its
own manpower requirements.

The Kemp-Jones Committee reported that in the 1960s 'the
arrangements for a return to the Civil Service after a break still
reflect the attitude that such a thing is exceptional and that nothing
in particular should be done to encourage it – rather the reverse'.
They made several recommendations designed to increase the ease
with which women could return: only one recommendation, that
there should be a regular competition run by the Civil Service
Commission for former civil servants for reinstatement to the
Executive Officer grade, was not implemented. In fact as will be
seen in Chapter 4, the intention of this recommendation was
eventually achieved as the result of an Industrial Tribunal ruling,
under the Sex Discrimination Act 1975, over age-limits. In the 1970s
the number of reinstatements being made annually amongst middle
and higher administration grades has been very small. Several of the
major departments contacted in the course of the research could not
produce annual totals of reinstatements made or of initial enquiries
received from individuals.

By 1978 one of the women leavers contacted in the 1968 study had
been reinstated as a Principal after twelve years' absence from full-
time employment. Two features of her history are of interest. First,
she had kept herself in part-time employment during the years of her
absence. She worked mainly on Civil Service assignments including
interviewing for the Civil Service Commission and preparing case
studies for the personnel and training sides of the Treasury in the
1960s. This interim employment had, she felt, a considerable
influence on the decision to reinstate her. Second, a little more than
a year after her reinstatement she was promoted to Assistant
Secretary, having served, in all, nine years as a Principal. She said
that the boost to her morale occasioned by this was enormous and

that she subsequently experienced less of a sense of a gulf between her rank and that of her former contemporaries.

It is worth pointing out that when she was reinstated there was no discussion whatever of her promotion opportunities as a mature re-entrant. She did not broach the subject as she did not want to be seen to be 'pushy'. As it happened, she was able to capitalise on the experience gained through her part-time employment and to apply for an Assistant Secretary post with very relevant specific responsibilities. She saw this as a stroke of luck: few Assistant Secretary posts are advertised, 'trawled' is the Civil Service word, and she had in fact been previously interviewed by a general Assistant Secretary board and had not gained promotion. Reflecting on her experience, one would have thought that all parties to the reinstatement decision would benefit from a thorough and realistic discussion of future promotion possibilities.

Working full-time with children

Some women administrators leave when their children are born: some remain at work. All of the women interviewed in 1968 and 1978 who continued to work stressed that, given their initial inclination to remain at work, the encouragement and support of their husbands was vital; the husbands' support often seemed to play a crucial role in tiding them over periods of exhaustion when pressure at work or at home made the women themselves question the benefits of the combination. The 1968 study remarked that the basic factor determining a woman's decision whether or not to continue working after the birth of children was the attitude of man and wife as to what constituted acceptable patterns of married life and child rearing, for such is the nature of work in Civil Service administration that a woman with children who continues to work must hand over the bulk of their care to someone else. The 1968 study compared the information on leavers and stayers that was available from its cohort investigation and came to the conclusion that there was no clear association between the decision to continue and the occupation, income level and place of work of the husband. It seemed that even given broadly similar circumstances between couples in terms of social background, age at marriage, occupation of both spouses, assessed competence at work and expressed interest in it, the outcome in terms of the wife's continuation at work may well differ. For the women who continue working it seemed that their relationships prior to and including their marriages make the pursuit of their careers answer an important need in their own lives and sometimes in their husbands' lives. The late 1970s is a very good time at which to review the experience of women administrators with children. There still are in the service women who entered in the late 1940s who were amongst the first in peacetime conditions to combine full-time careers with motherhood. One also has at the younger end and now starting to have children the women administrators who entered in the late 1960s and early 1970s when the women's liberation movement was affecting women's intentions and aspirations.

The experience of women entrants between 1947 and 1954 still serving in 1978 indicates that women with children can forge successful careers in Civil Service administration. There was no difference between women with children and women without children when it came to the proportion of them holding Under Secretaryships and the average age at which promotions were gained. Equally some women with children as well as some without thought it likely that they themselves would attain Deputy Secretary ranking by the end of their career. But, this said, the one or two women identified amongst the 1951 and 1954 cohort of entrants as having a serious chance of being Permanent Secretaries in the near future were women without children. Thus it would seem that the observation made of women civil servants in 1968, namely that the responsibilities of family life take the ultimate competitive edge off work performance, continues to hold in their later career.

Amongst these older women administrators with children who had continued working there was a very keen perception that the difficulties involved in providing adequate substitute care for their children did not lessen when they reached school age. Indeed, there were ways in which providing care became a more complex task. Pre-school it was a matter of finding a reliable mother substitute; during the school years it became more a matter of providing the necessary support for a child to start building a life outside the home. Amongst the women contacted it was noticeable that very few of them sent their children to boarding school. Thus they faced over the long term the need to provide the kind of care that enabled their children to invite friends home to tea, travel to music, swimming lessons, etc., and to avoid having, during both health and sickness, too much of the feeling that their children were being 'farmed out' to the care of others. There were some very successful arrangements involving nannies, relatives, neighbours and friends. But the energy expended in creating a network of help and making it work did lead a substantial minority of the older women who worked whilst having two, three or four children to wonder whether, in the end, full-time work had been worth it.

The forty to fifty-year-old married women with children who, in the late 1970s, were very satisfied with the combination of career and family life that they had created had been clearly distinguishable ten years earlier when they were Principals and Assistant Secretaries. At that time they were characterised as experiencing 'very stable combinations of family and career'.[3] Ten years on there was every indication that their equable, successful journey had continued; all were now Under Secretaries, with the majority of them strongly expecting to be Deputy Secretaries before retirement. One of these women generalised from her own experience in the following terms:

> There need be no problem in the Home Civil Service in combining a career with marriage and if one plans from the start to combine a career with having a (small) family, it is possible to do this though I suspect that the problems of employing paid help will increase, not decrease, as time goes on. The husband's co-operation and genuine goodwill is probably one of the most significant factors but I think that one needs a professional approach to the organisation of one's life both at home and the office and a very careful selection of priorities in the light of the time, money and energy available to deal with what has to be done. It is pointless to expect other people to be particularly sympathetic if one has family problems which could have been foreseen and guarded against.

The other successful women subscribed to her emphasis on the need for cool professionalism on home and work fronts, though interestingly one of them had a large rather than a small family.

In addition to these women there were several who in the first Women in Top Jobs report were characterised as having unstable accommodations between career and family. These women appeared to fall into two rather different groups when interviewed in 1968. One set, when talking about their work, emphasised their high commitment to it but expressed a sense of unsatisfied ambitions and frustrations. They felt that their family commitments had led to difficulties in their work and indicated that at times they had been seriously at odds with other people in the work environment. The other set of respondents were accounted highly competent by people at work and conveyed a sense of managing their lives well. But at a deeper level they felt a basic lack of commitment to their work and in this they differed from the two sets of women administrators discussed above. They had invested a lot of time and energy in their work but after something like twenty years they strongly wanted more time to spend with their families and to develop other aspects of their lives.

Ten years on in the 1970s it was notable that much of the sense of dissatisfaction and discomfort felt by these women had not disappeared. One now expressed herself in less frustrated terms, perhaps influenced by now being an Under Secretary and only two years off retirement. Another had left the Civil Service shortly after 1968. The other women had experienced considerable frustrations in their careers post-1968: these frustrations they attributed to the interrelation of their own family circumstances with the limited options for married women administrators prevailing in the 1950s and early 1960s – full-time work or nothing. One of these women was highly committed to working full-time but in the late 1950s a domestic crisis stretching over a year had forced her to resign, there being no possibility at that time of part-time employment or special leave without pay. She was later reinstated but her absence for several years then left her feeling behind in the career stakes. When contacted in 1978 she was irritated by the fact that she had not yet been made Under Secretary: so much so that she decided to apply, successfully, for a job outside the Civil Service.

Another 1978 respondent saw herself as having suffered from the 'all or nothing' option open to her in the 1950s and 1960s. By the end of the 1960s heavy family and work responsibilities culminated in her feeling exhausted and after many years full-time employment she requested work that was three-quarters or four-fifths of a full-time appointment. She secured this in the early 1970s but found this arrangement very difficult to operate, her explanation for this being that her superiors and the personnel side of the department refused to broadcast news of the arrangement and that, therefore, her colleagues continued to expect full-time availability from her. Her dislike of this situation led to her resuming full-time status in the late 1970s and at the same time increased her desire to find a job outside the Civil Service which gave her greater freedom to manage her work schedule.

The 1968 report suggested that the women administrators interviewed might be divided into two groups. On the one hand, there were those who perceived and spoke of their work and family lives as a successful resolution of a number of challenges; because they both had this experience and perceived it this way, they inspired confidence in their colleagues and were in turn psychologically supported by this confidence. In 1978 the same behaviour appeared to be there. These women felt successful in their work, and they were the women who broke through to appointments of Under Secretary and above. On the other hand, there were women who found the going much tougher, who communicated in much more harried terms about the pressures involved in their dual commitments. Amongst this category of women both in 1968 and 1978 there was a much stronger desire for part-time working: they saw this as a mode of working that, had they been able to engage in it over a period of ten years or so, would have helped them resolve the persistent and gnawing sense of overload that they experienced.

In 1978 the researcher re-encountered, in addition to the above respondents, younger women who in 1968 were just married or had very young children: by 1978 their families were larger and older. These women too could be placed on either side of the line that divided the older respondents. There were those who were successfully proceeding up the administrative ladder but there were also those with whom the costs of their work weighed much more heavily. One Principal in her mid-thirties with two young children said:

> I think that over the last ten years the Civil Service has become generally busier, more stressful and more competitive . . . Personally I am beginning to feel that the Service is no place for any human being, male or female, who doesn't want to work fourteen hours a day, six days a week, most of the time high on adrenalin.

It must be stressed that these women are not failures, except by some very high estimation – including probably their own. They are intelligent, capable and resourceful, but their own experience has led them to the conclusion that the opportunity to work part-time in Civil Service administration is from the point of view of a woman with children a desirable and legitimate option.

Part-time work

What moves has the Civil Service made in the last ten years to develop this option? It was the conclusion of the 1968 study that:

> given the will the Service could go further than it does at present in the direction of creating part-time employment for married women administrators.

This too was the conclusion of the Kemp-Jones Committee. In its report, the committee referred to the issue of part-time work in the Civil Service as the most important and far-reaching of those that it considered. It was noticeable, it said, that in the letters which it received:

> the most frequent request was for part-time work to enable women with family responsibilities to overcome two major problems – how to fit into their out of office hours the work they must do at home and how to give adequate attention to the children . . . Various patterns of part-time work were suggested, such as mornings only and afternoons only, alternate days or weeks, and 10 a.m. to 3 p.m. each day, the pattern depending on the woman and on the job concerned. Some letters indicated that part-time work would be acceptable even if it conflicted to some extent with, for example, school hours because the problems would not be so difficult as those caused by full-time working.

The Committee's investigations revealed virtually no part-time work in 1970 and it insisted that, whilst its provision would mark a major departure in the assumptions and practices of the Civil Service, many more part-time posts at all levels of the Service should and could be provided.

Following the acceptance of the Kemp-Jones report's recommendations by the government of the day, part-time working in the Civil Service was organised on a more secure basis. Both full-time and part-time employees now have the same security of tenure. The Civil Service goes further than the Employment Protection legislation which restricts the operation of the national appeals machinery against unfair dismissal to those who work for more than sixteen hours a week. Part-time Civil Servants who work for less than 18 hours per week are, however, not included in the Principal Civil Service Pension Scheme. Part-time work is still today a rare occurrence in the Civil Service. In 1978 there was a total of 4,934 part-time posts in the Administration Group as against 250,053 full-time posts. Most of these part-time posts were held by women in the clerical grades. In the higher administrative grades the number of part-time posts is negligible – 13 posts in the Principal grade, of which seven were held by women.

Two women working as part-time Principals were amongst the 1978 respondents. Both were currently working eighteen hours a week, negotiating with their superiors on whether they arranged these hours into two and a half or five days a week. Both described their jobs as 'back room jobs', in one case acting as secretary to a permanent advisory committee and in the other case as a member of a research and planning section. One of these respondents had resigned from the Home Office in the early 1970s following the birth of her first child. After that she worked on a casual basis for the Home Office, being paid hourly on the lowest point of the Principal scale and working for about ten hours a week on a number of background papers. In 1976 the supply of assignments started to dry up and the Home Office would only consider reinstating her to a full-time post; via the Civil Service Department she was directed to the Department of Employment where she was reinstated to occupy a permanent part-time post. Not all who seek part-time employment are able to obtain it, as is shown by the following comment made by an informant:

> I like many others of my intake was keen to continue working after the birth of my first child but doing less hours than I had done. The Department was not interested – there was a widespread dislike of such arrangements at all levels. So instead I've decided to have my two children as close together as possible and hope that I can get back when the younger is nearly five.

In the 1978 study enquiries were made of several government departments about the current incidence of part-time working in the Principal grade and the general departmental policy regarding part-time working. Their replies, some of which are quoted below, revealed uniformly a very low-key approach to the question, treating it as a distant issue of no great concern to anyone:

> Over the last five years there has been only one case of part-time employment of a Principal and that was of an officer over retirement age. Going back further than five years, the very few cases of part-time working have been mostly the re-employment of officers over 60 for particular assignments. The use of flexible working hours in this Department makes it easier for staff to adjust their time in the office to enable them to cope with personal and domestic problems without any loss of salary. (Ministry of Agriculture, Fisheries and Food).

> Our guidelines as regards part-time working would be those in paragraph 38 of the 1971 Report of the Committee on Women in the Civil Service . . . This is the theory, but in practice there has been no part-time working in the Principal grade in this Department during the last five years nor have there been any applications. We do, however, have one part-time Executive Officer and a number of other part-time staff, mostly in the clerical typing, etc. grades. (HM Customs and Excise).

> Our Staff Associations do not favour the employment of part-time staff where full-time officers are available. Part-time staff other than in secretarial work are therefore comparatively small in numbers, widely dispersed geographically and split between various non-mobile groups and classes which would make promotion procedures difficult to operate. We do not therefore promote officers who are only prepared to work part-time. (Department of Health and Social Security).

> Over the last five years five Principals have undertaken some part-time work . . . the work offered has been on special short term tasks. The recruitment of part-time clerical staff was tried experimentally in one part of the Office where the type of work made it possible at a time of severe staff shortage. However, the use of such part-timers was found to be costly administratively and in the provision of accommodation, and recruitment on a part-time basis was brought to an end on completion of the experimental period. (Home Office).

About half of the administrators, men and women, who featured in the 1978 enquiry were in favour of a more vigorous attempt by management to provide more part-time work: several of them specified that these posts should be available to be requested by both men and women with responsibility for caring for dependants. One woman informant underlined this by mentioning the instance of a male colleague whose working wife was reluctant to have children because she could not count on his playing a direct role in their care.

The informants in favour of part-time work were convinced that all levels of the Administration Group have potential part-time posts that do not compromise the efficiency of the service. Several of them referring to the Principal grade were prepared to argue that efficiency did not mean confining part-time posts to work that was of a more long-term, research-orientated nature. There were Principal posts in most Divisions which carried a number of responsibilities which, as one woman Under Secretary put it, were 'at the sharp end of administrative work', i.e. carried policy responsibilities that involved rounds of meetings, responding to political pressures, which could be split and carried by an individual on a less than full-time basis. This same woman, an Under Secretary in the Ministry of Transport, detailed the way in which a large administrative post in her Division had been split into one-and-a-half jobs with the part-time post involving what she called much of the active policy end of the work, held by a married woman. One woman Assistant Secretary pointed out that:

consultant medical staff whose responsibilities are still more immediate than those of administrators, habitually have part-time appointments and in the case of a married woman a lot of care is taken to fit their work to individual needs.

A woman Principal wrote:

In general I think the difficulties of creating part-time posts are greatly exaggerated. Most Principals are not on tap all the time – after all if they are at a meeting they are not available to anyone else are they? I've never found any difficulty caused by a day or half day's absence and most patterns of part-time work don't involve longer absence than this.

Several informants gave instances from their acquaintance of line managers refusing to accede to a suggestion from personnel officers that they create part-time posts for particular individuals who had requested such employment. Two examples were given from the Customs and Excise Department: in one instance, a suggestion from personnel that executive officer posts in VAT offices could be worked on a part-time basis was met with resistance by local managers. In another, Customs and Excise solicitors resisted the suggestion that their work could be run on a part-time basis, the reason given in the latter case being that legal work in Customs and Excise could broadly be divided into two kinds: advisory work which was located in the London headquarters and prosecution work, which involved very immediate deadlines and frequent travelling. Personnel argued that a woman solicitor wishing to return on a part-time basis could be given such a post in advisory work: the solicitors section argued that such work was the 'plummy end' of legal work in the department. It had the greatest interest and most contact with the top of the department. To assign some of this work to a part-timer would, the lawyers argued, diminish the career interests of the full-timers.

These were respondents who were sure that part-time work could be institutionalised so as to provide career mobility between part-time postings and advancement from the Principal to the Assistant Secretary grade. Currently in the Civil Service the career development processes aiming to take people to beyond Assistant Secretary are not seen as able to embrace more than a very short period of part-time working. One woman in a small department where promotion was tight and where she was not a clear front runner said, 'The year I spent working part-time between my two children was a serious mistake in career terms: while the Civil Service can organise part-time working in some posts one's credibility declines very markedly'. Another woman, clearly a high flyer in a department known for its rather traditionalist approach, remarked that she had never risked a period of part-time working, feeling that it might count against her. A woman in a large social services department had had early promotion to the Assistant Secretary grade despite a number of years part-time working. Currently she was working in a heavy full-time Assistant Secretary posting and, though she felt her family life was still best suited by a less than full-time commitment, she was reluctant to go out on a limb and try to negotiate a part-time Assistant Secretary posting.

According to the Civil Service Department the policy of central Civil Service management has been 'to remove all possible obstacles to part-time employment in the Civil Service and to encourage Departments to examine the organisation of their work to see whether part-time work could be provided for serving or former women civil servants who wanted to continue but were prevented from doing so on a full-time basis'. That such encouragement has resulted in so little provision is disappointing. There has been little pressure to extend part-time working from the unions which appear to prefer strongly the recruitment and action base of full-time work. During the 1970s unions have co-operated with Civil Service management in devising flexible working schedules (FWH).[4] In 1979 it was estimated that 40 per cent of non-industrial civil servants were working flexible hours. The schemes were mainly confined to executive and clerical grades and mainly in regional and local offices; headquarters offices and higher grade administration personnel are rarely at present incorporated into FWH schemes. For those covered by them FWH schemes give some leeway in managing the integration of work and domestic commitments, and the advent of such schemes has probably tended to reduce the interest in extending part-time working amongst the big battalions of the lower executive and clerical grades. Given the limited approach to part-time work that has characterised the 1970s, the recently formed women's groups in the Civil Service see themselves as having an important role to play in articulating the issue.

Maternity and special leave

During the 1970s the Civil Service has sought through its leave arrangements to ease the pressure on women civil servants with new babies and young families. Following Kemp-Jones' recommendations paid maternity leave has been extended to three months and an unpaid entitlement of three months has been created. By the standards of some other public sector employers the paid leave allowance is small and suffers from the disability that pay for the third month is withheld until the woman returns to work for three months. Until recently maternity leave was reckoned against sick leave entitlement, but any leave taken beyond the three months for reasons of sickness due to maternity could not be treated as paid sick leave. Currently the relationship between sick leave and maternity leave is being reviewed by Civil Service management. The impetus for this has been provided by an Industrial Tribunal judgement in late 1979 that the Civil Service had discriminated against a woman civil servant by observing its rule that no paid sick leave was to be granted to a woman immediately following the expiry of paid maternity leave.[5] Two recently organised groups of women civil servants, the Civil Service Women's Rights group and Women in the Civil Service, are campaigning to improve maternity provisions.

In 1980 they hoped to get motions accepted by the conferences of the Civil Service unions, instructing the unions to press the National Staff side to negotiate for 'an end to the present retention arrangement so that a woman receives her three months maternity pay on her normal pay dates' and 'a discontinuation of those conditions of service which reckon maternity leave against sick leave entitlement'. Also included in the draft motions were pleas for 'the provision of six weeks paid paternity leave and consideration of arrangements whereby maternity leave entitlement may be shared between parents as family circumstances dictate' and 'the right for a woman to return to the same type of work up to five years after the birth of a child without loss of seniority'.

The Civil Service does have provisions for various periods of paid leave for several domestic circumstances, e.g. bereavement and marriage. It has, subsequent to Kemp-Jones, allowed departments to interpret domestic crises more widely and to grant unpaid leave to help cope with school holidays. It also has the provision that up to three years unpaid leave should be available to a woman whose services her department wishes to retain if she accompanies her husband on a move required by his employment to a place where she cannot continue her own employment in the Civil Service. There do not appear to be provisions enabling women to negotiate lengthy periods of special leave in order to care for their children when young, but there do appear to be one or two instances of this occurring as the experience of the following informant illustrates.

> When I was pregnant I asked if I could have two years special leave (unpaid), which was at once agreed to. After eighteen months I was asked about my plans, and I asked whether there was any chance of part-time work. The answer was no, but they offered to extend the special leave for a year. Subsequently the Treasury put me in touch with the Civil Service Selection Board where I now do some work as an assessor. But this suggestion came from me not from them. And, while the work I am doing suits me very well at present whilst I have two very young children, I do not regard it as an ideal permanent solution. But the choice I am faced with is this or a heavy full-time job. And unless I resume the full-time within the next six months I will have to apply to be reinstated. I have been told informally that the Treasury would in practice be willing to reinstate me barring unforeseen circumstances, and that they would take account of my experience when it came to promotion – but none of this is in any way binding.

Several women who had had children during the last few years and continued to work full-time emphasised during interviews the amount of consideration that they were shown by colleagues during their pregnancy and after their immediate return to work: they noticed attempts to limit the travelling they had to do, and after their return found themselves being consulted about their posting and being offered a post where they could count on getting home at a regular hour. One woman recorded that she was asked whether she would have any objections to a quiet post: another said that her boss kept saying during her first two or three weeks back in the office, 'What, are you still here?', when seeing her at her desk at 6.10 in the evening, 'No need for this'. It is common for administrators working in central London to be away from their homes from 8.30 in the morning to 7.30 at night. Most of the women with small children had a daily fixed point of contact with their children such as giving them breakfast or reading them a story at bed-time but their major time with their children was at weekends: women with children recorded themselves as doing no work at weekends much more frequently than married men or women without children. According to the women concerned they dispensed with weekend work by working intensely and efficiently through an eight- to nine-hour office day, taking only short lunch breaks and working some evenings at home.

Some departments have begun to experiment with allowing some women with children to re-organise their work loads and their working hours. The purpose of this, according to the three women encountered with such arrangements, was to enable them to see more of their children than the normal organisation of work permitted, and at the same time to retain them in quite demanding administrative posts. The women themselves made the point that management considered them amongst the ranks of the able and that it was prepared to be flexible in order to retain the use of their ability. Two of the women in fact gained young Assistant Secretary appointments. There was, said one of the women, nothing in writing and, were she to try to get it, flexibility of attitude would evaporate into thin air: what she had was the clear understanding amongst the Establishment section that she had latitude to negotiate with colleagues that meetings involving her be held only at specific times, that colleagues were to contact her at home, and that subordinates had to hold the office in her absence. Both women reporting this arrangement emphasised that it worked best if they came into the office every day, except when travelling: generally they hoped to leave the office by 4 or 4.30 pm. The women agreed that the success of the arrangement depended on their ability to count on the goodwill of colleagues and that the goodwill depended on their being seen not to be cutting corners. The result was that they purchased their flexibility at the cost of intensive work both in the office and in the evenings at home.

Comparing the women working with children who were interviewed in 1978 with those interviewed in 1968, there was amongst the former a greater sense that the Civil Service was backing them and wanting them to succeed in their dual responsibilities of family and full-time work: regarding part-time work, however, the younger women had much the same sense as the older women that it was often difficult to obtain, with some departments being unprepared to contemplate the possibility. Amongst the younger women who stayed working full-time there were a few in their early to mid-thirties whose family responsibilities had not prevented their attaining early Assistant Secretary appointments. But, comparing older and younger administrators, it is quite possible that one of the most significant contributions to assisting women's combination of work and family is being made by the women themselves; on the evidence of the questionnaires completed for the 1968 and 1978 enquiry women administrators now in their thirties seem to be heading for having fewer children than their older colleagues. The evidence indicates no appreciable difference between, on the one hand, 1940s and 1950s entrants and, on the other hand, 1960s entrants concerning the age at which they have their first child: in both cases the majority of the women had their first child when they were between twenty-six and thirty-five years of age. Where there does appear to be a difference between the two groups is in the rate at which they add to their families. All but one of the older women had a second child within two years of the birth of the first. This only happened with one-third of the younger women and several of them with one child made the point in interviews that they did not intend having additional children. Even should they have children, the evidence on the spacing of births indicates that the younger women are likely to have smaller families than the older women, half of whom had three or more children.

Nursery and day-care provision

In 1978 as in 1968 women administrators with small children almost invariably employed full-time paid help in their homes to care for their children: paying, in 1978, about £60 a week for the help. A high proportion of them when questioned expressed general support for the provision by the Civil Service of crèches at or near work places. Many said that had these been provided they would have been prepared to use them at full economic cost. They acknowledged many of the problems associated with nursery provision by the employer: the high cost of central city premises, the difficulty of gauging real demand except over a long period of operation, the decisions as to what level of income to subsidise, the negative aspects of nursery day-care a considerable distance from home. Many of these women, however, attached a high symbolic importance to the Civil Service providing nursery care: to them such provision indicated a substantial commitment by the employer, and more indirectly society, to the reality of women working. To date the Civil Service has not been prepared to act in a manner bespeaking such commitment: it *has* ventured into day-care provision, but in a hesitant and low-key manner.

In 1971 the Kemp-Jones Committee made a very definite suggestion about the provision of care for pre-school children, namely that:

> at least one nursery should be set up for an experimental period of four years for the children of civil servants in an area other than London: fees should be fixed in relation to salary but with a maximum equivalent to economic cost: if the experiment proves to be of value to the Civil Service it should continue and other nurseries should be set up on a similar basis.

Action on this recommendation was positive and immediate, but in the event did not survive the experimental stage. In July 1973 a purpose-built nursery, agreed by all to be splendidly equipped, was opened on the site of government offices in Llanishen, Cardiff. The nursery was situated about eight minutes' walk from most of the offices and was intended to help retain the service of young women tax officers (Clerical and Executive Officer grades) in the Inland Revenue. Training for these posts was reckoned to be relatively complex and expensive and the Inland Revenue was experiencing difficulties in recruiting and retaining sufficient staff.

The Civil Service Department put the running of the nursery in the hands of the local health authority – though in fact this particular authority had no nurseries of its own. In its first year of operation (1974) the nursery had 32 children aged between two and five, and a ratio of children to staff of 4.5 to 1.

In March 1976 the Civil Service Department announced that they were going to close down the Llanishen nursery and that it would be phased out in two years. They also stopped the preparation for another nursery in Croydon. The major reason for this action was a government policy of public expenditure cuts. In addition the Inland Revenue, and the government service generally, was finding recruitment easier and that the total costs of training an officer were not significantly above the annual cost to the employer of providing a nursery place. In these circumstances the Llanishen and Croydon nurseries came to be seen as experiments that were too costly. This is certainly how they are recorded in Civil Service memory. An external account of the experiments has, however, urged that the record of the costs should be carefully scrutinised, there being grounds for arguing that staffing was over-generous. As Peter Mottershead wrote in an account[6] for the Equal Opportunities Commission:

> It seems unfair that this experiment should cease with the general impression that employers' day-care facilities are prohibitively expensive. As I have tried to show, I think that substantial savings could have been made which would have been perfectly consistent with adequate standards of care. As far as I know, no evaluation of the exercise has been undertaken, and it would seem premature of the CSD to decide that the experiment had proved too expensive without at least some attempt to assess the benefits in terms of training and recruitment.

According to the Society of Civil and Public Servants,[7] strong union objections to the nursery closures succeeded in convincing the Civil Service Department that there was still a need for some day-care provision. From 1976 onwards the Civil Service Department started to promote locally organised day fostering schemes involving the use of supervised child-minders. The broad intention has been to reduce the cost per child compared with day nurseries, whilst ensuring a good standard of care and providing a scheme of care that can incorporate supplementary care for school-age children.

The three schemes that have developed have been very much the product of joint central and local initiative: the Welfare Division of the Civil Service Department has researched the idea and drawn up a guide to procedures and organisation, *Day Care for the Children of Civil Servants*, which was circulated to departments at the beginning of 1979. The policy of day fostering received the qualified approval of the unions:

> The National Staff Side recognises the merits of the Family Day-Care Schemes as proposed, although it reserves the right to continue to campaign for provision of other forms of day care for civil servants' children. It also asks that local staff sides participate in the design of local schemes to protect the interests of both care-parents and parents.

In essence the proposal is for management and staff in government offices (i) to form Steering Groups to find out the extent and nature of the demand for child care amongst their staff and to decide whether the demand is sufficient to proceed with organising a scheme, (ii) to create in outline a scheme of care and to recruit a paid, experienced part-time organiser who would carry out the detailed work of recruiting carers and parents to the scheme, (iii) with the scheme's organisation and finances approved in principle by the department, to form themselves into a Management Committee with responsibility for working with the organiser to establish the scheme and then keeping an overall review of it. It is agreed Civil Service policy that personnel and financial resources are devoted to child-care schemes: thus Steering Group/Management Committee 'must be given permission to meet in official time and to use official facilities. One member, e.g. an executive officer from Personnel or Welfare who is personally in favour of such a scheme, should be designated Secretary to the Group. He or she must be given official time to initiate and co-ordinate the Steering Group's activities'. Further, the cost of the organiser during the setting up of the scheme will be met by the department and 'it is envisaged that there will be a phasing-in period where the department will share the cost of the scheme with these first parents already using it. The department will also provide finance for certain contingencies and unforeseen problems'. The eventual aim is for schemes to become self-financing but none of the existing schemes has yet achieved this.

Of the three schemes at present in existence two, in the Office of Population, Census and Surveys at Fareham and the Department of Employment at Runcorn, have found the greatest demand to be for holiday care schemes and they have concentrated on organising these. The third scheme, in the Department of Health and Social Security at Newcastle, has developed an emphasis on day-fostering, placing seventeen children in all and currently supervising the care of twelve children.

The position taken on day-care by the Civil Service Department is that they are prepared to aid schemes started and run on a self-help basis. The problem from the parents' point of view is that the degree of co-operative effort needed to initiate and sustain such schemes makes them often seem less certain and manageable than bilateral arrangements they can make for themselves.

References
(1) For an account of numbers and how chosen see earlier pp. 48–49.
(2) Civil Service Department, *The Employment of Women in the Civil Service*, HMSO, 1971.
(3) Fogarty, Allen, Allen and Walters, op. cit., pp. 294–295.
(4) Civil Service Department, *A Guide to Flexible Working Hours*, 1979.
(5) For further details of judgement see Chapter 4, pp. 79–80.
(6) P. Mottershead, *A Survey of Child Care for Pre-school Children with Working Parents: A Report prepared for the Equal Opportunities Commission*. Manchester, EOC, 1978.
(7) *Child Day Care*, Research Paper, 9 October 1978, EC 561/78.

Current Policy to Eliminate Discrimination

Over the last hundred years the Civil Service has developed a set of procedures for recruitment, evaluation and promotions, and the granting of job-related benefits, which aims to ensure impartiality of treatment to all applicants and all employees regardless of social connections, religion, race and sex. During the 1970s national legislation has created specific responsibilities for employers to avoid action that is directly or indirectly discriminatory on the basis of sex, marital status and race. In implementing these specific responsibilities the broad policy of the Civil Service has been to assume that the general procedures aimed at ensuring impartiality of treatment to all comers are the best safeguard for eliminating specifically sexual or racial discriminatory practices. At the same time, the treatment of women has become a highlighted issue and the Civil Service is faced, within the present legislative context, with deciding on the extent to which it should specifically address itself to scrutinising and affecting women's careers. This chapter seeks to establish the means at present used to eliminate sex discrimination and to discuss what further action is being suggested to the Civil Service. The policy pursued by the Civil Service stems from a two-fold impetus: the recommendations of the Kemp-Jones Committee and the obligations engendered by the Sex Discrimination Act 1975.

During the lifetime of the Civil Service Department there has been a branch within it concerned with implementing the principle of equal opportunity for women in the Civil Service. It is manned by a Principal and two Executive Officers who report to an Assistant Secretary with a general responsibility for considering Civil Service personnel matters. The Principal and Executive Officers also have responsibility for developing and implementing Civil Service policy on race relations and the employment of handicapped people. The written advice that the branch gives to departments on the subject of recruitment, promotion boards, training and postings, etc. is as follows:

Staff should be made aware that considerations on grounds of sex or marital status must be ignored in considering promotions, training, etc., except where special training is provided for one sex for work which they have not previously done. Particular care should be taken to ensure that staff are aware that discrimination on the basis of marital status is unlawful, as well as discrimination on the basis of sex. Departments should ensure that staff engaged on these areas of work are well briefed on the need to avoid discrimination in the context of the general definition of discrimination in the Sex Discrimination Act.

Such injunctions abound and there is a widespread belief amongst civil servants that they are generally observed. There are in addition mechanisms available for checking on the operation of the system. They divide in terms of whether scrutiny follows from the registering of a complaint by a particular individual or whether it involves, from the beginning, a systematic review of a general category of decisions; though, as will be indicated in this chapter, particular cases brought under the Acts governing sex equality[1] can result in general rules being scrutinised. The following discussion considers (a) how individual civil servants are able to have cases reviewed and (b) how general scrutiny of Civil Service practice is implemented.

Individual cases
There are within the Civil Service internal appeal procedures whereby a civil servant can seek consideration by superior officers of a grievance that he or she has about their employment: it can be specifically about treatment in relation to promotion or more generally about other aspects of employment. These internal procedures have been supplemented by the external procedures which are available under the sex equality Acts. The Civil Service Department recorded a total of 32 complaints about job opportunities, recruitment decisions and pay which invoked these Acts in 1976, 1977 and 1978. Few of these complaints went beyond the initial registering of a grievance and a formal reply by the department to which it was made. In two instances, however, the cases went before Industrial Tribunals and the decisions given there have had significant consequences for Civil Service employment practice.

These cases tend to be known by the names of the complainants, Belinda Price and Linda Coyne. In the Price case the substance of the complaint was that the age restriction on eligibility applied by the Civil Service in recruiting Executive Officers was indirectly discriminatory to women. Eventually,[2] the applicant's claim was upheld by an Industrial Tribunal sitting in London in 1977. A recommendation was made that Civil Service management and unions use their best endeavours to agree in time for implementation in the competition year of 1980 what upper age limit, if any, other than that which existed in 1977, ought to be applied to candidates for direct entry to Executive Officer posts in the Civil Service. Late in 1979 the Civil Service revised the upper age limit for the Executive Officers Entry Competition to 45 years of age, and commenced a review and consultations with the staff side on the very sizeable list of other recruitment age limits. When questioned, in the course of the research project, about the outcome of this process a senior official with the Civil Service Commission said:

> I think the only forecast I could safely make at present is that the next few years are likely to see a movement towards higher age limits at the top end of a number of Commission-run competitions, and a gradual change in the traditional assumption that the Civil Service should recruit primarily for a life-time career. This is, of course, no more than a personal assessment of a likely trend: there could well be a number of obstacles in the way.

The Coyne case was heard in October 1979. The claimant held that her employers, the Exports Credits Guarantee Department with whom she was an Executive Officer, was ignoring the equality clause deemed to be in her contract by virtue of the Equal Pay Act. The substance of her claim was that they were treating her less well than men by not allowing a state of illness arising from the birth of her child, and which delayed her return to work beyond the expiry of her three months' maternity leave, to be covered by paid sick leave. The Civil Service did this under paragraph 8479 of its maternity provisions which stated that 'further paid sick leave following maternity leave may not be allowed within a woman's normal allowance'. In its decision[3] the Industrial Tribunal made the following statement about this paragraph:

> the fact remains that the sole substantive effect of the paragraph is not to confer any rights in relation to maternity upon a woman, but on the contrary to deprive her of rights to sickness benefit to which she would otherwise be entitled (i.e. six months on full pay in any period of twelve months) on the

grounds that the sickness is connected with her confinement. Far from being a provision which affords women special treatment, or special rights, in connection with maternity, it is a provision which deprives them of their otherwise existing rights to sickness benefit. Paragraph 8479 must be treated as so modified that the provisions relating to sick pay are not less favourable to the applicant than they are to male employees . . . and should in future be treated as if it read simply as follows: 'Further paid sick leave following maternity leave may be allowed within a woman's normal allowance'.

After the decision, a senior officer of the Civil Service Department was quoted in the national magazine *Now* as saying:

The problem is if we accept the ruling it could end up with thousands of women taking their full sick leave entitlement after having a baby.

The extra leave – both in actual wages and working hours lost – would cost God knows how much. And it would be the tax payer who would have to pay for it. We'll study the published findings word by word, clause by clause, and if there is a chance we'll fight for that one paragraph all the way to the top.[1]

In the event, however, the Civil Service Department decided not to appeal against the decision.

The outcome of these two cases does serve to emphasise that provisions of the prevailing sex equality legislation can have a very significant impact on general organisational practices that affect women's working lives. This is particularly so where the employer is a bureaucracy given to defining minutely its employees' rights and obligations. The cases further emphasise that the pursuit of a point is dependent on the alertness and persistence of individual women, although eventually two organisations, the National Council for Civil Liberties and the Equal Opportunities Commission, helped to sustain the appellants in their challenge to the Civil Service. The two cases illustrate that even in the case of an organisation committed to being a good employer regarding women there can be impediments to the achievement of non-discriminatory practice. There were in the case of age limits and maternity provisions strong pressures for maintaining the *status quo:* age limits had the support of the relevant union, the Society of Civil and Public Servants, and the maternity provisions were potentially less expensive for management than their more generous non-discriminatory amendment.

Procedures for general scrutiny

These are initiated by the Civil Service. Thus the Service has procedures for reviewing posts for which sex stands as a general occupational qualification: the need to do this stems very directly from the Sex Discrimination Act. The Civil Service also has some procedures for monitoring the progress of women through the grade structure: the development of such procedures is in line with the Equal Opportunities Commission's suggestions for monitoring the effectiveness of an equal opportunities policy.

The Kemp-Jones Committee tackled the question of jobs restricted to one sex and recommended that:

> it should be open for both men and women to be considered for any job, and appointments should be solely on the grounds of suitability and qualifications.

In a letter advising departments on the implementation of this recommendation the Civil Service Department wrote in March 1972:

> Departments are asked to ensure that all non-industrial posts in the Home Civil Service are now open to both sexes, except in those cases where there is a statutory bar on the employment of men or women. Some Establishment Officers have drawn attention to accommodation difficulties which could prevent the employment of either men or women at present: departments should take all practicable steps to eliminate these as soon as possible. Departments should let the Civil Service Department know of any posts which cannot be opened now to both sexes, together with the reason for this. The fact that either men or women are unlikely to have the qualifications for a particular post does not constitute a sufficient reason for excluding them from consideration altogether. For example, although women are unlikely to be able to do heavy work many men would not be capable of this either. In all cases of this nature individual ability should be the determining factor in selection.

Information sent from departments to the Civil Service Department in 1973 specified 25,854 posts that were restricted to men and 1,015 posts that were restricted to women. After the Sex Discrimination Act departments were told that they had to seek the approval of the Civil Service Department before recruiting to a newly created post that they considered they were legally entitled to restrict to one sex. In the last two years there have been two instances in which approval has been sought and given. By 1978 the total number of posts so restricted was 14,500, a reduction of 13,000 since 1973.

Whilst many posts have been formally de-restricted during the last few years, the Civil Service Department has no regular means of knowing whether a member of the sex previously disqualified for a post is in fact ever appointed to it. This particular lack of knowledge is part of a wider lack of systematic information about the sex of incumbents of specified posts.

The general recording system of annual reports, promotion reviews and promotion boards in the Civil Service provides considerable information on the evaluations made of women civil servants by their superiors and enables the analysis of promotion decisions to be made on a sex basis. During the 1970s the Civil Service made a start on this, though at present the overall picture is patchy: a few departments have gone considerably further than others in analysing material and the information available on a service-wide basis lacks much of the possible detail available. Monitoring appears to be an active issue in the Civil Service at the moment, with management considering what level of information should be sought about promotion decisions and how much of the analysis should be made available to unions, staff or outsiders.

Monitoring

The Kemp-Jones Committee scrutinised promotion rates. They published no findings for the upper administration grades, stating that statistical analysis was compromised by the small numbers of women involved: their figure for the junior executive grades, however, where there was a substantial minority of women, revealed female promotion rates significantly worse than those of men.[5] The Committee do not appear to have pursued very far the search for evidence to assist the interpretation of these findings; they cited complaints of bias against women, they also mentioned departments having some evidence that more women than men refuse promotions. At that point they left the issue: in their various recommendations they made none about regular statistical analysis or the collection of data relevant to the promotion rates of men and women. They did, however, feel sufficiently convinced of the possibility of prejudice operating in promotion procedures to recommend a corrective: namely, that wherever practicable women should form part of promotion boards. They were not explicit about their reasons for this recommendation except that it might help to change long-held attitudes: not did they make any explicit recommendations as to how the women should either seek to establish an instance of prejudice or seek to correct it. One is left wondering how effective a mode of general scrutiny and remedial action the mere presence of women on promotion boards can be.

Subsequent to the work of the Kemp-Jones Committee the Civil Service Department published statistics in 1975 on some annual rates of promotion from Executive Officer to Higher Executive Officer.[6] The commentary accompanying the tables confined itself to the following observation:

> For executive officers although the overall relationship between the percentages promoted for the two sexes has remained more or less unchanged, for those officers with five to nine years seniority the proportion of women promoted appears to have increased more than for men.

In pointing to the limited improvement the commentary acknowledged the possibility of improvement but gave no indication of either curiosity or concern with what changes had effected the improvement.

In 1979 the Annual Report of the Supplementary Benefits Commission[7] broke new Civil Service ground in terms of the amount of information on men's and women's promotion rates that it made publicly available. The SBC explored women's careers because of its concern with the effect of staff turnover on the quality of service offered in local benefits offices. It dealt with and clearly identified one department, the Department of Health and Social Security: it gave promotion statistics up to the level of SEO to Principal promotions with no qualifications about small numbers and it broke down the promotion sequence into a number of stages. The tables in the report clearly revealed that, at the higher levels of promotion (HEO to SEO and SEO to Principal), women eligible for promotion were much less likely than their male counterparts to be invited before a promotion board and also, in one of the two years in question, much less likely to be approved for promotion.

A civil servant involved in the analysis and presentation of the DHSS information said that, in deciding to publish, the Supplementary Benefits Commission took the straightforward view of the matter: viz., that widespread dissemination of the information assisted the formation of informed opinion about the degree of similarity or difference between men's and women's rates of promotion and possible explanations of observed differences. But a more cautious view of the consequences of publication was attributed to management by this civil servant and several others. The view was broadly that the Civil Service system of personnel evaluation went to great lengths to identify merit and to reward it. To quote one Establishment Officer contacted in this investigation:

> It is my strongly held belief that people should be selected for posts within the Civil Service solely on the basis of their ability to perform the job, and on no other criterion whatsoever. I also believe that, while we are not perfect, we are pretty close to this position . . . if adoption of the right criterion, as set out above, results in posts being staffed by bug-eyed monsters from outer space, or women, that will be O.K. by me (and, I think, all my colleagues).

However, it was argued that it was not completely certain what the figures showed; officials in departments where most analysis was going on invariably emphasised 'there's a lot of debate amongst us as to what these figures mean'. The debate tended to highlight two points of view and two sets of observations: (a) women's 'reluctance' to accept more responsibility and the observation from the data that larger proportions of women than of men declined invitations to promotion boards at higher executive levels; (b) the tendency of the selection process at the higher executive levels to 'prefer' men to women, the relevant data being the lower proportion of women invited to boards and, in one out of two years, approved after interview. Notwithstanding these qualifications, however, it was felt that the figures could support the interpretation that the system of evaluation was unfair to women and could give rise to pressure for more emphatic emphasis on the promotion of women. Such pressure might, it was argued, upset the 'delicate balance' of the evaluation system since it could promote 'backlash' from other groups. Such thinking tends to be inhibiting in its effect not just on publication but indeed on the internal process of scrutiny and enquiry, for it tends to see scrutiny as implying that the institution of evaluation is not working as it should and therefore calling the legitimacy of its current operation into question.

Women's groups

The two women's groups in the Civil Service, both formed since 1978, tend to be viewed within the framework of thought outlined above as threats to the 'delicate balance'. The groups broadly recruit from different levels of the Civil Service hierarchy: Women in the Civil Service draws most of its officers from higher administrative grades and their equivalents, whilst the Civil Service Women's Rights Group is primarily sustained by women from executive and clerical grades. Both groups are in early stages of development and are concerned not to demarcate ground but to pool information and combine efforts. Both groups see their role as two-fold: seeking to act as a pressure group on management and unions, and more broadly sustaining women in their working lives in the Civil Service. Open meetings of the groups reveal a range of attitudes and assumptions amongst the women present as to the forces moulding women's careers and what constitutes appropriate action. There does, however, seem to be a widely shared opinion amongst the members that there should be within the Service much more systematic information on and general discussion of women's careers.

In developing their pressure group role the two groups have had to tread very carefully. Management-staff relations in the Civil Service are structured through the Whitley system of joint management and trade union committees, and both sides have fired shots over the women's groups' bows warning them not to seek any special place in the system of consultation, discussion and negotiation. The women's groups recognise that they must channel demands for change through the trade unions. As indicated earlier, they have sought to get a specific set of resolutions on maternity leave, paternity leave, reinstatement and part-time work adopted by the union annual conferences. Recently the Women in the Civil Service group drafted a letter seeking from Principal Establishment Officers up-to-date information on aspects of departments' employment of women. The group's members were urged that 'it would be preferable to persuade Departmental staff sides to put forward this letter rather than to write it as individuals'. As a way of ensuring the active commitment of trade unions to the pursuit of women's interests, the women's groups are pressing Civil Service unions to appoint women's rights officers. The Civil Service Women's Rights Group records itelf as beginning as:

a spontaneous expression of anger and frustration at the blatant sexism and disregard for women's rights shown at CPSA[8] Conference in 1978. The dismissive attitude to women which exists throughout CPSA and the Civil Service unions in general was thrown into sharp relief at that conference, where debates on crèche provision and on the pay and conditions of typing machine operator or secretaries' grades were a signal for most delegates to leave the hall and for speakers to indulge in jokes and cynicism which implied that it was impossible to take such issues seriously. And this was a union whose membership is over 70 per cent female.

Women activists in the group see some improvement taking place in the attitudes to women's concerns displayed by union officials and activists: in 1980 the First Division Association has given one of its women departmental representatives responsibility for women's rights. But in general the attitude of these two groups is that both management and unions have consigned the issue of women's careers to the margins of their concern and that pressure from women is needed to bring it closer to the centre of attention.

In its conclusion the 1968 study characterised the Civil Service as being silent on the issues of women's employment. It said that:

> having granted women formal equality of opportunity with men in entry, promotion prospects, pay and the combination of work and marriage, the Service now assumes that it can, in its formal rules and procedures, treat men and women as indistinguishable employees . . . one result of the eventual granting of formal equality was that organisations specifically concerned with women – the women's organisations and the ad hoc sub-committees on the Whitley Council on the 'Treatment of Women' quietly dissolved.[9]

The 1968 study went on to advocate that the silence should be broken and there is certainly evidence of this happening in the 1970s. The Civil Service Department appointed the Kemp-Jones Committee and accepted nearly all of its recommendations. Since the Sex Discrimination Act came into force the Civil Service Department has had six-monthly meetings with Equal Opportunities Commission officials to discuss matters of mutual interest. There is, however, some justification in characterising the overall Civil Service approach to women's employment as 'low-key': it does tend to imply that at any one time the situation is 'close to perfect', though never completely shutting the door on new measures: such an attitude accomplishes gradual change, whilst defending each position along the way as good in the circumstances, and not warranting change. Such a 'low-key' approach breeds its own form of opposition; one that tries to puncture complacency and perhaps over-emphasises the degree of inertia prevailing during a span of time. Whilst there does seem to be a general Civil Service attitude, the Civil Service is not monolithic. The 1978 study encountered three departments actively scrutinising women's career progress. In each instance the department was responding to initiatives considered in the Civil Service context as 'rather radical about women'. Significantly enough, in each instance sufficient grounds were revealed for the personnel managers involved to be convinced that there was cause for concern over women's promotion chances, from the point of view of equality of opportunity and the Service's commitment to promoting the best individuals. There was, moreover, general agreement that the most appropriate action was to urge the managers to guard against the possibility of 'unconscious discrimination'. The phrase is an interesting one which both acknowledges the existing discrimination and disclaims it at the same time.

The question for the immediate future seems to be whether the present readiness of a few departments to explore further issues of women's employment can become a Service-wide readiness. The 'low-key' approach will certainly gain sustenance from the present political and economic climate of constraint affecting the Civil Service. But notwithstanding the present political climate, there is in society today compared with the late 1960s a more general commitment to scrutinising and improving women's achievements in employment. Within the Civil Service the recent development of women's groups is witness to such commitment. As yet, these groups have had little time to make an impact, though within two years of their foundation they do appear to have played some part in persuading the Civil Service to review (in 1980–81) what has happened to women in the Civil Service since the Kemp-Jones Committee reported.

Looking at the last ten years, it is the conclusion of the present research that, whilst in the Civil Service there have been small incremental changes to enable women to combine work and family life, big significant changes still need to be made. The key to these changes is shaping ways in which Civil Service careers can embrace divergence from what is still the dominating model of life-long, full-time, continuous service. The creation of diverse career patterns allowing for periods of part-time work, systematic re-entry and late entry and appropriate schemes of career development could benefit both men and women and the Civil Service as an institution, but it would seem that really strong pressure from women and their supporters is needed to bring these changes about. In the 1970s management, in consultation with unions, has supported the principle of part-time work but done little to ensure that it is a real option, has founded nurseries but quickly closed them down, has assumed rather than checked the impartiality of promotion procedures, and has had two of its practices, namely a narrow youthful age limit for the recruitment of Executive Officers and the refusal to allow paid sick leave to follow on directly from maternity leave, judged discriminatory. Thus it would seem that in the Civil Service in the 1980s important steps remain to be taken in the implementation of the principle of enabling women with children to work at levels commensurate with their ability.

References

(1) The Equal Pay Act, 1970, the Sex Discrimination Act, 1975, the Employment Protection Act, 1975.
(2) *Industrial Relations Law Review*, 1978, pp. 3–8.
(3) Decision of the Industrial Tribunal, November 1979.
(4) *Now*, 2 November, 1979, p. 59.
(5) Civil Service Department, 1971, op. cit., p. 46.
(6) Civil Service Statistics, 1975, p. 33.
(7) Cmnd. 7725, HMSO, 1979, pp. 67–74.
(8) Civil and Public Servants' Association.
(9) Fogarty, Allen, Allen and Walters, op. cit., p. 308.

B. Women in Two Industrial Companies

Introduction

When we looked at the careers of women in industry in 1968, two large firms agreed to participate in the study by allowing us to examine their organisation and structure, to look at the career paths of their managers or employees of equivalent status, and to interview small samples of men and women, including those responsible for personnel policy and its implementation. Both companies agreed to our publishing our findings on condition that they remained anonymous, and this practice has been followed in the present report.

We approached both companies in 1978 to see whether they would agree to our carrying out a follow-up study to *Women in Top Jobs*,[1] and both gave us their fullest co-operation. The interviewing for this took place during 1979, so that the material was collected eleven years after the previous study.

Most of the statistics and studies of the position of women in management and industry since the end of the 1960s have confirmed what we found in 1968: that women tend to occupy the more junior posts in the management structure, that the path to the top is very tough, and that a combination of past attitudes and a continuing failure to deal in a practical way with the problems of combining children with a career have limited women's chances of moving up the promotion ladder. In spite of the fact that there has been some evidence of a gradual change in attitudes towards equal opportunity for women, reinforced by the Equal Pay and Sex Discrimination Acts, nevertheless it has been indicated that there is still widespread misunderstanding of the legislation and the way in which certain practices may still include elements of 'indirect discrimination' against women.

This report is intended to look at the changes over the past eleven years and the effects of the legislation to see to what extent they have

affected women's opportunities to reach the top in the two organisations. The need for anonymity in this particular report has meant
that it has been necessary to present tables and figures mainly as
percentages, with less detail than in the case of the other reports in
this book. Anonymity also means that the companies cannot be
described in the published report in as much detail as the other
organisations studied, nor can as full an historical account be given
of how women's opportunities have fared over the last eleven years.
These companies are also different from the BBC and the Civil
Service in that there has not been the same public interest in them or
the same amount of available material resulting from this, since they
are not seen to be publicly accountable in the same degree.

Reference
(1) M. P. Fogarty (ed.), Isobel Allen, A. J. Allen and Patricia Walters, *Women in Top
Jobs – Four Studies in Achievement*, George Allen and Unwin, 1971.

CHAPTER 5

Structure and Organisation

Both companies have remained essentially in the same lines of business in which they were engaged in 1968, although Company B has undergone considerable internal reorganisation.

Company A is a large international organisation, covering a number of smaller companies, departments and divisions, which are involved in manufacturing, marketing, sales, distribution, market research, scientific research, advertising, personnel, finance and other service departments. It has a large central staff, although many of its subsidiary companies and divisions have a great deal of autonomy. Although managers are employed by the subsidiary companies and divisions, they are regarded as a total group for career development purposes. Some managers move around the organisation while others spend all their working lives within one company or division.

Company B is also a large organisation with international links, but is still a much more directly science-based organisation. As in 1968, a much higher proportion of its non-manual staff is engaged in scientific research than is the case with Company A.

Women in senior posts in the two companies

(i) *Company A*
In 1968, women accounted for 2.7 per cent of the total number of managers, and by 1979 this proportion had risen to 3.3 per cent. The number of women managers had more than doubled (from 104 in 1968 to 228 in 1979) but, of course, they remained only a tiny proportion of the total number of managers. In 1968, we found that women accounted for less than 1 per cent of the managers at the most senior level, 1.6 per cent at the middle management level, and 3.3 per cent of junior managers. By 1979, these proportions had risen to 1.3 per cent, 2.2 per cent, and 3.8 per cent respectively.

It would be hard to argue, on the basis of these figures, that the level of women's achievement has changed more than minimally in the last eleven years. We made some analysis to see whether there had been any movement in where the women were within the organisation, particularly as one of the themes which recurred in our last study was that women were unlikely to reach senior management since their experience tended to be confined to certain areas, which meant that they did not usually have the breadth of experience thought necessary for top management.

In 1968, we found that women accounted for 2 per cent of all the managers in the operating companies of the organisation, which were mainly concerned with manufacturing and marketing. By 1979, this proportion had increased to 2.9 per cent. Women had not really made any significant breakthrough into these companies, since they were still mainly to be found in certain areas. For example, there were eleven operating companies, and more than half the women managers who worked in an operating company were employed in only three of these. In the market research company, they accounted for as many as 40 per cent of the managers, in another company engaged in the manufacture and marketing of products bought mainly by women they accounted for 10 per cent, and in the third company for nearly 5 per cent. In the other eight operating companies, the proportion of women managers was negligible, even though some of the companies were engaged in the production of consumer goods bought mainly by women.

Outside the operating area, women tended to do fairly well in certain service departments of the head office, for example in personnel, as they did in 1968. However, the proportion of women managers in scientific research had fallen slightly from 5 per cent in 1968 to just under 4 per cent in 1979. There were eighteen main companies or divisions in Company A, and in one-third of these, women accounted for 1 per cent or less of the total managers.

These figures must be looked at against the profile of men and women managers in the organisation as a whole. As in the other organisations studied, the lack of women in senior posts was said to be mainly attributable to two factors – first, that women had not been recruited in large numbers to management in the past for a variety of reasons, so that there were likely to be very few women in the age-groups from which senior managers were drawn; and secondly, that the majority of women left the company either when they got married or when they had a baby.

Table 5.1 shows the proportion of women amongst the managers by age and grade.

Table 5.1 *Percentage of women among Company A managers by age and grade June 1979*

Grade	Senior management	Senior middle management	Junior middle management	Junior management
Age				
20–24	—	—	25	32
25–29	—	0	11	14
30–34	0	4	4	7
35–39	5	2	2	5
40–44	0	2	2	5
45–49	0	1	2	4
50–54	3	5	0.5	7
55 plus	0	1	0.5	1
All ages	1.2	2.3	2.7	6.8

The numbers in the 20–24 age-group were very small, but it can be seen that it was here that the women were doing best, with a third of the junior managers in this age-group being women. In the next age-group, they still accounted for over 10 per cent of all managers, but above the age of thirty, there was a steady decline in the proportion of women. If the figures are analysed in another way, it can be shown that 48 per cent of the women managers were under 35, compared with 22 per cent of the male managers. The crucial question is whether these young women managers will stay in the organisation and work their way up.

The importance of children can be seen most clearly in Table 5.2 which shows the proportion of male and female managers in each grade by whether they were married or had children.

Table 5.2 *Percentage of male and female managers in Company A married and with children, by grade June 1979*

	Senior management		Senior middle management		Junior middle management		Junior management	
	Men	Women	Men	Women	Men	Women	Men	Women
Married	96	63	93	46	88	42	83	47
With children	92	50	82	14	71	4	62	4

This table shows quite clearly that the higher up the ladder the men went, the more likely they were to be married and to have children. This was, of course, partly related to age, since the younger men were more likely to be unmarried and in the more junior jobs. The profile of women shows that among the junior and middle managers, although over 40 per cent were married, only a very small proportion had children. Indeed, although nearly 50 per cent of the women managers under the age of thirty were married, none of them had children. The exception to this situation was among the senior managers, where nearly two-thirds of the women were married and half had children. The numbers involved were tiny, but the implications are interesting, and will be discussed further in the chapter on women and children.

The main point to emerge from these tables is that the women managers in Company A tended to be young and childless. Only 7 per cent had children, and, as we have seen, 48 per cent were under the age of 35. It remains to be seen whether these young women will have children, and, if so, whether they will leave.

(ii) *Company B*

The company as a whole has contracted slightly in the United Kingdom since 1968, largely because of rationalisation and internal reorganisation. In 1968, our study of women was largely confined to the research division, since that was the only part of the company where women were to be found in any significant numbers in senior posts. The number of qualified staff in the research area has not as yet been much affected by reorganisation, although, at the time of writing, there was a move towards some reduction in scientific staff.

In 1979, we looked in detail at the women in two of the major parts of the company, in which about two-thirds of the total staff, and the vast majority of women in senior posts, were employed. These were the research area and the main operating area, which covered most of the primary and secondary production of the company.

In 1968, we found that 3 per cent of the top management in the research division – the Executive grade – were women. Women then accounted for approximately 10 per cent of the next grade (Senior Scientific Officer 1), 10 per cent of the next grade (Senior Scientific Officer 2), and 11 per cent of the next grade (Scientific Officer). At the next grade, Junior Scientific Officer, they accounted for nearly 50 per cent. Some of the scientists on the top scientific grades were also classified as managers, depending on the extent to which they were responsible for other staff rather than their seniority in the company.

In 1979, we found the situation in the research division little changed. Women accounted for 4 per cent of the Executive grade, 10 per cent of Senior Scientific Officers 1, 15 per cent of Senior Scientific Officers 2, and 32 per cent of the Scientific Officer grade which had changed since 1968 to include many more junior scientific and technical staff. In the research division there were very few senior administrative staff, but women accounted for 20 per cent of the highest administrative grade (below Executive level) and 33 per cent of the next level down. Overall, they accounted for 21 per cent of these scientific and administrative grades in the research area.

In the operating area, women accounted for 1 per cent of the Executive grade, 1 per cent of the SSO 1 grade, 2 per cent of the SSO 2 grade, and 7 per cent of the SO grade. They accounted for 3 per cent of each of the senior administrative grades below the Executive grade. Overall, they accounted for 3 per cent of these scientific and administrative staff in this part of the company.

In Company B, the profile of the managers, scientists and senior administrators shows similarities to the other organisations studied. Again, the women tended to be concentrated in the more junior posts and in the younger age-groups, as Table 5.3 shows. For these purposes, both the research area and the operating area are combined.

Table 5.3 *Percentage of women among Company B managers, scientists and senior administrators by age and grade June 1979*

Grade	Executive	SSO 1	SSO 2	SO	Senior administrative	Middle administrative
Age						
20–29	—	—	15	26	—	—
30–39	—	—	7	9	—	7
40–49	—	4	7	—	8	4
50–59	5	12	3	—	6	12
60 plus	—	—	—	—	—	—
All ages	2	5	7	22	4	7

Table 5.3 shows the expected pattern of young women in junior posts, with women accounting for over a quarter of the scientific officers under the age of thirty. It also shows the fact, which will be looked at in more detail later in this report, that there were a number of senior women in the 50–59 age-group for whom there were no obvious successors within the company. Company B had very few women in the 30–50 age bracket. If the figures are looked at in another way, it can be shown that 60 per cent of the women working in the research and operations areas in these grades were under the age of thirty. As with the other organisations studied, it remains to be seen whether they will stay.

Table 5.4 shows the proportions of men and women who were married, and the proportion of women who had children.

Table 5.4 *Percentage of married male and female managers, scientists and senior administrators in Company B and of women with children, by grade June 1979*

	Executive		SSO 1		SSO 2		SO		Senior admin.		Middle admin.	
	Men	Women	Men	Women	Men	Women	Men	Women	Men	Women	Men	Women
Married	94	33	92	44	88	47	55	48	90	33	91	50
With children	n.a.	33	n.a.	11	n.a.	20	n.a.	0	n.a.	0	n.a.	0

The table shows the same pattern as found in Company A and in the BBC, that the higher up the ladder the men went, the more likely they were to be married. Figures for children were not available for men from Company B, but there was no reason to suppose that they were very different in this respect from the men in Company A. The women in junior and middle posts showed a similar pattern to the women in Company A, with over 40 per cent being married but very few having children. Again, it is interesting that the young women tended to be childless. For example, nearly half the women scientific officers under the age of thirty were married, but none of them had children. In the most senior grade, a third of the women were married and had children, but the numbers were so tiny that very little can be deduced from this.

The same pattern found in Company A emerged in Company B. The women tended to be young and childless. Only 5 per cent of the women managers, scientists or senior administrators had children and, as we have seen, 60 per cent of the women were under thirty.

The people interviewed in Company A

In 1968, twenty women managers in Company A were interviewed. Three were senior managers, five were women under thirty who had entered the company on its management trainee scheme, and the rest were junior or middle managers, mainly aged between 30 and 45. When we returned in 1979, we found that only six of these women were still working for the organisation. Very little was known about what had happened to the women who had left the company, especially the management trainees interviewed in 1968, all of whom had left the organisation by 1969.

In 1979, we drew a new sample of nine women aged 30–45. They represented all the women in middle management and two of the four senior managers in this age-group. Two of this new sample had entered the organisation as management trainees, four as clerks, typists or secretaries, one as an assistant manager and two as specialist managers. We interviewed a new sample of five women under 30 who had entered the organisation as graduate management trainees, of whom four were junior managers and one was a middle manager. We interviewed five of the women we had interviewed in 1968, four of whom were over 50 and senior managers and one of whom was between 45 and 49 and a middle manager. We interviewed one other senior manager who was over 50. Of the twenty women, ten were married, nine were single and one was divorced. Three of the women had one child and three had two children.

Five men were interviewed, two of whom had been interviewed in 1968. They were all senior managers.

The people interviewed in Company B

In 1968, fourteen women were interviewed in Company B for *Women in Top Jobs* and one woman was interviewed for *Dual Career Families.*[1] Eleven of them were aged between 35 and 50 and one was over 50; the other three were under 30. In 1979, we found that seven of the fifteen women were still working for the organisation, of whom six were now over 50 and one was between 35 and 45. Two of these were on the Executive grade and the others were Senior Scientific Officers. Most of them were doing the same jobs they had been doing in 1968, and they were all re-interviewed.

We drew a new sample of seven women, aged between 32 and 47, five of whom were Senior Scientific Officers and two on a senior administrative grade. In addition, we interviewed the only other woman in the company on an Executive grade, who was over 50.

Twelve of the women worked for the research division of the organisation and the other three worked for the operations division. Those interviewed from the research division represented just over half of the women on the Executive and Senior Scientific Officer grades in that part of the organisation, while those interviewed from the operations division represented well over half the women in those grades in that part of the organisation. Six of the women were married and eight were single. Only one woman, who was over 50 and had been interviewed last time, had any children.

Seven men were interviewed, four of whom had been interviewed in 1968. They were all on the Executive grade, and were senior managers or directors.

Reference
(1) R. and R. Rapoport, *Dual Career Families*, Penguin, 1971.

CHAPTER 6

Career Opportunities for Women between 1968 and 1979

There can be little doubt that the period from 1968 to 1979 was a time in which the subject of women and their role was discussed to a much greater extent than at any time since that of the suffragette movement. Not only was there public discussion, but legislation on a number of issues affecting women was passed, including the Equal Pay Act, 1970, the Sex Discrimination Act, 1975, and the maternity provisions of the Employment Protection Act, 1975. At the same time, there was evidence of an increasingly difficult economic situation and increasing unemployment. British industry was not in an expansionist mood, and by the end of the period was making very gloomy forecasts about the future in terms of growth and employment. Against this background we asked our respondents about the effects of any changes within their organisations on the career opportunities for women.

Effects of changes in recruitment

In both companies recruitment of young graduates was considered a very important source of senior management of the future. Although people were recruited when older, training within the company was given a great deal of priority by these firms. Most of the women interviewed in 1968 had spent all their working lives within their companies, and this was also true for the women interviewed in 1979. We were therefore very interested to see what had happened in these companies as far as recruitment of qualified women was concerned.

Company A had a management training scheme, with very rigorous selection procedures. Graduates were recruited as trainees and given as much experience as possible in different types of work. They were usually sent to one company or division and tended to stay there until they were 'developed' into another part of the organisation. The women graduate trainees interviewed this time, like their 1968 counterparts, had, with one exception, spent all their time in one part of the organisation.

In Company B, the women usually came in as graduate scientists, although some came in as specialists in personnel, accountancy or some other administrative function. More women biologists than chemists were recruited, because it was said that women tended to study the biological sciences rather than chemistry at university and the recruitment reflected this.

In Company A, more than half the respondents said that the recruitment of qualified women had improved since 1968, while in Company B the majority of respondents thought that it had stayed about the same. Certainly in Company A, there had been an increase in the number and proportion of women taken on the management training scheme since 1968. From 1961, when women were first taken on as graduate trainees, until 1972, they rarely accounted for more than 10 per cent of the intake, but from 1973 onwards they have accounted for between 16 and 21 per cent. It was pointed out that of the 56 women management trainees taken on between 1961 and 1971, only two were left in the company. But, although women's track record until 1971 looked poor in comparison with that of the men, nevertheless, of the trainees recruited between 1961 and 1978, 43 per cent of the men and 38 per cent of the women were still working for the company. It was the most recently recruited women who had stayed, and the record for the women in the last three years had, in fact, been better than that of the men.

It should be stressed that the graduate trainee scheme is by no means the only way to reach senior positions in Company A. Of those entering management in any year, they account for less than 10 per cent. About a third of those entering management are recruited from outside the company; they include new graduates, recruited directly to individual parts of the organisation, and people with specialist knowledge or expertise. The system of internal promotion is favoured. The recruitment of qualified women, other than through the management trainee scheme, was not closely monitored so that it was difficult to tell how successful they had been and what proportion had stayed or left.

It was generally agreed in both companies that the quality of women applying or being interviewed was very high, and in many instances higher than that of the men. Nevertheless, more men applied and more men were recruited, even if the overall calibre of the women was higher. The situation was thought to have improved in both companies since 1968, when it was said that certain parts of the company would simply not recruit women, however high their calibre. However, there was still a general consensus among those recruiting women that they had to be better than the men. One senior woman pointed out one of the reasons: 'I have a reputation for being harder on the women at boards than the men are. But if she fails, all women will suffer.' Another senior woman pointed to the fear expressed in 1968 that, if too many women were taken on in certain areas, these areas would be devalued in terms of influence and also as places for good career experience. Certainly, there were examples of men senior managers who had had a number of women in their departments and thought that this had affected their own credibility as top managers. It had made them reluctant to 'over-recruit' women, however good they were.

One senior manager in Company B thought that there were still certain prejudices at work, especially in certain functions:

> This time last year, one of my colleagues said he'd seen a first-class candidate on the milk-round of the universities. We said, 'Wheel him in'. He said, 'You won't want to see her . . .' He'd just assumed we wouldn't want her. But it was a job any graduate could do. She wanted to be a Production Manager, and we said OK, but she didn't come. She was absolutely first-class – gave all the right answers. But she was the only woman to come through for that type of work in the time I was in charge . . . Perhaps the other women had been filtered out at a lower level or by those who do the milk-round. . . . I think we should actually send a senior woman on the rounds of the universities. Her presence would make us look attractive to women graduates.

In scientific research in general, the trend towards demanding higher qualifications, especially a PhD, from new recruits, was thought to be increasing. Some people thought that this was likely to lead to fewer women being recruited, since they were less likely to stay on at university to do a PhD.

Although some people were worried about recruiting too many women since so many of them left, others thought that it helped to solve a problem since not everyone could become Chairman of the company.

You can take the cynical view and take on women for the younger managers' jobs. If they only work for ten years, and you take on women in the proportion 50:50, how lucky those fellows are. They can go up and up more quickly, and you'd solve the problem that the young men leave because they don't have the quick opportunities they want.

The high quality of the young women was certainly recognised, but there was no chance of their being taken on in equal proportions to the men. Even in areas where women applicants outnumbered the men, there was an increasing reluctance to take them on in proportion to their qualifications and applications, since the senior management were worried about the future holes in their manpower planning. Perhaps they were also worried about the possible devaluing of these areas because of the proportion of senior women.

Effects of structural changes

Both companies had undergone changes in organisation in the previous eleven years. Certain parts of Company A were seen to have expanded while others had remained static or contracted. The respondents were fairly equally divided on whether any structural changes had affected women in particular. The general view was that any expansion in the earlier part of the period was being matched by retrenchment at the end. There was certainly a very strongly held view that the future structure of the company was going to be less favourable to the promotion and prospects for women than the past, particularly since there was an increasing trend towards trimming the number of management jobs to what one of the respondents described as the 'bare boards'. He thought this likely to militate against the recruitment or promotion of women, partly because there was going to be an increasing need for manpower planning which was thought to be difficult with women because of the fact that the majority left when they had babies, and partly because the removal of the 'fat' of the company meant that many of the peripheral, possibly specialist jobs, traditionally done by women, were going to disappear.

If you've got two people of equal calibre – a man and a woman – if you take on the girl you've got to take the risk that four years from now you're not going to have a developed manager to fill an important hole. If you have too many men you're not going to worry, but if you take on too many women, it's no good.

This view was certainly reflected by one woman who had an overall view of recruitment of graduates. She thought that if a company or division was not in an expansionist mood, this was shown in their lack of willingness to consider women among their management trainees.

It was pointed out by some of the respondents, particularly those working in marketing, that the wastage among young male management trainees was as high in these areas as among the women, but that it looked as though the wastage of women in general was higher mainly because a higher proportion of them were taken on in these very areas. Some of the women interviewed thought that the high turnover among young managers working in marketing had given them opportunities at an earlier age than they had ever expected. But these were the only women who thought that changes in the employment structure had helped their careers. Most other women thought that, if there had been any structural changes, they had not been personally affected, while a small number considered that reorganisation had either hindered their career prospects or increased their workload without improving their position.

In Company B, there had been several bouts of reorganisation over the past eleven years, with renaming of divisions and rationalisation of subsidiary companies. However, the respondents were much less likely than those in Company A to consider that these changes had had any effect on the careers of women. In fact, although there had been a lot of internal reorganisation, the numbers of jobs had remained much the same. It was said that the proportion of really senior jobs had declined while the next layer of management had increased. It appeared to some of the women interviewed that this had meant that men had been appointed over their heads into this expanding level of management.

Changing policy and management attitudes

Policy was seen to be made by senior management, so that any changes in company policy towards women were seen as stemming from the top. There were considerable differences between the two organisations on this question. In Company A about a third of the women thought there had been some change in company policy towards women, while none of the respondents in Company B thought there had been any change.

In Company A it was said that at the most senior level there was a definite interest in having more senior women within the company, and that over the years there had been committees considering the subject, including the possibility of running special training courses for women, which had been discounted. The effectiveness of changes in policy was seen to be much more debatable. Some women with very long service within the company remarked that although there was 'apparent sympathy' from the top, this did not work out 'down the line', and that the number of women in top jobs had changed very little from the time they had joined the company.

Changes were often thought to be reflected in attitudes, but there was much disagreement on the extent to which the attitudes of those responsible for promoting women had, in fact, changed, let alone whether any changes had made any difference. In both companies, there was a very strong feeling that policy had not changed, and part of this was attributed to senior management. This view was held by some women in both companies: 'There will be no policy changes towards women until they've moved out the entrenched conservative senior management.'

Nevertheless, there were certainly some women, particularly in Company A, who had benefited directly from the policy and personality of very senior managers. Some were reported as being very much in favour of promoting women, and, more important, facilitating this process, as one woman reported: 'It would have been much harder for me if our Chairman had left five years ago. It was made much easier because there was someone at the top of the business who believed in giving the girls a go.' But the importance of having someone who believed in giving opportunities to women was remarked on in 1968, and there were certainly women interviewed then who attributed an important part of their success in reaching a senior position to the help of a senior male colleague.

One woman in Company A indicated how she had observed that senior management were concerned at the shortage of women in senior posts:

As far as this company is concerned I'd have said there is no policy, *but* when I went on my last course, it was intimated that the company is desperately looking round to find women to place in senior management positions. On the course they were looking closely at the women. They may think there's going to be a shortage of men, but I think they like to be seen to be being fair and doing the right thing. They maybe think the men managers are blocking women's promotions – it's the men managers who produce the women's reports.

Her view was confirmed by a male senior manager, who thought that the pressure for more women stemmed from the top:

The Personnel Director is persistently nagging top management about appointing women to senior posts, but at senior management and the level below you never get a proposal from anyone to promote any woman to anything . . . That may be because of the area that I'm in.

However, if there was some disagreement on whether policy had changed at senior management level, there was less disagreement about what was happening further 'down the line', where the day-to-day decisions on promotion and recruitment were taking place. The personality and attitudes of individual line managers were seen to be the most important factors affecting the prospects for anyone, and women in particular. A certain personnel policy could be laid down from on high, but the implementation of this policy was usually in the hands of individual heads of department or managers at a lower level. Women's careers were seen to be as dependent on individual attitudes as they were eleven years before; and the influence of the line manager in determining future career prospects was seen as vital: 'Promotion is very dependent on heads of department, and if there's a job which is applicable to both sexes, there are many heads of department who would choose the man rather than the woman – both being equal.'

Some respondents thought that there were indications that things were changing and that the attitudes of younger managers were less entrenched, but they found it difficult to point to examples of promotion for women stemming from this. And not everyone thought that younger managers were necessarily any more enlightened as far as women were concerned: 'The more brash young executives are coming in now. Our directors used to be kind, friendly men.'

Although in Company A rather more than half the respondents thought that opportunities for women had improved in the last eleven years, the vast majority of respondents in Company B thought there

had either been no change or the situation had got worse. About a
third of the respondents in Company A thought that encouragement
or positive management policies for women had improved, while
none of the Company B respondents did. However, among the
people who thought there had been an improvement in Company A,
several thought that only small things had changed. For example, it
was said that the advertising of more jobs up to senior management
level had opened up the field to women more, even if they did not
apply. Similarly, when lists of people eligible for promotion were
compiled, women's names were much more likely to be included
than they had been in 1968. One senior woman thought that actual
opportunities were now much better at the lower levels of management:

> I wish I were starting now. They are much more accepted by their
> intellectual equals. There is a consciousness about management trainees
> and their first appointments. It is a great deal easier there now. Then it
> depends on the individual. I think there is still a feeling, if there are two
> equal candidates, of 'Let's have the man'. There is still a feeling that
> women leave 'undesirably' to have a baby. People accept that men leave.

Another woman from the 1968 sample thought that opportunities
had improved although not necessarily for very good reasons:

> The concept has been so much discussed. I think it gives a feeling of
> conscious virtue to a manager who promotes a woman . . . It used to be
> thought that one appointed or promoted the best people, and that meant
> men. It wasn't discussed. Now it is discussed, even if it is not reflected in
> more women at the top.

And a senior man in Company B thought that opportunities for
women had improved, even if most of the women there did not think
so:

> I think there would be far fewer people today who would take the view –
> 'We can't possibly give her the job – she's a woman'. That was a common
> reaction ten years ago among senior staff. Or they said, 'We can't give it to
> her – the other men wouldn't like it'. Among people in their thirties and
> forties now, I can't think of anyone who would think like that.

Positive management policies or encouragement for women were
another matter. Some people interpreted positive management

policies as positive discrimination, and the women were all very much against that. Their views were summarised by this senior woman:

> I think that would be a disaster. Women have got to do it on their own merits. If a woman is appointed beyond her status, it does nothing but harm. It puts shells in the guns of those who say, 'Look'. But my own favoured route has shown very slow results.

But the thought that management could actually identify its women and perhaps encourage them a bit more was accepted by some, but by no means all, women:

> It could help much more in career development – as a policy. If you are sent for training, it should be done with the aim of promoting in a certain line and pushing you in that direction. Young graduates, when they reach junior management, should be channelled. They do it for certain men – give them more experience at a younger age – move them around. You can't get promotion if you haven't had experience in a variety of fields.

It certainly did appear that career development was sometimes a rather haphazard matter, and the companies did not appear to have come to terms with the different way in which many women view their careers. One senior woman thought there was a need for action on the part of the companies:

> One of the most important things we should do for women is to give them an idea of career patterns earlier and in more detail. The girl has less idea of her future than a man and doesn't know what she can do. If one wanted an active policy of helping women to stay, do it in terms of information so that she can plan the future.

In both companies, the comment was heard from men and women alike that both sexes were treated the same and that there was no need for any particular policy for women. They had equal opportunities, the annual appraisal of their achievement and potential was conducted in the same way, and as one senior male manager said: 'The girls all get the same crack of the whip as the boys'. Another senior manager in Company B agreed that women were treated and should be treated in the same way as men, but that the experience might be tough: 'If we employ a woman with the right potential or the right expertise, she will get developed, provided that she is tenacious enough to overcome the ups and downs of industrial life. It's not an easy life.' But undoubtedly, if a woman found herself in a job where her senior management was in favour of women getting on in principle, it was certainly made much easier for her to rise in practice: 'The chap I work for is very well predisposed towards me. His wife works in a senior job, and men like that realise the problems.'

One aspect of positive management policy which could be furthered was mentioned by some respondents, particularly men, and this was the possibility of encouraging secretarial or administrative staff to move into management functions. Two senior men, one in each company, said they had positively tried to do this, with very disappointing results. One of them described what he had tried to do by encouraging secretaries to go on a training scheme:

> We had very few internal applications. I wanted more. I said to them, 'Would you like to be a manager?' and they said, 'We don't want to be a manager. We like the one-to-one relationship in being a secretary.' They couldn't think of anything higher than being a Director's secretary.

Some of the women thought that there were many women in administrative or assistant manager jobs who would make first-rate managers, but their promotion came so late, if it came at all, that they were destined never to rise very far in the hierarchy, simply because they had started so much later and did not start with a degree or other qualification.

Women were frequently mentioned, both in 1968 and 1979, as being good in supportive roles, or in the number two job in a department. One senior woman thought that this had a number of implications, most of which were usually ignored. Among them was the possibility of using positive management policy to promote these women:

> In all businesses and organisations, each bit is headed up by a man and a very high proportion are seconded by a woman. She knows about the work and she's often the power. When that man is within a couple of years of retirement, they put in a young man to take over his job. My contention is that they should find that woman. I'm certain she exists in three-quarters of departmental structures. She should be plucked out and forced into doing the job. As long as you're behind her supporting her and giving

her confidence, she'll do it. If you did that, you could transform the position of women, rather than relying on management trainees. That's bound to be long-term. They could do it in five years by the other method.

Although anything that sounded like positive discrimination was greeted with horror by most of the women, there were obviously ways in which tacit discrimination in the other direction could take place. Some women in both firms pointed to ways in which certain assumptions were made about women which disqualified them from particular jobs or promotion prospects, without their being asked if these assumptions were correct. These were very important in depriving women of even the opportunity of refusing. For example, some women pointed out that it was simply assumed that women were not prepared to move around the country, and certainly not abroad, whether they were married or not. (They pointed out that it was generally accepted that married men were becoming increasingly difficult to move, partly because of their wives' jobs and partly because of schooling.) Similarly, some women felt that it was assumed that married women would not be prepared to go on residential courses, or would not be prepared to spend nights away from home. The assumptions reported in 1968, that the 'client' would not like being taken out to lunch by a woman, or that women were not accepted as salesmen, were thought still to be implicit in the thinking of some men, and to act as automatically discounting the possibility of considering a woman for certain jobs, without giving her the chance to discuss it or prove otherwise.

It was thought that a deliberate policy of seriously considering women for all jobs, courses, movement and training, and perhaps making extra efforts to see that line management was aware of the need to put this policy into practice at all levels, could be encouraged, without anyone putting forward any accusation of 'positive discrimination', which was such anathema to most of those interviewed. There were signs that top management and personnel departments in both companies were aware that something like this might be necessary, but there were not many signs that this view was reflected further down the line.

And it was certainly not reflected in all parts of the organisations. In 1968 we found that women did much better in certain parts of the organisation than others. This was generally recognised by management as well as the women themselves, and was reflected in the statistics. In 1979, it was universally held to be still true for both companies. However, in Company A, half the respondents thought that the situation was better than in 1968, while in Company B, the vast majority thought it was about the same as in 1968.

Where did the women do well? The views of the respondents were confirmed by the statistics. In Company A they were seen to be doing well in market research, some of the marketing companies, scientific research, personnel and, to a certain extent, in accounting. These were all areas in which they had been seen to be doing well in 1968, apart from marketing, where there had then been much more reluctance to take them on. It appeared that this had been a change over the last eleven years, even though there were still marketing areas which took very few women.

Some respondents thought that women were doing better in the areas where they had done well in 1968. This would obviously be a logical step, in that if they had already been recruited in larger numbers in some parts of the organisation and had risen to some of the senior positions in 1968, it would be very depressing for women if they were not doing even better by 1979. There was said to have been an improvement since 1968 because women were now being given experience or being recruited into some of the previously 'no-go' areas, like factories, sales, and to a lesser extent some of the technical areas. Certainly the views of some of the younger women were much more positive towards working in marketing areas than they had been in 1968:

> In marketing everyone is broad-minded and a graduate – it's quite unique. It's like a big university in a way because everyone's a graduate which makes it easier for a woman to be accepted . . . I found the sales force and the factory infuriating. They won't take you seriously. You have to build up a stone wall. You have to establish your credibility more strongly than a man has to do. They always assume that if a man is with you he's senior to you, even if he's junior.

It was remarked frequently that it was much more difficult for women in the north and in factories. In the past, this had been given as a reason for not sending them to either the north or factories, but this policy had changed in recent years. There appeared to have been a greater acceptance of women, but some of the pioneers had found it tough:

I believe a lot of men are prejudiced at the factories. There are very significant blocks there, partly because the managers are so much older anyway and attitudes haven't changed as fast as management here. At the factory they're still worried about women bosses and men workers.

This view that women and factories did not go together, particularly in management functions, was also generally held to be true in Company B as well. There the women were thought to be doing well in the same areas where they had been found in 1968 – in scientific research, more particularly in biological research, in personnel, and some of the 'creative' jobs in advertising or publicity. It was said that women did less well in chemistry research, partly reflecting the fewer numbers of women reading chemistry at university, in marketing, and most especially in the factories, in primary and secondary production.

Very little change was thought to have taken place in terms of women doing better and making any kind of breakthrough into new areas, although a few pointed to the fact that women were now accepted in the sales-force. In 1968, there was said to be a great resistance to having women as representatives, but, in the intervening period, women had been taken 'on in this capacity and demonstrated their effectiveness. Part of the reason was the large proportion of pharmacy graduates who were women. Some of the women, however, thought that this change had been forced on the company, since they could not afford to ignore more than 50 per cent of potential recruits simply because they were women.

The proportion of women on the production and marketing sides of Company B was very small, and the proportion actually working on factory sites was even smaller. Certain reasons were put forward for this, such as the legislation protecting women of child-bearing age from working with certain chemical substances, or the fact that many factories were in remote, rather inaccessible places, or the simple fact, as found in Company A, that most factory workers were men, and that women managers were said to be less acceptable to a factory force than men managers. And yet, in both companies, some of the most senior personnel managers, dealing with industrial relations as well as all the other personnel work in some of their northern factories, were women, and were said to be especially good at their jobs.

There was thought to be a case for taking women on in certain functions and giving them the chance to prove themselves. Undoubtedly if one woman is seen to do a job not hitherto done by a woman, others can more easily follow. One senior manager pointed to the great impact made by a very few individual women in his northern factory, which he was convinced would lead to a greater acceptance of women in those functions by their male colleagues. He thought that things were changing, but not all the women interviewed found themselves able to agree whole-heartedly with him, and certainly their views of the future and the possibility of women breaking into entrenched male-dominated areas at a time of increasing male unemployment were gloomy.

Career planning and women's own attitudes

As we have seen, in Company A there had been a tiny increase in the proportion of women both in the really senior posts and the next level down between 1968 and 1979. In Company B, there had been virtually no change in the eleven years.

What then did people think were the reasons for this apparent lack of any real improvement in the achievement of women, in spite of all the changes outlined in the previous chapter? One of the main reasons put forward for the lack of women in the really senior posts was that there were very few in the next level down, so that the pool from which potential top women managers could be drawn was very much smaller than that of the men. This was then said to be true of the next level down, and so on. Women were only to be found in fairly large numbers in the administrative, secretarial or clerical grades, and the proportion of women declined in each level above this.

Many respondents said that this was because the majority of women left when they had their first baby, never to return. They tended to have their babies when they were in their twenties, before they had been promoted off the lowest rung of the management ladder, which meant that the junior women tended to be young and childless, that the middle managers were usually childless, and that it was only at the most senior levels that there were examples of women with children having worked their way through, but again, in both companies, these could be counted on the fingers of one hand. Since the majority of women have babies, and the majority of the women in management or research in these companies apparently left the companies in their twenties, it therefore followed that the number of women who could be promoted to senior management was going to be much smaller than that of men.

But not all women left when they had babies, and not all women had babies. What were the factors operating which prevented them from reaching senior posts, and how were they different from those found in 1968?

One of the themes which emerged this time with much greater emphasis than in 1968 was that of career planning. This had been accentuated by what was seen as a tendency for firms to introduce more rigorous manpower planning, with much less scope for individual careers to deviate significantly from certain norms. There was little doubt in the minds of several respondents that this was a major factor in inhibiting the prospects for women and was an important reason for the small numbers of women in senior posts. It was said that the career patterns laid down by this type of planning made assumptions about the necessity of movement into certain types of job, by a certain age, with a need for geographical mobility, usually at least within this country, and for the more senior jobs, particularly within Company A, an essential spell abroad. Combined with this, there was a belief that the manager embarking on a career with the companies would very quickly understand that, to get on and up, there were certain career paths open, and that any move too far from these paths would mean a closing of doors to the top.

All this had very definite implications for women's careers. One of these was the difference in the approach of women to work right from the start, as this senior woman in Company A pointed out:

> The real difference between men and women is that men know that they are going to work for the next forty years. Even those women who know they are going to work don't know for how long. I always knew that I was going to work and I took a very long-term view . . . The single most important factor in my success is that I knew that I was going to do it for the rest of my life.

Combined with this shorter-term view of careers, it was thought that women had a different attitude towards planning their lives and work. One of the senior women interviewed in 1968 had her views on why women had not been more successful in the company:

Women don't think about careers. They think about jobs. They have a very short time horizon. Men think about the next job and the job after that. Women are much more open-ended. And men indulge in politics much more. They write papers with the aim of winning friends and influencing people.

And again, one of the younger women who had been very successful pointed out the difference between men and women in planning their careers and their attitudes to work: 'Men will do jobs for the short-term with a long-term view. Women's ambitions are not more than two jumps ahead . . . The majority of women work because they enjoy it and not because of any long-term ambition.' One of the management trainees gave an example of this view: 'I work for stimulation. "Career" is a horrible word. I'm not a career woman. It would be the same if I were a man. If I'm not happy, I'll move on.'

But not all women had the same view of their careers, and yet it appeared that most women were treated as though they had. One senior woman thought that one of the main reasons that there were so few women at the top today was because when the present senior women were starting their careers they did not receive early promotion like some of their male colleagues, simply because it was not expected that they would stay: 'Some of my peers are directors of this company. Their whole careers have been different from Day One.' She thought that the situation had not changed much since 1968, and, if anything, the future looked worse:

> I think you've got to look at the sort of women there are. Ahead of me they were maverick women – there for various reasons – chance presented certain opportunities and they took them. My generation was the first generation of specialist women with specialist skills. We were unique and stood out. Now women are equal in the race with men – competing equally. They're not being picked out and they're not so unique, so it may be worse for them.

Her views were echoed in Company B, where a number of the most senior women had risen very quickly as the research area in which they worked had expanded after the war. They were mainly going to retire fairly soon within a few years of each other, and there was little doubt in the minds of many of the respondents that they would not be replaced by other women. One younger woman viewed this with some pessimism:

There aren't very many women in the 35–50 age group at all. Probably quite a few of the older women will retire soon and I don't see where the next layer of senior women will come from . . . It's going to get worse once the older women retire and there are no more women to fill their shoes.

Women's own inclination was also thought to have been a factor in preventing more movement towards senior posts. One senior woman interviewed in 1968 said: 'Women are not their own best friends. They do chuck their hands in too easily. Maybe women don't like the business climate. A lot like to do vaguely social things – men too – like lecturing.'

In both companies, views were expressed that women lacked ambition and the total commitment and single-mindedness that were required to do well in senior management. This was frequently reported by women when describing themselves, and obviously affected the views of men when thinking of women in top jobs, as this senior man in Company B reported: 'Women would not be happy as directors. This company expects you to put the company before yourself, and there are not many women of my acquaintance who would be happy to do that on a long-term basis.'

The very fact that there were so few women at the top and that there was no real evidence of much change was also thought to be an inhibiting factor: 'Success breeds success. Until you get a lot of women about who've been manifestly successful there won't be much change.'

It was certainly agreed that if there were more women around at the higher levels it would make it easier, both for men to see that women could perform well in a range of senior jobs, and for women to have images to emulate so that they could be encouraged to think it possible for them to rise. Certainly the success of some of the younger women with children in Company A who had reached senior posts was seen as an enormous encouragement to some of the even younger women.

Nevertheless, it was undoubtedly regarded as very difficult to work and have a family. There were some women in all age-groups who had done it, and they were represented among the most senior women in both companies. Some of them had met considerable hostility, particularly the older ones. It was not surprising that so few managed to stay and rise to the top, as this senior woman, now in her fifties, commented: 'Looking back, I'm amazed at the number of people who disapproved of me working with young children. I've had strangers coming up to me and saying they disapproved. People were incredibly rude'. One younger woman said she too was not surprised that so few women got to the top. She pointed out some of the problems for young women today continuing to work with a baby:

> There are great difficulties financing the care of children. It's only open to people with highly-paid jobs. If you have a baby when you're in junior mangement and your husband is a teacher or a social worker you just can't afford it. At the same time, there is a tremendous social pressure on women not to do it – 'The children will suffer'.

One of the themes which was frequently mentioned in 1968 was that men did not feel comfortable in the company of senior women, either as peers within a group or as their boss. This type of comment was heard much less often in 1979, and there did appear to have been a genuine change of attitude, particularly among the younger men. Perhaps the type of women now reaching senior posts has also changed. There were certainly fewer comments about intimidating women frightening senior men. However, some women thought there were still subtle ways in which women were frozen out: 'There is still a social resistance to women who do well. Men don't know how to deal with senior women. You can watch them thinking. You can feel the waves sometimes'. Some of the women interviewed in 1968 had not gone as far as it appeared they might at the time, and it was clear that some of them thought this was because they did not fit into the male 'club' at the top. Even if they did not frighten the men, they did not always make them feel comfortable. Some of the younger women, commenting on this, thought it very depressing that certain women had not got further, simply because they had been blocked by an unspoken prejudice, where it would be impossible ever to prove discrimination.

Two women in Company A summed up their views on why women had not reached senior posts. The first one, a woman in her fifties who had reached a very senior level, thought it was mainly to do with women themselves:

> I don't really think this company's policy prevents women reaching senior posts. The doors are wide open. I have not seen any discrimination against

women in senior posts, provided that they have 100 per cent commitment. They can't do a 9–5 day; they must be prepared to travel; to do things in the evenings and at weekends. If they do all that, there's no problem.

And the second, who had come in as a management trainee and was in her twenties, thought there were a lot of other reasons, again implicit in the characteristics of women:

> Women leave to have babies and don't want to work. Or they're not aggressive enough. Or they don't like managing or being in charge of people. Or they like teaching or nursing where their special skills are used, like nurturing or caring. They want to be loved – and you're certainly not loved if you're a manager in this company.

In Company A, one of the senior men said that he thought that the performance of women management trainees could not have led to any increase in the number of women in senior posts. As we have seen, only two women were left of the 56 women management trainees who had been taken on between 1961 and 1971. Both of these had, in fact, done extremely well, and both had continued to work while having children. However, he pointed out that in 1979, if the company looked for people to develop to senior management among its management trainees from the period 1961–1971, it would only find two women. This was, for him, one of the main reasons why there had been so little change in the proportions of women in senior posts. He thought that if the track record of women management trainees was so bad, there ought to be more consideration of women who had not come in as trainees, and, of course, they made up the bulk of women in Company A in the more senior posts.

But why had the women trainees left? In *Women in Top Jobs*, one of the main findings about the female management trainees was that they felt frustrated and under-used; and they thought that the company was not fulfilling the promises it had made to them. When we returned to the company in 1979, we found that all these management trainees had, in fact, left within a year of our research, mostly with no reason given. They had been very bright, ambitious young women, who expressed the view to us that they were not going to be treated like some of the older women in the company. Evidently, they found that they could not change the company, and so, for reasons some of which could perhaps have been deduced from our report, they left.

The five management trainees interviewed this time presented a very different picture. They had been recruited between 1972 and 1975, and represented all the women who were left from the intake of 1972 (two out of four), 1973 (none out of eight), and 1974 (two out of eight); the fifth was one of the six survivors from the intake of 13 women in 1975. They were different from those interviewed in 1968, mainly in that they had had much earlier promotion. This was said to be due to a big loss of both male and female management trainees in the years in which they were recruited and the years before, which meant that they had been promoted into jobs which they might not otherwise have had the chance to fill. There was little evidence of the frustration and lack of job satisfaction reported by their counterparts eleven years before. However, these were the ones who had remained in the company, so that it was likely that they would be more satisfied than those who had left.

Part of the problem was a general one, as one of the people concerned with management trainees pointed out:

> We can prove that there has been a higher loss of women than men, *but* women are concentrated in marketing and market research, and the wastage rates in those areas tend to be higher in any case. Around the 25–26 age-mark there's a lost of head-hunting of both men and women. A girl will go where she gets the most money. These are short-term decisions. Some girls leave because they feel they're not getting promoted quickly enough. They take the short-term view.

Obviously a lot of men take the short-term view too, since the proportion of male management trainees who had left was, in fact, as high in some years as that of women. But, of course, there are more of them, so that the actual numbers who remain are likely to be greater than those of women.

One of the reasons for some of the women management trainees leaving was the fact that they appeared to be almost encouraged in their short-term view of the future, or at least, not to be presented with the alternative, as this senior woman pointed out:

> I'm afraid you would expect a big turnover in graduate trainees through a lack of explicit career planning. Very few women have had a specific career plan put in front of them. If you look at the management trainee scheme, there are expectations, but it is the system the men come up on.

And this argument was heard time and time again, that, if the women were prepared to follow exactly the same type of career pattern as the men, there was nothing to stop them doing as well as the men. There might be lingering prejudices, but these were dying out as older managers left, and the expectations of young women today could be identical to those of young men.

This, sadly, was obviously not true for the majority of women. Their initial expectations might be the same, and, indeed, the expectations of the management trainees interviewed were very high. They regarded themselves as equal to their male contemporaries, and were very determined to succeed. But then, so were their counterparts of eleven years before, even if they appeared more frustrated in their ambitions even then. It remains to be seen what happens to these management trainees, but, to judge from the movement of their contemporaries, even if they themselves stayed and rose to the top, they would still only comprise a tiny number of unusual women among a lot of men. The main problem remained, that, when and if women had babies, they either had to continue in their careers in exactly the same way as men or they had to leave. In these companies, there was virtually no opportunity for continuing in any other way, and certainly no other way to reach a senior post.

CHAPTER 7

Women and Children

The figures have shown that the number of women in the two companies who manage to combine work with running a family is extremely small. This is true of all age-groups and at all levels of seniority, although, of the tiny number of women in the most senior jobs, the actual proportion who have children is much higher than that at any other level. This suggests an interesting possibility that women who manage to continue work with small children are much more like their male counterparts than women who do not marry or do not have children. This may make them more, rather than less, acceptable to the male-dominated environment in which they have to operate. They have what was described in *Women in Top Jobs* as the 'measure of the man's world', and they bring to their work a dimension of shared experience which, perhaps, their single counterparts do not.

However, the vast majority of women entering these two organisations do not reach the top, and, it is said, most women leave, mainly when they have babies, and are then never seen again, at least not in the same company. Some respondents thought that they just gave up work, or, if they returned to work at all, they did not work full-time or did jobs which fitted in with their family commitments. There was a very considerable lack of knowledge, not only about what happened to the qualified women who had once worked for these organisations, but also about what could have or even what should have happened to them. Women who left these organisations were regarded in the same way as men who left them. They did not return, they did not ask to return, and if they had wanted to return it would have been surprising. The question of whether it might be a good idea to encourage them to return had only occurred to very few of the respondents, either male or female.

There appeared to be two areas for exploration. One was the question of whether there was anything that the organisations could do to help women to continue working while they had small children, and the other was whether there was anything they could do to help women to return after a break in which they were looking after their children.

Help for women to remain

Most of the respondents in both companies thought that their organisations could do more to help women remain working while they had small children, but there was a very definite question-mark over whether or not they should do so, or whether it was, in fact, practically possible.

The most common suggestions were to provide crèche facilities, to provide or allow more part-time work, to have more flexible working hours or arrangements for time off, to institute or encourage work-sharing, and to arrange more work so that it could be done on a freelance basis at home if possible. There was also a suggestion that, rather than provide a crèche, companies should contribute towards the child-care expenses of working mothers.

The question of crèche provision brought a mixed response, and none of the respondents thought it an ideal solution. On the whole, it was thought likely that most of the qualified women would prefer to make other arrangements for their children nearer their homes or in their own homes, and that they were usually in a better position to afford this than most working women. It was thought that the lack of a crèche might prevent clerical, secretarial or shop-floor staff from returning to work, but was unlikely to be the major factor in stopping a woman scientist or manager from returning. Central London offices were also thought to be unsuitable for crèches, and some respondents said that travelling with a baby every day in the rush hour was not an attractive prospect. Some respondents thought that the existence of a crèche would mean that women would be tempted to go and spend part of their working day with their child or children, and that they might not be able to give their whole minds to their jobs. But, basically, the main objections to a crèche were that it was expensive, that there was no guarantee that it would keep women working within the company, and that it was a lot of bother which was of questionable cost-effectiveness. It was also said that, if special child-care facilities were offered to women, the argument would be put forward that they ought also to be offered to men, and the implications of that were very far-reaching. Both firms had considered the possibility of providing crèches, although the retention of qualified women was obviously not uppermost in their minds when doing so. Neither firm had put it at the top of the list of priorities and it was suggested that, in the present economic climate, there were far more pressing problems than the potential provision of a crèche.

None of the women who had continued working with small children thought that the provision of a crèche would have made much difference to them, although they pointed out the expense of adequate help with small children. One of the respondents thought that her firm might look seriously at the possibility of going into the day-nursery business, since present facilities were so obviously inadequate for so many people. She thought that perhaps the firm's employees could 'get a cut-rate' at one of these nurseries. Perhaps because they had had to make arrangements for looking after their children, these women were not convinced of the need for a crèche. This reaction was fairly typical of women who had children: 'I don't think it's up to the employer to look after you and your children. It's up to the employee and most will find a way. Self-motivating women will sort out their own domestic problems'. It was evident from the numbers of women with children in these two companies that it was not perhaps terribly easy to be self-motivating in this way.

In Company A, it was thought that there was more scope for part-time work or job-sharing of some kind, although in Company B this was thought to be much more difficult, mainly because so many of the jobs held by women were in scientific research which was said to require full-time attendance because of the nature of much of the work. One of the general arguments put forward against part-time work was that line management jobs could not be performed on a part-time basis; decisions had to be taken and, if part of the chain of decision-making was not there for some of the time, the business could not function efficiently. But not all the women were in such a structure and, even if they were, they could cite other jobs which could be done by people with their qualifications on a part-time basis. Even within the scientific field, there were said to be jobs which could be done less than full-time. There was an immediate reaction among men that senior jobs could not be done part-time or by two people sharing responsibilities. But at the age when most women have babies, they are not in senior posts in any case, and it is quite possible that those who were in line management would consider working in a less demanding job which allowed more flexibility. Several of the women said that the situation at the moment was one of 'all or nothing'. One woman said that this had been made very clear to her:

> I've thought a lot about freelance or part-time work. I've had discussions about it, but it was made very clear to me that it meant no more promotion . . . One has to be seen to be demonstrating commitment – you've got to be around and stay late. The business needs reassurance all the time that you're committed to the business.

On this basis, which was generally accepted to be true by both men and women, it was not perhaps surprising that so many women left. The provision of part-time work, although many women thought that it would be feasible, was not thought to be worth the bother, and men said that it would have to be demonstrated that it was in the company's interests to redesign jobs so that women could continue to work.

In terms of manpower planning, it was also thought to be difficult to create or redesign jobs at a junior or middle management level, since they were needed for training junior management or scientists, or they were regarded as jobs for older people who were unlikely to go very far in seniority. Having bright young women part-time in such jobs was regarded as potentially creating problems about what to do with the not-so-bright men who were not going to go any higher.

The inflexibility of big organisations was puzzling to some respondents who thought that large firms like theirs ought to be able to accommodate a number of different ways of working:

> They could be more flexible in their attitudes and have different attitudes to suit different situations. There are certain kinds of jobs where you don't have to be in the office all the time and you could easily work at home, but I don't think they look at it that way. A man would never work from home – but then, it's not necessary for them.

In some areas, for example in market research, women who had once worked for the organisation and then had babies were used on a consultancy or freelance basis, and did work from home. They were highly valued, did not clog up the promotion ladder and were said to have a great deal of job satisfaction. This seemed to be a situation in which everyone was happy, but it appeared to be almost unique.

One senior woman who had worked with small children thought that one of the main problems was coping with the sudden crisis. This could be children's illnesses or the collapse of child-care arrangements. In such cases, she thought the companies could be more flexible in allowing time off work to sort out problems of a temporary nature. A senior man thought that, in fact, this kind of thing did happen; albeit unofficially.

The question of fitting in women who came back after maternity leave was raised. Some respondents said that there was always a doubt about whether a woman was actually going to come back, even if she said she was going to. This meant that someone had to fill her job, which nevertheless had to be kept open for her. This was thought to be especially difficult in scientific research, where there was great stress laid on continuity. Some of the women who had had children thought, however, that the maternity provisions of the Employment Protection Act had made it much easier for women to come back. They thought that having the legal right to have their jobs held open made all the difference to some women who might otherwise have found it difficult, since the fact that the employer had a legal obligation removed any barriers that might have existed before. This meant that women were presented with a real choice, and that if they then decided not to come back, they could feel that it was their own decision and not forced on them by their employers.

There was evidence of some change in attitudes towards women with children working, but there was still a very ambivalent feeling towards them, even from people who were very much in favour of women being able to progress more quickly and further up the ladder. This was expressed by both men and women, and explained in some part why there was such an emphasis on the 'all or nothing' job for women who continued after having a baby:

> You can't expect the best of both worlds. Either you have a child and devote your energies to it or you have a job. To do this sort of job is physically and mentally demanding. You have to be very very dedicated to do the two together . . . I wouldn't want to.

The women who continued working certainly found themselves under greater scrutiny after their return to work, which may have acted as a spur to some, but was not likely to help everyone.

One of the big problems was undoubtedly that of being able to work after having a baby without being under pressure while the children were small and yet being able to rejoin the promotion race after a few years. Any kind of level-pegging for a few years was regarded as an almost automatic disqualification for promotion, since the structure for promotion in both companies was geared so much to age and salary. Some senior managers, particularly in Company A, said that this was not true, and that there were plenty of examples of people being promoted at later ages, with the opportunity of moving up to the most senior levels of management. But this had not happened with women, and it was certainly not how the majority of women in both companies saw the situation. There was no doubt in their minds that, if they missed the boat at the age at which people moved from junior to middle management, they would never find themselves in senior management.

One of the results of this was that, unless women were determined to stay in the mainstream of the promotion race, the figures suggest that they decided, for one reason or another, that it was not in their interests to continue to work in these companies, if at all. This could have been because they could not afford the necessary help with their children since they were not senior enough, it could have been that they wanted to stay at home with their children, or it could simply have been that only the most highly motivated women will stay working after a baby, and they will rise because of this very high degree of motivation. For the women who are not determined to rise to the top at the time they have their first baby, all the other factors stacked against working mothers appeared to have encouraged them to leave, and undoubtedly one of the most important factors was the 'all or nothing' attitude towards jobs within the two companies. Several senior women within these companies thought that career alternatives were not presented to women, and that no attempt was made to persuade them that it might be in their interests to stay. One senior woman thought that this would always militate against any increase in the numbers of senior women, unless the policy was changed: 'They have babies and go off. They might have had other ideas or made other arrangements if they thought there was something worth staying for. Unless you can see career patterns ahead, you don't stay.'

Help for women to return

Although the majority of respondents thought that their organisations could do more to help women continue working while they had small children, they were certainly not sure about whether the companies could do more to help them return to work after a break to look after their children, if that break was longer than the statutory maternity leave. Oddly enough, it was the senior men rather than the women who thought their companies could do more to help women return after a small-child break. Almost all the men interviewed thought that their companies could do more, while in Company A less than half the women thought they could, and in Company B only two women thought they could.

The main objection in Company B to women returning after a break was that they would have lost expertise and knowledge, particularly in the field of scientific research, even if they had been with the company for some time. As this senior woman pointed out:

> They're out of touch. If they leave as a Section Head in their late twenties or early thirties, five years later they can only come back as a technician. You could establish a training system, but it would be unlikely because of the odd numbers, and people would ask whether it was worthwhile.

And within this company, it was also thought difficult to come back even if one had had expertise of another kind: 'It's also difficult with general management. Look at all the legislation. Managers are now saying they can't keep up with all the legislation. Women would be out of touch with that.'

It seemed to be particularly ironic that women graduates were, in fact, considered more dispensable than women with lesser qualifications, as this senior woman pointed out:

> They do it with more junior women and with the packing people and secretarial staff. They will allow seasonal and part-time working . . . I think we've suffered from a lot of male unemployment in the graduate area. And we've got a grading system, by which we pay a salary based on age, experience and grade. If you've got people in their twenties, a person

of forty is a pain in the neck in the grading structure . . . Here's a person who's badly out of age and step . . . A person who leaves for purely domestic reasons – when they come back they must accept the penalty. It's very difficult to fit them in.

And a senior man who was very much in favour of the company doing everything it could to help women also pointed to the difficulties:

We've got many examples of secretaries coming back. They're very valuable – a lot better than the young ones. But there's a problem with qualified women. They've probably stepped out to have their families at an age when the man is leaving the bench to become a manager . . . If they come back as a bench researcher, they're less useful than a fresh person out of university.

The question of whether it was worthwhile was the main factor in the minds of management: 'We've got enough people without tapping this source. If we ever got really short of people we might do it from our own point of view.'

If some people had seen a problem about fitting women back in after maternity leave, or had pointed to the difficulties of providing part-time work for women who might then be competing with men who were not going to progress very far, certainly far more saw the problems of fitting in women who came back after a number of years.

We have a culture of promotion from within. It's a kind of psychological contract that we don't bring people in above them. We develop an internal culture. If you start monkeying with that, you're in trouble.

There were certainly seen to be jobs at middle management level which were earmarked for men who were not going to the top. The prospect of bringing back women at that level did not appeal to those who were responsible for fulfilling the expectations of these men:

The culture of internal development militates against the external applicant and therefore against returning women . . . We do take people back, if they've gained in experience or qualification, but there is a re-entry problem.

There was a general acceptance that a woman who had had time off to bring up a family had not gained in experience or qualifications, or at least that, if she had, they were not particularly relevant to doing a job. One woman who had had a baby commented on this:

> The ability to manage resources is not something people lose. You don't need any technical skills to do my job. You need organisational ability, clear-thinking, the ability to get on with people. I'm not going to lose those qualities by being at home with a baby. I think that's just an excuse.

Fitting women back in meant that there had to be a slot for them, and this was regarded as very difficult by some of the respondents, particularly at a time when many saw redundancies for men looming up, as well as little recruitment taking place:

> Those people who've done a very good job and everyone regrets them going – we tell them there will always be an open door. We've said we'll be delighted to welcome back able people. But it may not be that easy when they want to come back – you can't *manufacture* jobs.

One senior woman thought that it must be in the interests of the companies to welcome good women back:

> They have to define where their interests lie, and they won't do it for idealistic reasons. If it's cheaper to re-employ women after say three years away – and I calculate it must be cheaper to have them back than employ someone new – the company should see how they can benefit from that. Being a realist, I can see mutual advantages . . . Is it good business to have young graduates leaving? These women are more loyal, they have greater stability and reduced expectations.

This may well be true, but it was precisely because of this greater loyalty and possibly reduced expectations that management shuddered at the thought, it sometimes appeared:

> You have to accept the fact that the company has to be run economically and you have to have due regard to the staff. If a woman leaves and a man is promoted to her job, it's very difficult if she wants to come back after a couple of years. You would always have to have certain openings at a certain level, and that would create bad feeling from the men below. Why should businesses do that? It would create personal problems as well as not being an economic proposition.

There sometimes appeared to be a conflict between getting the best person for the job and keeping the existing workforce happy. It seemed that management often took the easy way out, since they had no guarantee that a returning woman who had been first-class when she left would be any better than a second-class man who had stayed in the business and for whom they had to find a slot in any case. Again, there was a certain amount of ambivalence, even among those who said that they could see the advantages in helping women to return:

> Why should I do it unless I haven't got the managers I need? I don't know whether it is a legitimate objective for a competitive business to construct a structure to claw women back . . . But where we are perhaps shortest is in people with a few years' management experience. I am sure that most parts of the company would look favourably at women with a good track record who had had a three to four years' break. I think I would regard having a baby as nearly as good as having been overseas for that time, but it's subordinate line management who need convincing of that.

It was frequently said that no woman had ever asked to come back, and that none had intimated when they left that they might ever want to come back. Men thought that the qualified women who had worked for the company over the years and who had left to have a baby were not really interested in returning, although virtually nothing was known about what had happened to them, whether they were working or not, or, indeed, whether they might be interested in returning to the firm that had trained them. The widespread assumption, however, was that they would not. This view was held among young women as well as among the senior management:

> I've never known anyone come back . . . People feel reticent. Perhaps the same people aren't there. Perhaps they move on. Perhaps women want to work nearer home. In today's world, people aren't thinking of going back. People are looking for jobs which are interesting but not very demanding. They're not interested in careers when they're married with kids. They're interested in supporting the household budgets.

If this view can be held by a young woman in her twenties, it is perhaps not surprising that it was so prevalent among older men. But how true was it? It was remarkably difficult to find out, particularly since there was no evidence of anyone having done it. One woman who had thought of the possibility pointed out some of the problems:

It will only happen if someone makes it happen. I don't know anyone who's asked. It's a very competitive environment . . . There has to be positive encouragement from your husband. You need a combination of support from your husband and people at work. Not many women get that.

And a senior woman who looked favourably on the idea in principle, reiterated some of the practical problems:

In theory you should be able to come back to an organisation like ours. I can't think of any who have . . . The age thing operates here. Everything is dominated by promotion. There's no continuity. When you move you take it with you . . . The woman would need a patron to say, 'I remember her . . .' but ten years on – where is he? Probably when she returned she'd be in competition with younger people – ten years younger. The whole of the motivation of this company is to get on and move up. They always want someone with potential and don't want to get landed with people.

This was a very definite factor operating against returning women. If people were expected to get to a certain point at a certain age, if promotion and movement were paramount, there was certainly no room for a returning person who might gum up the works, and certainly no room for someone who might come back and expect to take up where she left off, if that meant competing with younger people for a limited number of jobs further up the ladder. Either way, the returning woman could not win.

All this was, of course, extremely theoretical since the problem had not arisen, and it looked unlikely to arise since all the cards were seen to be stacked so neatly against it. Any woman leaving either of these two organisations could not have had many illusions about the possibility of returning after a break to be greeted with open arms.

And yet, it was in this area that some of the senior men thought that there might be room for improvement, and there were signs that the question of re-entry for qualified women with a 'good track-record' might be examined seriously. It was recognised that the present loss rate on women graduate trainees made the scheme look uneconomic, and that re-training was cheaper than training, particularly where an investment had already been made. The problems of internal promotion were thought to be less acute if a woman had been employed in the organisation before, although these were matters to be discussed further. It was stressed by both men and women that if the scheme were to work women would have to be made aware of the possibilities, both when they left and at continuing times after they had left. It was clear that the present *ad hoc* arrangements and relying on people remembering were not effective, and that some properly institutionalised scheme would have to be worked out, so that it could be properly monitored.

CHAPTER 8

Effectiveness of Agencies of Change

Internal pressure groups

We were interested to see whether there had been any pressure brought to bear over the last eleven years by any formal or informal pressure groups within the organisations as far as the employment or prospects for women were concerned, and, if so, what were the circumstances and what had been the effects.

In Company A, managers had formed themselves into a house union shortly before our interviewing took place. One woman pointed out that there was not a single woman among the national officers of this union, which was restricted to junior and middle managers. The respondents in Company A were unanimous in their feeling that there had been no pressure brought to bear from any internal pressure group as far as women's careers were concerned.

On the whole, the women interviewed were very much against any idea of bringing pressure as a group. There was a widely-held belief that membership of any group or being seen to be pressing for women's rights would be interpreted as conduct unsuitable for a manager, as this woman pointed out:

> A lot of successful women won't band together. One of the things that has made these women successful is that they've got there on their own merits. They can't see the problems. There is still a tremendous feeling that, whatever else you think, whoever you're going to be complaining to will be responsible for your promotion. Women just don't want to kick the boat out too far.

There was an impression among respondents that very senior women had had such a struggle themselves to make it that they were either too exhausted to fight for their younger colleagues, or that they felt that, if they had made it, there was no reason why others should not follow. Some of these women were, in fact, more active on behalf of younger women than was generally recognised, but some felt there was a limit to what they could.do.

Some of the younger successful women reiterated the point that it was not wise to make too much fuss about things: 'I think I would know if any pressure had happened. The women are around but they very rarely talk to each other about rights. People take the lead that I have given – get on with it and not talk about it.' There was a general tendency to dislike group involvement of any kind, as this young manager pointed out: 'Women tend to like to fight for themselves. They're more individualistic than men. There's no need here. I don't think anyone feels hard done by.'

Although it was quite clear from our research that a great many women did feel 'hard done by', there was obviously a tacit acceptance of the fact that it was better to keep quiet about such feelings, or, at least, not to band together with other women, whether to air an individual grievance or to encourage examination of the status of women in general within the organisation.

In Company B, all but one of the respondents said that there had been no pressure brought to bear as far as women were concerned. The company had moved from being an almost entirely non-union company to being almost entirely unionised in the early 1970s, with the lead being taken by the scientists. Many of those interviewed, particularly those who had been with the company for a long time, were very much against this, and their knowledge of union matters was very limited.

The only respondent who knew of any pressure, in either company, said that there had been union discussion in Company B about the question of providing crèche facilities, for which it had been agreed there was little or no demand, and of extending pension rights to widowers of employees as well as widows, which had been of interest to a very limited number. There was no other evidence of any discussion by any group of the position of women in Company B.

Internal pressure had not been brought to bear on the companies in 1968 and the situation had not changed by 1979, in spite of the fact that there was much greater organisation of managers and scientists in both companies by that date.

The Sex Discrimination Act, 1975

The majority of respondents in both companies thought that the Sex Discrimination Act had had little or no effect on their companies, although some thought that it had some effect on the country as a whole. One of the main reasons cited for this lack of impact was that both companies had been forward-looking employers before the Act, so that it was likely to have had less effect on them than on other less enlightened companies.

Among women, there were frequent references to what was seen as the difficulty of changing attitudes by legislation, and one woman summed up the view of her colleagues: 'Legislation isn't going to get women to the Boardroom.' Some respondents questioned the need for any legislation at all, but there were comments that it had been effective in 'making people think twice'. Some senior women thought that the existence of the Act would lead to a gradual erosion of prejudice. However, the fact that both companies had always been regarded as enlightened employers led some respondents to think that the legislation might mean that, instead of leading the way in the removal of discriminatory practices, the companies might now say that they observed the law and that that was sufficient.

In both companies, considerable emphasis had been placed on informing managers about the legislation, and respondents agreed that the law was being strictly followed. However, there was some doubt expressed about how and if the companies took any very active part in implementing the recommendations of the Act: 'Probably they have had to be careful what they do so that they obey the letter if not the spirit of the law. But there are still a lot of people who just pay lip-service to it.' And again, the importance of individual managers in executing the law was stressed by this woman: 'They made a law saying you mustn't be seen to discriminate, but it's in the hands of the individual.'

Very few respondents had any idea of what was contained in the Act, and many of them thought that the maternity provisions of the Employment Protection Act were contained in the Sex Discrimination Act. Among the few people who had any knowledge of the Act, this woman was the only one to make any positive suggestions of how the companies could actively implement it:

We should start by having an informed audit. They should appoint a few people to have training in the Sex Discrimination Act, and what is perceived as good practice internationally as well as in this country. We could get a centre of expertise on what we should be doing. We could take a look at all the signs and portents whether current practices were having any effect in the use of women. You'd get some anecdotal evidence of individual successes, but you'd also get some evidence of the attitudes of men and women . . . Quite a lot of what we need to do is in information and training and we'd find practices that needed to be changed . . . For example, people accept certain structures, but if they're not producing the right number of people with specific skills, they're not the best. There's nothing wrong with positive training according to the Act. It would help to get the balance right.

Some respondents, both male and female, thought that the Act had possibly worked against the interests of women. It was suggested that legislation of this kind could have a 'back-lash' effect in making people less sympathetic towards women. From both companies, women expressed this fear: 'It's made some men more anti-women. They think we're being over-protected and so women have to work that bit harder.'

This question of protection, emphasised in the maternity provisions of the Employment Protection Act, was thought to have made men think twice before taking on women. One senior woman went much further:

The Sex Discrimination Act is terrible for women – it's terribly counter-productive in helping women to get on. It's saying in effect that we're all the same. It's mechanistic in its effects. At a time of high unemployment it makes it worse. It leads to counter-reaction. It makes people more sensitive and careful and there's a kick-back effect.

There was still a very strongly felt view that a woman had to be better than a man to be appointed to a job in direct competition, and this view had not changed since 1968.

Nevertheless there was evidence that both companies took the legislation seriously and made every effort to ensure that it was being implemented at every level in the companies:

The company genuinely tries to stay within legislation. I am sure that company policy would not condone any attempt to wangle round it. We can't afford to be caught out and we would be very tough on anyone caught out of line on this.

However, the majority of respondents thought that the legislation had made little or no difference to their companies or the prospects for women within them, and their views were summarised by this senior male manager in Company B:

The Sex Discrimination Act has made no difference, because I don't think that the factors which determine whether women rise to top jobs are affected by policies which could be changed by legislation.

The Equal Opportunities Commission

Although some of the younger respondents thought that the Equal Opportunities Commission had had an effect in general, the majority of respondents in both companies thought that it had little or no effect on their organisations, and indeed, in Company B, nobody thought that it had anything other than a negligible effect. The main reasons given for this almost total lack of impact on the companies were similar to those given for the relative lack of impact of the Sex Discrimination Act. The companies were seen to be anxious to comply with the law, and therefore there was no need for the Equal Opportunities Commission to become involved with them. One woman thought that the EOC had had more impact elsewhere: 'It's needed because there are unscrupulous employers who would *not* implement the Act without such a watchdog commission to oversee legislation.' In general, most respondents knew very little about the Commission, and were certainly not aware of any particular way in which it was affecting their organisations.

Rather more than half the women interviewed in Company A said that the EOC had had an effect in general. However, most of these thought that the effect had been negative rather than positive, citing what they considered to be poor publicity as having contributed towards a rather unfortunate image, and some women thought that it had gone about things in the wrong way, particularly through tackling the wrong issues. Some women thought that the EOC had got off to a bad start, and that the poor press it had received had not been entirely of its own making. There were also some questions about the reasons for its existence: 'They've had a very funny press and I don't suppose they enjoy it. They've got labelled with fighting cases. I think they would wish their more positive stance were publicised.' The question of the role of the EOC was one which puzzled some of the respondents who were concerned about the future: 'I think its role is to be a catalyst. It can precipitate things. It can stir things up. I don't know whether it has achieved enough to justify its existence.'

Grave doubts were expressed on whether the EOC justified its existence by most of the men interviewed, and it did seem very clear that there was a need for the public image of the EOC to be brushed up if it were to be taken seriously by employers.

Very few respondents in Company B could think of anything they would like to see the EOC doing, although some of the men said they thought it ought to be abolished. One woman thought that it ought to encourage women to stay at home and look after their children, while another thought it ought to ensure that companies took a certain quota of women when recruiting, although she feared that firms might get round this requirement.

One of the men in Company B thought that the EOC could be the right vehicle to stress the openings for women in engineering:

> There still seems to be a national image that girls play with dolls and boys play with Meccano sets, and that if a girl wants to play with a Meccano set she's unfeminine. A woman who goes into engineering has to be very strongly motivated to get in and on, and to withstand all the pinpricks and succeed. I think most managers would not mind whether it was a man or a woman. They'd say, 'We need people – it doesn't matter who'.

His view on the possible role of the EOC in helping to educate people on the potential job opportunities was shared by several women in Company A. Schools were thought to give girls very inadequate advice on possible careers, as this young manager thought:

> Girls are doing the wrong 'O' and 'A' levels. The careers people are very bad, especially with girls. They tend to push them towards traditional careers, and the girls don't realise what they could do. Both boys and girls know very little about industry. And the girls are not thinking of taking economics or the sciences. The jobs problem being what it is, employers are not going to take people with non-useful subjects. Teachers haven't got a clue about what goes on in industry. The EOC should do something positive in educating schools to develop the careers education they give girls. They should run courses for careers, especially in all-girls schools.

Some of the women thought the EOC should encourage people to think about the role that women will have in the future. It was thought that it could do more to help women with children work, not only through concentrating more pressure towards achieving better child-care facilities, but also in changing the image of a working mother being in some way a 'bad' mother.

There was a general feeling among those who thought the EOC could achieve something that it ought to concentrate on issues like mortgages, tax, pensions, child-care and education, and take a positive lead, rather than get tied up in cases and tribunals, which were thought to help foster a rather negative image. Certain criticisms were made of what was considered to be a rather middle-class image surrounding the EOC, which was thought to be a bit too 'ladylike'. But against these views of what the EOC could do must be placed the views of the majority of those in Company B and a substantial minority in Company A, as reflected in this comment: 'I don't think you can change attitudes through legislation or the Equal Opportunities Commission. You can't *make* people change attitudes. You've got to break down barriers through women doing things themselves.' This comment epitomised a common thread running through interviews with many women in the two companies – that women had to be judged on their own merits and achievements, and that this would change attitudes, and not legislation or commissions or pressure groups.

The women's movement

The majority of respondents in both companies thought that the women's movement had had some impact and effect on public opinion over the past eleven years. There was a fairly even division among the women on whether the effects had been negative or positive.

Some women said that the women's movement had made the public more conscious of women's rights and had publicised some of the discriminatory practices which were in existence: 'It's highlighted some very definite abuses, such as not being able to get mortgages and having to have male guarantors. It's done very valuable publicity work in these things and the situation has improved.' Some women saw it as having had an enormous impact on society as a whole, although this view was by no means widely held:

I think it has been a great force for the better in our society. The tremendous acceptance of a woman prime minister wouldn't have happened ten years ago. The women's movement has affected whole attitudes of whole generations, especially the younger generation. It's a splendid advance. There's a changing attitude of men towards women. The movement has accelerated a natural evolution.

This was an older woman, nearing retirement, speaking, and her views were certainly not shared by most of the younger women interviewed. It was particularly interesting that among the women under the age of 35 the majority thought that the women's movement had either been irrelevant or had had a negative effect. In fact, some of the greatest hostility to the women's movement came from the younger women in Company A:

The women's movement and feminism actually do damage to women's cause. They actually want their cake and eat it. I don't see why. One should be talking about equal opportunities for both men and women. Women can only be expected to be treated as equal if they behave as equal.

One younger woman expressed another view:

I think the effect of the women's movement is dissipating now, primarily because now the younger and more modern women regard women's rights as automatic and not something to fight for. Women of over 35 or over 40 still show some appreciation or surprise when women's rights are granted. Under that age-group women *expect* to do everything men do.

Some women thought that one of the main effects of the women's movement was in raising the consciousness of women themselves. It was perhaps odd that, among women who stressed the importance of the individual so much, there was not more emphasis on this: 'It's helping to change attitudes, especially among women themselves. It's increasing their self-esteem.'

Against this was the view that the women's movement made women look 'ludicrous'. Even among those who thought that it was a good idea in principle there were several who had grave reservations about the 'extremists'. There were criticisms of the bra-burners and it was thought that many of the activities had brought a counter-reaction from men: 'At present, it's seen as an image of extreme actions. Men don't like aggressive women and it's done women a disservice.'

Within the organisations themselves, it was thought that the women's movement had encouraged an existing tendency not to take women seriously: 'As a serious woman in business, I get fed up with all the jokes.' However, some of the younger women thought that the women's movement had had very little impact on their companies:

> I don't think much affects this company. They plough their heavy ponderous way along. The women's movement is a little irritation which they wipe off like a flea. With their paternalistic approach, they set the rules and you like it or leave.

And another younger woman was even more forthright: 'Any effect on this company? No way. It's like a castle. They send people out to find out what's going on, but any trouble and they'll just pull up the drawbridge.'

Some women thought that the women's movement had probably been necessary and was similar to many movements which sought to bring pressure. This older woman thought the main effect had probably been positive: 'It has added impetus to the acceptance of women in areas where they would otherwise not have been accepted. Many things have been counterproductive, but someone has to be militant. I think it has stimulated general interest.' Others thought the general effect had probably been negative:

> I think it's had *some* impact – probably on younger women, as it should. The problem about the women's movement is that there is too much aggression which has to be let loose before it can come to grips with the issues. The revolutionary thing is probably necessary, but a state of conflict does not produce positive things. I think it's backfired. It's shown the worst of the frustrations and this had led to more conflict. But there are beginning to be some attempts of a more sane and sensible approach recently.

It was obviously very difficult for some of the women interviewed to understand what all the fuss had been about, either because they did not feel frustrated or discriminated against: 'It's irritated a lot of people, partly because any movement like that will irritate. A lot of what it's trying to do is pushing against doors that are already open.' Or because they did not think that this type of pressure would make any difference in the work environment:

The only way a woman will get on is to put her head down and do the job.
I don't want to be an agitator. There's nothing to be gained. The only way
is for me to do my job very well and to be seen to do it very well. That will
give other people the chance.

Or because they found activities which highlighted women's
problems unattractive: 'I don't have any sympathy for them. I
would still prefer to see a return of old-fashioned chivalry. All these
young men in tube trains never get up. No one offers to do anything
for anyone.'

Other external changes

A wide range of external factors were thought to have made some
difference to the prospects for women's careers. One of the most
important influences was said to be the economic climate over the
previous eleven years, which had led to increasing numbers of
married women going out to work to help achieve what they
considered to be a reasonable standard of living. Some respondents
pointed out that this had become an acceptable thing to do among
middle-class women as well as among working-class women, and
that, in fact, it was increasingly regarded as an economic necessity
by women in all sectors of society. Some thought that this would
make a difference in the future: 'Women *have* to go out to work
nowadays. The more women there are employed, the more there will
be in senior positions. Women are *expecting* to spend a large part of
their adult life working. It's going to be the norm rather than the
exception.'

This expectation of working for much of their lives was thought by
some of the younger respondents to have affected women in other
ways: 'The economic situation has ensured that more women work
than used to, and more women have opted for a career rather than a
job. Marriage isn't considered the be-all and end-all of a woman's
life as it used to be.' The importance of marriage, and particularly
children, was thought by some respondents to have declined as
women saw that they could be more economically independent:

The economic climate has forced women to work to the age of 28 or 30 and
then they decide *not* to have a child. People realise that when women take
on responsible jobs they aren't going to throw them up. It's partly the
economic climate and partly unemployment. Women are now taking on
jobs for the future.

One of the younger women in Company B thought that the effects of
this could have generally beneficial effects all round:

> More women have been forced to go out to work and women feel less
> guilty about taking jobs and continuing their careers. They're more equal
> in their own minds and have more self-esteem. They realise it's very
> important to keep themselves up-to-date, so their relationships develop on
> all levels. In marriage it makes them more equal partners.

Obviously an important factor in women's being able to plan whether
or not, or when, they will have children has been the introduction of
increasingly efficient methods of contraception, notably the pill,
which was cited by a number of the younger women. The increase in
the incidence of divorce and separation over the period was thought
to have led to a greater necessity for women to have some earning
capacity so that they could be independent if their marriage broke
down.

The increase in the number of married women with children
working was brought up by some respondents, who thought that
some women felt a great ambivalence towards working while they
had small children, even though they might feel a strong economic
need to do so:

> I think the social climate has accentuated the difference between those
> who think women can work and leave the kids and those who don't
> because they think that's being a 'bad mum'. Everyone wants to be a
> 'good mum'. They want to be liked and approved of. If they work, they're
> made out as being selfish and that's not a nice thing to feel. A lot of young
> women are worried when a family comes along because they think they
> will be bored, but they feel guilty about going out to work.

The maternity provisions of the Employment Protection Act met a
mixed response. Some of the men in particular thought that the
provision had acted against the interests of women, particularly the
more senior their jobs when they became or were likely to become
pregnant. Some people thought that employers would think very
hard about promoting a married woman in her late twenties, and
that the situation had become worse because of the legislation, since,
if she became pregnant and exercised her right to return, the job
would have to be held open for her. This was thought to be unacceptable, especially in the scientific research field, where continuity was

said to be essential. Even in management, grave difficulties were foreseen in holding jobs open, and it was interesting to note that the very few women interviewed who had returned after maternity leave had, in fact, returned to different jobs in the organisation.

The only respondents who thought that the maternity provisions of the Act had improved the situation for women, particularly in removing barriers, were those who had returned to work after taking maternity leave: 'Before, the business would have felt if you were having a child you should look after it. A responsible manager would have felt it his duty to encourage a woman to look after her child. It wouldn't have been a negative "Thank God we've got rid of her", but a concern about whether she could run a job and a family.'

The effects of more women having a better education were thought to have made some difference to the prospects for women and made them 'less of a novelty and more of a general theme'. It was thought that at the recruitment level there had also been a significant change over the previous eleven years: 'The fact that there are more women graduates is putting pressure on organisations to take them. There is a shortage of good graduates, and there is pressure to take the women.'

However, there were increasing fears that the future economic situation was so gloomy that prospects for women were actually going to become worse rather than better. These two women expressed the views held by several men and women:

> Unemployment will grow and there will be a criticism of women in the labour force and a resistance to women being employed. There are signs of antagonism growing.
> I suppose if there are redundancies it'll be the women who go first. The economic situation may affect women adversely. Unemployment will see men rather than women chosen for jobs.

It seemed very ironic that at a time when women did appear to be poised for making some kind of a breakthrough, because of greater numbers, because of more qualified women coming into the labour market, because of the pill, because they were tending to postpone having their babies or were not having them at all, and because there was a general feeling that men's attitudes might be changing, the economic climate was such that opportunities in real terms for women were contracting rather than expanding.

CHAPTER 9

Views on the Future

In 1968, many of the respondents, both men and women, thought that the situation could only improve for women. There was a general air of optimism that the entrenched attitudes of older male management would disappear as that generation retired, that the pressure of numbers and the quality of more young qualified women would ensure a push from below, that the numbers of women in middle management ought to ensure that some of them would rise to the top and that, in general, things looked rosier for women in the future. This report has indicated that much of this optimism appears to have been misplaced.

What did people now feel about the future? There have been indications throughout this report that pessimism is the order of the day, particularly since it has been seen that in spite of all the legislation, changes in attitudes, and increase in numbers of qualified women, the actual position of women within these organisations has not changed much. Some women retained some optimism, like this woman also interviewed in 1968:

> There will be evolution. The young men working with girls will be more ready to accept them and appoint women . . . I don't know about the proportion of top jobs. I can see women here who could do more senior jobs and a lot of jobs in this company go to people with potential. Maybe it's more difficult to recognise potential in women. Many women are stuck in supportive roles – not given the opportunity.

How could they be given the opportunity? Some women thought that the policy ought to come from the top, and that it should be put into action with real backing from senior management:

> They should take a totally different view of the problem. How can we make better use of female talents in career development? I'd appoint a committee – make the blokes sit down and think about it. At the moment they sweep it under the carpet and pretend it doesn't exist. It leads to untapped talent which they're not using, which is a shame commercially

and economically . . . They should totally rethink their policy – try and be constructive. They should rethink work patterns and how people deal with work. But first they have to have the will.

It would be unfair to say that senior management was not aware of the fact that the proportion of women in senior posts in their companies had hardly changed, and that there was not much evidence that it was going to change in the near future. The extent of their concern about this varied, but there was a strong impression that there were people among top management who would very much like to see more women in senior posts. However, their analysis of the situation also varied, which meant, inevitably, that no easy solutions were suggested. Their views were shared by some of the women, of course.

Some people thought that the answer lay with women themselves. This was expressed by one senior man who said that it would add to the prestige of men if they could be seen to be helping more women reach senior posts, but nevertheless:

> The instruments of change are the women themselves and not the men. If women wanted to run this organisation, they could do so. There's no obstacle within the system. We have an obligation to develop the girls and put them in the right slot but the people who get to the top don't get there through other people. They will get there if they want to . . . The initiative lies with the women.

There was an assumption in both companies by many respondents, even by those who thought there was a real problem, that opportunities were the same for both men and women, and that if women did not take their opportunities, there was little that could be done. Some people challenged this assumption, and said that the statistics showed that it was wrong. Although most people were against positive discrimination, some thought that the only way to have more women in senior jobs in the future was to recognise that there were differences between the careers of men and women.

One of the main factors was still seen to be the way in which jobs were designed:

> There is still an attitude that management jobs are as men created them. There are too many excuses and too many pressures on business. In another five years when there are *patently* more women around, there will

be a need for looking at the problems of motherhood and working, but there will be no system for doing so. It requires a flexibility of attitude that people haven't got because they don't believe that it's really necessary.

Other changes were thought to be necessary if more women were to reach senior jobs. One of these was the insistence on mobility as a pre-requisite for top jobs: 'This organisation will have to realise that progression through a single company is as good as going through a number of companies. That militates against women.' Another was the 'all or nothing' syndrome:

> They've got no imagination in how they employ people. It's nonsense to say that jobs come in conveniently labelled boxes. We have got room for a good deal more idiosyncratic management, so that people can work for a few hours a week . . . I know I'd be in a minority of one if I suggested that. A lot of managers need structuring and supporting.

Some women thought that there ought to be responsibility taken for women by one person in senior management, as suggested by the EOC's Code of Practice. It was feared that unless someone took this on, the desire by top management for more senior women would remain a rather woolly ideal, which was not, in fact, being put into practice except by a few individuals. There was a recommendation that a much more thorough examination of situations in which women had done well, and the factors affecting their success, could be a useful exercise in indicating what could be done.

There is, of course, a danger in this. The fact that women have done well in some areas at some time is no guarantee that women will continue to do well there. In Company B, for example, women had done well in a certain area at a time of expansion when, almost by accident, a number of women happened to find themselves, partly because of their qualifications, in a certain place. It has been pointed out that, when these women retire, they will not be replaced by women. Although it was argued that having a senior woman in an area of business can pave the way for others, the reverse may be true, and a pioneering woman may not always be followed by other women, for a number of reasons.

Some women thought there ought to be more monitoring of women and where they were, combined with more positive career plans laid before the high flyers. However, others thought that there were so few women around that everyone knew their careers off by heart.

On the whole, the women were more pessimistic about the future than their counterparts had been eleven years before. One young woman said:

> I suppose inevitably more women must get to more senior roles. I'd give it fifteen years – even here. But I'd have a bet that it will be twenty years before there's a woman on the board – and that will be a Personnel Director. There's a solid block of men at the top and no woman will get through that.

In the end, women thought that companies had to have the will to have more senior women, and not many thought that the will was really there to the extent that any positive attempt would be made to encourage them. The harsh realities of the economic situation and the business climate were thought to be the final factors operating against any real change, and this woman summarised the views of many: 'Why should they want women when there are so many men who are simpler to employ? In the end, what do women have to offer that's different? If it's only a question of equality, it's easier and simpler to stick with men.'

It is clear that there were certain changes between 1968 and 1979 as far as women in industry were concerned, even if there was little or no change in the proportion of women in top jobs in these two organisations. One of the most encouraging signs was that, at least at the time of interviewing in 1979, recruitment of qualified women looked better than it had in 1968. A much higher proportion of the management trainees taken on in Company A were women. There were no longer parts of the organisations which categorically refused to take women simply because they were women, and there appeared to have been some breakthrough into parts of the organisations which had been less than enthusiastic about women.

This was reflected in the job opportunities of women after recruitment. We heard less of frustrated women graduates who could not move out of their first job, and, indeed, some of the management trainees interviewed this time had had very rapid promotion, completely in line with that of their male counterparts. There were also signs that there was a much more favourable attitude towards promoting women among the most senior management, and, although not everyone thought that they were 'desperately looking round to find women to place in senior management positions', nevertheless one senior manager in Company A spoke of the Personnel Director persistently nagging top management about appointing women to senior posts, and it was clear from our interviewing that there had been a very definite shift at the top towards a more genuine desire for women to succeed and to be seen to succeed.

There was much less evidence of direct discrimination, even of the more subtle kind. Women's names were more likely to be on lists eligible for promotion, and the advertising of more senior posts meant that women could at least apply for them. There was said to be more discussion of whether to appoint women to senior jobs and not the almost automatic disqualification on the grounds of their sex which was one of the features of our 1968 research.

There was less discrimination of the type which cited society's attitude towards women as a reason for not promoting them or giving them certain types of job, for example, the 'client wouldn't like it' syndrome, or 'women and factories don't mix', or 'women don't make good salesmen'. However, there were still instances of indirect discrimination, based on assumptions that women would not want to do certain things, like going on residential courses, or working abroad, or being prepared to move around the country. Things were changing, but entrenched attitudes take a long time to eradicate.

Job opportunities for women joining the company were different from those experienced by the women we interviewed in 1968. Graduates joining these organisations today would be unlikely to say of their male contemporaries, as one of the older women interviewed did about hers: 'Their whole careers have been different from Day One'. And some of the management trainees in their twenties sometimes gave the impression that they did not know what all the fuss was about, since they did not feel in any way discriminated against and felt that they had kept pace with their male counterparts in every way.

How far was this a trend which was likely to continue, and how far were the careers so far of this tiny handful of women indicative of a real breakthrough? There were plenty of reasons for a cautious appraisal of the evidence.

One of the major themes which emerged in both organisations was the increasing emphasis on career planning and manpower planning. These had several important implications for women's careers. It was often stressed, by both men and women, that women had a completely different approach to work from men, particularly in the initial stages. They were thought to have less of a commitment to a career spanning forty years, since few thought that this would be the pattern of their lives. They were said to be much more interested in immediate job satisfaction, and to take the short-term rather than long-term view of jobs, which meant that they were much less likely to be prepared to take a job they didn't like even if it meant potentially greater long-term job satisfaction. Women were said to have much less idea of planning their careers, which meant that unless they followed exactly in the male career patterns, they were never likely to get anywhere near the top.

But following exactly in the male career patterns was precisely what most women could not do, because the majority of women got married and had babies. And even among those who did not have babies, or who continued to work after a baby with the minimum of interruption to their careers, the male pattern of total career commitment for those who were going to the top was often unacceptable to women because of its intrusion on other aspects of life.

This adherence to the concept that the male career pattern was the only path to the top was the main factor in many people's minds which prevented more women from reaching senior posts. It was said almost to encourage women in their short-term view of the future, since none of the conventional career plans in these organisations could be tailored to fit their requirements. As manpower planning became a more impotant part of the thinking of these organisations, so the prospects for women if they did not conform to the male career pattern became more gloomy.

There was evidence that senior management would find it very difficult to fit in women who wished to return after a break to look after small children, in the same way that they would find it difficult to fit in women who wanted to work less than full-time or who wished to level-peg for a while but to come back into the promotion race a few years later. The lack of flexibility of large organisations was commented on as being astonishing, but there was little doubt that both these organisations, in spite of a long-standing tradition of being 'good' employers, found it difficult to envisage any way of helping women who wanted to get to senior posts or even middle management without sticking very tightly to the rules.

The 'culture of promotion from within', the adherence to a grading system based on age and experience, and the problem of what to do with all the men who were not going to the top, all conspired to make women who wanted unusual career patterns unattractive propositions. Although management stressed that really good women would be welcomed back with open arms, it was significant that no one could remember anyone coming back, and there were obviously doubts about how older women who had once been first-class would fit back into a structure which did not really have a slot for them. 'Granny' secretaries or middle-aged packers were encouraged to return but scientists or line managers were quite a different kettle of fish. It was not surprising that management were seen as taking the easy way out by not encouraging deviations from the normal career pattern. Nor was it surprising that so few women working in these organisations in management or research posts had children.

The previous chapter indicated the general gloom which was felt in both organisations about any real likelihood of improvement in the prospects for women, particularly in the light of the economic circumstances. Since this interviewing was completed in 1979, the employment situation has grown worse, and it is even more unlikely that women's careers will be a priority in manpower planning in the 1980s. Therefore, in spite of the changes in the general climate, in spite of the legislation, in spite of obviously genuine shifts in attitude, at least at the top, in spite of more qualified, ambitious, articulate women entering industry, the prospects for women in these two firms do not look much brighter than they did in 1968, and, indeed, in some respects, they do not look as bright.

C. Women in the BBC

Introduction

The purpose of this study is to examine what had happened to women in the BBC in the eleven years between 1968, when we first looked at women's careers for *Women in Top Jobs*,[1] and 1979, when the BBC agreed that we could come back again and see what had happened in the meantime. Our brief was therefore confined to the experience of women working in the BBC and their future prospects. However, the power and influence of the BBC as an arbiter or leader of public taste and attitudes cannot be ignored, and, since this was one of the matters which preoccupied many women in the 1970s, this was also considered. The study called on the available material on broadcasting where necessary, but it should be stressed that it is intended to be an up-to-date report about women working in the BBC, and not an analysis of broadcasting in the 1970s.

Reference
(1) M. P. Fogarty (ed.), Isobel Allen, A. J. Allen, and Patricia Walters, *Women in Top Jobs – Four Studies in Achievement*, George Allen and Unwin, 1971.

CHAPTER 10

Structure and Organisation of the BBC

The most detailed account of the current structure and organisation of the BBC is given each year in the *BBC Handbook*, which contains a wealth of information, not only about the administrative structure, but also about the output and other activities of this highly complex organisation. Since 1968, when we first looked at women's careers in the BBC, there have been major changes in the organisation of the Corporation. We reported on some of these in *Women in Top Jobs*, which was published in 1971, when the BBC was in the process of streamlining its structure and organisation following some of the recommendations of the management consultants, McKinseys, who examined its workings in 1968. There were further changes in the early 1970s as a result of *Broadcasting in the Seventies*,[1] in which major changes for regional broadcasting had been suggested.

There are twelve Governors of the BBC, usually appointed for five years by the Queen in Council. There is then a Board of Management, which is made up of the most senior BBC executives – the Director-General, the three managing directors of radio, television and external broadcasting, and five other directors for engineering, finance, personnel, public affairs and news and current affairs. The Board meets weekly and is chaired by the Director-General, the BBC's chief executive and editor-in-chief.

Under the Board of Management are two Chief Assistants, a director of programmes for radio, a deputy managing director for television and a deputy director and an assistant director for engineering. In 1978, there were twenty-four controllers and beneath them came assistant controllers. The BBC has discontinued its former practice of listing senior staff with divisional and departmental responsibility in its annual *Handbook*. In 1969, we found that of 211 posts listed, five were held by women. The last time that the *BBC Handbook* listed the Board of Management and 'some other senior staff', stating that the list was not comprehensive, was in 1978. There were 54 posts on the list, none of which were held by women. The link between the senior management and the rest of the staff is the head of department or division, whose job it is to interpret general policy and pass on decisions made at a higher level.

The management structure of the BBC was discussed in some detail in the *Report of the Committee on the Future of Broadcasting*,[2] chaired by Lord Annan, which published its findings in 1977, and gave much consideration to the BBC's future management. The Annan Committee found what they called an 'organisational malaise' which they thought had begun to afflict the BBC, and they recommended the remedies of clearer lines of decision-taking, fewer chieftains and better communication.

This 'organisational malaise' has some relevance to the position of women in the BBC over the period since 1968. It arose in part from the tremendous expansion in the late 1960s, after the opening of BBC2, followed by stagnation or even contraction during the 1970s, combined with the fact that many of the bright young producers taken on in the expansionist times were getting older, and that there was beginning to be a block of people in their late thirties and early forties, who could not all be promoted. At the same time, many people reported to the Annan Committee that the BBC was becoming top-heavy with bureaucracy, termed by the Association of Directors and Producers as 'non-creative and non-productive staff'. There can be little doubt that this divide in the BBC between the production staff and those who can loosely be called management, noted by the Annan Report, has implications for the aspirations and employment of all staff, not least of them women.

Perhaps one of the reasons for the sometimes barely concealed hostility between production staff and 'management' is that, although responsibility for each programme is delegated to the producer, one of the changes made in 1969 was to delegate more but to insist on managerial accountability down the line. One of the most interesting sections of the Annan Report shows how different the BBC is from other industrial concerns of its size and complexity:

> The BBC told us that McKinseys, after some weeks of analysis, were surprised that they could not identify the seven or eight decision takers they expected to find in any organisation of comparable size. Instead there seemed to be not less than 1,400 people each properly identifiable as decision takers – and necessarily so. McKinseys told us that, compared with a commercial organisation, a very high proportion of the 25,000 staff

of the BBC were 'management personnel' who were actively involved in planning and controlling resources to produce a particular programme. Once decisions had been taken to make a particular programme, the structure of the BBC enabled programmes to be planned, created and executed by and large independently of each other; and this permitted a greater degree of delegation than could be found in comparable industrial companies.[3]

And so this curious structure meant that television producers could be managing budgets and facilities beyond the wildest dreams of some middle managers in industry, and yet regard themselves as 'creative' people and not managers. For example, we interviewed one woman who had a budget of £1m. for making a series of prestige films, and another who was responsible for an annual budget of £¼m. for making children's television programmes. And yet these women were not in managerial posts as such but were television producers – of a high grade and experience, but nevertheless still television producers.

We have laid some stress on this aspect of the structure of the BBC, described so clearly in the Annan Report, because of its implications for women's careers. It was frequently said, both in 1968 and 1979, that one of the reasons that women did not rise to the top in the BBC was that they wanted to stay close to the production or to the creative role. It can be seen from this brief sketch of the role of the producer how much management is involved, and it is this that must be borne in mind throughout this report.

References

(1) BBC, *Broadcasting in the Seventies: The BBC's plan for network radio and non-metropolitan broadcasting*, 1969.
(2) *Report of the Committee on the Future of Broadcasting*, HMSO 1977.
(3) Ibid., p. 101, para. 9. 15.

CHAPTER 11

Developments since 1968

In *Women in Top Jobs*, the report on the BBC ended with the words:

> In general, the BBC ought not to assume that it has equal opportunity for
> women, but should examine what it means by equal opportunity. It
> cannot ignore the long-term consequences of losing or not recruiting high
> calibre women . . . There can be little doubt that the BBC has great
> responsibility as one of the most prominent showcases for the policy of
> public enterprises on equal opportunity and the conservation of man-
> power resources. In addition, in examining its attitude towards women, it
> might be able to recruit or keep some top-quality talent which it has
> hitherto neglected.

After *Women in Top Jobs* was published in 1971, pressure on the BBC
to examine what it meant by equal opportunity grew from a number
of sources. The Association of Broadcasting and Allied Staffs (ABS),
the union recognised by the BBC as the negotiating body for all
categories of staff, started to press for some action on equal opportunities for women. At the same time, 'Women in Media', which had
been formed in 1970 by women working in newspapers, radio,
television and other media, took on a campaigning role and started
to press the BBC to use women newscasters on radio and television.
In the early 1970s, the Association of Cinematograph Television and
Allied Technicians (ACTT), the union to which some BBC and
most ITV production staff belong, although it is not recognised by
the BBC, started its own investigation into the position of women in
films and television, which was published in 1975.[1]

There was mounting interest in the problems of women's role in
society at large, and the likelihood of anti-discriminatory legislation
was growing. It was against this background that the BBC held its
own internal inquiry into the position of women in the Corporation,
which culminated in a statement in 1973 that the BBC recognised
that there was a problem as far as women's careers were concerned,
that in future all jobs would be open to both sexes, and that positive

encouragement would be given to women to advance their careers in the Corporation, both by applying for jobs in areas which had hitherto been male preserves and by applying for jobs in management.

In October 1975, the BBC made a further statement to the unions, spelling out in detail its policy on equal opportunities:

> The BBC's personnel policies and practices are based on the principle of equal opportunity for all. Thus the appointment, terms of employment, conditions of service and opportunities for training and promotion for a particular member of staff are unaffected by such personal characteristics as sex, colour and race. Any member of staff who has a grievance relating to equal opportunities may raise it under the Grievance Procedure set out in Staff Instruction 330.

In the meantime, Women in Media had been mounting their attack on another front, mainly concerned with how women were presented in the media. They conducted a spirited two-year correspondence between 1971 and 1973 with the then chairman of the BBC, Lord Hill of Luton, who assured them that if suitable women applied for jobs as newscasters on radio and television they would be considered. The campaign continued when Sir Michael Swann became chairman of the BBC. The story is told in *Is this your life?*:[2]

> It is important to recognise here that the effort was not just to stop job-discrimination and get jobs for the girls. As Women in Media explained in a letter to Sir Michael on 28 March 1973: 'Our chief concern is that the present conditioning of people, children in particular, towards the view that women are seemingly incapable of certain work, for example, news-reading, should be put right'.

Is this your life? found that women were not helped by entrenched attitudes in the BBC, and reported the then presentation editor of BBC Radio Four as saying in 1973:

> If a woman could read the news as well as a man there would be nothing to stop her doing it. But I have never found one who could . . . A news announcer needs to have authority, consistency and reliability. Women may have one or two of these qualities, but not all three . . .

By July 1974, a woman was reading the major news bulletins on Radio Four, and a few months later was joined by another. Today, a woman reading the news on radio and television is so commonplace as to be unremarkable, and it is difficult to think that this battle was won so recently. In 1974, Radio Four also appointed its first woman staff reporter in the newsroom. It is astonishing that such a fuss was made about appointing women reporters and newsreaders. But the prejudice was very deep-rooted, as one very senior BBC executive pointed out to us in 1979: 'There used to be a great myth that if you hadn't got a baritone voice nobody would believe what you said'. That myth may have been partially exploded, but it is still true that although women read the news, and there has been a woman lobby correspondent, there are no women's voices to be heard on the news as correspondents for any other subject, for example, education or social services.

Women in Media also attacked 'the BBC's predilection for the token woman' – the need to have one woman in a programme with perhaps three or four men. *Is this your life?* reported Sir Charles Curran, then BBC Director-General, defending this by arguing that the ratio of one women to four men 'represents the participation of women in public life'. The author comments:

> He was not concerned about reflecting the ratio of women in our society. And he seemed unaware that the prejudices against women taking a more active part in public and business life are being reinforced as long as the media project the image that only a handful of star women are capable of having an opinion worth voicing.

In 1977, the Annan Report contained a section on 'Policies on Employment of Women, Racial and Religious Minorities'.[3] How had things changed by then? One of the points raised concerned the criticism by some of those submitting evidence to the committee that too few women appeared on radio and television. The report says:

> Some of us felt that there is a built-in assumption that a man knows how to address an audience composed of men and women, but a woman does not. We also noticed that when there were discussions on radio or tele-vision there would be a token woman with three men, but that women would equal the number of men, or even outnumber them, only when the topic dealt with women or children. No wonder women complain.

But it was not only tokenism or their image about which women complained to the Annan Committee. Several organisations complained about the lack of women executives in broadcasting, and the ABS reinforced the view of Women in Media that many women graduates were recruited as secretaries with promises of a career in broadcasting which practically never materialised. The ABS made the very important point which Annan reported: 'Women generally started their careers lower down the hierarchy than men did and took longer to reach the point where they were competing on equal terms with the men, who had entered at the same time but at a higher level'.[4]

At the time of the Annan Report, only 12 per cent of the BBC's management and production staff were women. The Director-General, Sir Charles Curran, told the Annan Committee that the number of women recruited and the number who stayed was smaller than he would have liked them to be. The report continued: 'He wanted to find more women to fill top jobs and to join the BBC when their children were older, but once someone, whether a man or a woman, left the BBC it was difficult to re-introduce them at a senior level'.[5]

This problem had been referred to many times in *Women in Top Jobs*, and we commented in our conclusions:

> If the BBC wants more top women managers, it ought to find ways of encouraging some of its potential talent to stay with it, if only in a part-time or freelance capacity for a number of years, and then giving women with this talent the opportunity of coming back into the promotion race.

Annan takes up our point, only reinforcing that little, if anything, had changed between the time that we did our research in 1968 and 1977:

> More sympathetic attention could be given to women who are trying to combine work and family responsibilities. A woman once trained, who again becomes a viewer and is brought into prolonged contact with the wider community while her children are young, might be a help rather than a hindrance, since we believe that one of the problems facing the broadcaster, given the pressure of work, is isolation from the audience. Some posts, at a relatively senior level, could be held by women working part-time, though we recognise that this cannot apply to the most senior positions. These arrangements may call for additional training and even additional expenditure. There should be a more flexible approach to working conditions to make it easier for women to take maternity leave and to work part-time.[6]

Women in Media told the Annan Committee of their concern about the lack of women in top jobs in the BBC, giving their reasons which had much wider implications than whether women were doing well within the BBC itself:

> Firstly, by and large, it is people in top jobs who hire the other people in broadcasting. There are hardly any women on appointments boards. It is largely a question of men hiring other men . . . Secondly, people in top jobs are in a position to influence programme content and to determine which programmes get space on the networks. Over 50 per cent of the viewers and listeners are women, but when it comes to the people who choose what they should view or hear, not a woman in sight.

Annan commented that many employers now realised that they had a social obligation to adopt more positive policies as far as equal opportunities were concerned, and said:

> What is needed, first and foremost, is information. The virtuous refusal to identify often abets a disinclination in another quarter to deal with inequalities . . . We recommend that clear policies on the employment of women and ethnic minorities should be formulated and promulgated throughout the organisation. It has been suggested that one senior person should be made responsible for seeing that the policies are carried out and that the board of the organisation is kept informed periodically. We recognise that there is a risk that such special responsibility will come to be regarded as exclusive responsibility and that everyone else will feel that they need not take any action themselves. These matters should be the concern of all managers. So long as this risk is recognised, it would be helpful to have responsibility designated in this way.[7]

And finally, Annan concluded that an articulated programme of action was needed:

> Between positive discrimination on one hand and indifference on the other, there is room enough for policies which will encourage women and people from minority groups to seek careers in broadcasting, confident that they will be given equal opportunities of progress to the top positions.[8]

Since Annan reported in 1977 there has been some movement towards implementing some of its recommendations, although by the end of 1978, when we were starting our second study in the BBC, the ABS was still showing concern about the Corporation's record on the employment of women. In a letter to the BBC's Director of

Personnel, published in *ABStract,* November 1978, the General
Secretary of the ABS referred to the BBC's 1973 statement of policy
on equal opportunities:

> Since 1973, the ABS has sought evidence from the BBC that it is doing
> everything possible to ensure that its equal opportunities policy is being
> implemented and that there is a statistically significant improvement in
> the unequal position described in the 1973 promulgation. At no time has
> the BBC approached the union to discuss its apparent failure to improve
> the situation nor has it been able to demonstrate that any real progress
> had been made.

The General Secretary then drew the attention of the Director of
Personnel to the Equal Opportunities Commission's booklet
Guidance on Equal Opportunity, Policies and Practices in Employment,
which stated that the recognised trade union should be involved in
equal planning, that detailed practices and procedures should be
instituted to ensure that an equal opportunities policy was carried
out, and that progress should be regularly reviewed. The General
Secretary asked that a joint equal opportunities committee should
be established as soon as possible to monitor progress on the implementation of the BBC's equal opportunities policy.

The Director of Personnel replied at some length, suggesting that
there might be 'room for exchanges of information and ideas at a
higher level and on a more regular and wider basis', although he
pointed out that the union already received relevant statistical
information from the Appointments Department. He gave some
details on the employment of women in the BBC, which will be
looked at in the next chapter, and said:

> I would therefore agree that no employer, ourselves included, has any
> cause to rest on her (or, of course, his) laurels. But I hope that you would
> accept, as I do, that the position in the BBC has in fact improved. It may
> be that we should do more positively to encourage women to apply for
> senior posts even though this could enlarge the area of disappointed
> aspirations.

By May 1979, the ABS was rather more cheerful, and under a
banner headline in *ABStract* – 'A few small steps for womankind' – it
reported that there had been some 'encouraging recent developments' resulting from the first of a regular series of meetings between

the ABS' Advisory Committee on Discrimination and a BBC central management team headed by the Assistant Controller, Employment Policy and Appointments. The BBC had agreed to provide the union with regular information on the breakdown of men and women postholders in the operations and management and production areas. It had also agreed to look at a number of other topics, such as the male/female success rate in promotion among news trainees since 1971, a new look at engineering recruitment, and a statement on the eligibility of both men and women for jobs advertised on notice boards.

So the BBC had implemented one very important recommendation of the Annan Committee by giving responsibility for seeing that equal opportunities policies were carried out to someone as senior as an Assistant Controller. It had then followed the advice given in the EOC's guidance on equal opportunities and had involved the union in regular meetings on the subject, at which information was given and practices and procedures were discussed. Not many organisations have gone this far. But these are still early days, and these practices have only recently been instituted, after what *Is this your life?* called the BBC's 'years of benign neglect of women', resulting in a 'talent gap'. There is a long way to go to fill that 'talent gap' as the following chapters will indicate.

References

(1) ACTT, *Patterns of Discrimination*, 1975.
(2) Josephine King and Mary Stott (eds.), *Is This Your Life? Images of Women in the Media*, Virago, 1977.
(3) Op. cit., pp. 440–442, paras. 28.21–28.27.
(4) Op. cit., p. 440, para. 28.21.
(5) Op. cit., p. 440, para. 28.22.
(6) Op. cit., p. 442, para. 28.26.
(7) Op. cit., p. 441, para. 28.25.
(8) Op. cit., p. 442, para. 28.27.

CHAPTER 12

The Present Position

In December 1979, there were 27,569 staff working for the BBC, of whom 17,622 were men and 9,947 were women, representing 36 per cent of the total. There were nearly 22,000 people in monthly paid jobs. These included the Management, Professional and Editorial grades (MP), Operational (OP), Administrative Support (AS), Secretarial and Clerical (SC) and Clerical Operators (CO). Women accounted for 38 per cent of the monthly paid staff, but, as might be expected, were concentrated in certain areas. For example, 86 per cent of the SC staff, 82 per cent of the COs, and 66 per cent of the AS staff were women. However, they accounted for only 17 per cent of the MP staff, which includes producers and middle management staff, and 18 per cent of the OP staff, which includes the technical and engineering staff without managerial responsibility. Within the grades there were certain areas where women were only to be found in very small numbers and these included the engineering field.

At the time of our 1968 research, the grading system of jobs had just been revised. At the present time of writing, it is about to be revised again, but the intervening period has seen the same grading system used, so that direct comparisons can be made between the situation in 1968 and that in 1979. In 1968, there were 4,681 people in the MP grades out of a total of 23,376 working for the BBC, thus representing 20 per cent of the staff. By 1979, the MP grades accounted for 26 per cent. Our 1968 report was largely concerned with the careers of people in the MP grades, and we have followed this pattern in this report.

The top management jobs in the BBC were classified as A and A plus until recently, when they were reclassified AMP. The MP grades range from MP1 at the bottom to MP7 at the top, with AMP above this. Senior posts are defined as being in grades MP5 and above, and Table 12.1 shows the proportion of women to be found in these grades in 1969 and again in 1978, when we returned to the BBC. The 1979 figures are given in Table 12.2.

Table 12.1 *Post occupancy by sex 1969 and 1978*

Grade	1969				May 1978			
	Total	Men	Women	% Women	Total	Men	Women	% Women
A and A+	102	101	1	1	151	149	2	1
MP7	122	116	6	5	168	166	2	1
MP6	378	361	17	5	551	511	40	7
MP5	493	459	34	7	702	640	62	9
Total MP5 and above	1,095	1,037	58	5	1,572	1,466	106	6.7
Total MP5–MP7 (not including) A and A+)	993	936	57	5.7	1,421	1,317	104	7.3
Total MP grades (not including) A and A+)	—	—	—	—	6,159	5,248	911	15

Note: This table shows the distribution of men and women according to the grade of job they were doing, rather than their own particular grade, which could be a personal grade awarded for individual merit.

The BBC was concerned that these figures might not represent the fact that women were doing better in some areas than others. For example, although they represented 15 per cent of the MP staff (excluding A and A plus) in May 1978, the BBC's Director of Personnel pointed out in his letter to the General Secretary of the ABS[1] that they constituted 32 per cent of the MP staff involved in management support and administration, and 17 per cent of the category of staff which included producers and production assistants.

However, we found that even within these two categories, women were concentrated at the lower end of the scale, and the proportion within the MP5 to MP7 bracket was not much above the average for the MP structure as a whole. The big gap was, of course, in engineering, where there were 1,159 jobs in the MP structure in 1978, of which one was held by a woman. The Director of Personnel pointed out that this reflected the situation in the country as a whole, where 'women form something under 1 per cent of the electrical and electronic engineering students at universities; and the minority studying physics gravitate in the main towards atomic and nuclear physics'.

In 1978 and 1979, there was some evidence of an improvement in the position of women in the MP5 grades, and by September 1979, women accounted for 10 per cent of those holding MP5 jobs. However, in the autumn of 1979, there was a general upgrading of engineers, which resulted in the situation as given in Table 12.2.

Table 12.2 *Post occupancy by sex, December 1979*

Grade	Total	Men	Women	% Women
AMP	163	160	3	1.8
MP7	233	230	3	1.3
MP6	646	593	53	8.2
MP5	896	819	77	8.6
Total MP5 and above	1,938	1,802	136	7.0
Total MP5–MP7 (not including AMP)	1,775	1,642	133	7.5
Total MP grades (not including AMP)	6,627	5,515	1,112	16.8

However these figure are looked at, there remains the fact that women in the BBC had not reached the top jobs between 1969 and 1979. In 1969, there was one woman in the A and A plus grades, in 1978 there were two and in 1979 there were three. The proportion of women in these grades has crept up from 1 per cent in 1969 to just under 2 per cent in 1979. At the next level down, the MP7 grade, they are doing much less well than in 1969, when there were six of them accounting for 5 per cent of the people at this level. In May 1978, there were two women and in 1979 there were three women, accounting for just over 1 per cent of the posts at this grade. The AMP and MP7 jobs in the BBC cover the most senior management jobs and the departmental heads, and these are the policy-making posts. There were 396 people in these posts in December 1979, of whom six were women – 1.5 per cent. In 1969, there were seven women out of 224 people at these levels – 3 per cent – so that the position of women at the top of the BBC has actually deteriorated in the last ten years.

It is in the next two categories that women can be seen to be doing rather better than in 1969. In MP6 jobs, the proportion of women has risen from 5 per cent in 1969, to 8 per cent in 1979, and, in MP5 jobs, the proportion has risen from 7 per cent in 1969 to 8.6 per cent in December 1979, having reached 10 per cent in September 1979.

Overall, in 1969, women held 5 per cent of the posts in grade MP5 and above and this figure had risen to 7 per cent by the end of 1979. The proportion of women in the MP grades as a whole has gradually been creeping up in the 1970s, but over two-thirds of the women in the MP grades are in MP1 and MP2, compared with just over a third of the MP men in these two grades.

The change between 1969 and 1979 in the proportion of women holding senior posts can only be described as minimal. The slight movement upwards from May 1978 to September 1979 in the MP5 and MP6 jobs has been obscured by the regrading of the engineers, and it is impossible to detect any long-term trend from the figures. The prospects of a dramatic increase in the number or proportion of women in the AMP grades look slim, and it could not be argued that the prospects for a great increase in the number or proportion of women in MP7 jobs look much better. Even when the MP structure as a whole is examined, there is really no indication that younger women are moving up the promotion ladder, ready to make the break-through to the top in the next ten years or so.

The fact that there are now fewer women in the top management posts in the BBC than ten years ago was forecast in *Women in Top Jobs:*

> . . . it is significant that most of the women in positions of any real seniority today seized the opportunity offered to them during the war to prove their ability to hold senior posts. It is also significant that when this small group of women retires within a fairly short time, there are no obvious women successors to them and, in fact, the number of really senior women will probably fall sharply within the next few years.[2]

It certainly seems extraordinary that thirty-five years after the end of the war, in spite of the enormous increase in the numbers of highly educated and qualified women and in spite of the big upturn in women's aspirations and the increase in the numbers of women at work, there have still been no successors to the women who 'seized' their opportunities during the war. It looks as if Women in Media may have been right in complaining of 'years of benign neglect' of women. They have certainly not seized any opportunities in top management in recent years. There was no reason why the senior women in 1968 should have been replaced by women, but no other top jobs were filled by women either. The BBC argues that in its open competitive system for jobs, everyone, regardless of sex, has a chance, but that women either did not apply for the senior jobs, or, if they did, were not considered to be the best candidates.

Some indication of whether women stay when they get married or have children is given by the profile of the MP staff by grade and marital status, as shown in Table 12.3.

Table 12.3 *MP staff by grade and marital status, March 1979*

	Men % single	Women % single	Men % married	Women % married	Men % widowed/ divorced	Women % widowed/ divorced
A and A +	4	67	95	33	1	–
MP7	9	67	91	33	<1	–
MP6	14	52	84	41	2	7
MP5	18	56	80	42	2	2
MP4	19	50	79	43	1	7
MP3	22	55	77	41	1	4
MP2	30	51	68	43	2	6
MP1	39	61	59	35	2	4
All grades	23	53	75	41	2	5

The proportion of men who are married rises steadily through the grades, so that 95 per cent of the AMP grades are married. With women, just over 40 per cent are married in all grades apart from the highest and the lowest. No figures are collected on whether BBC staff have children, but it seems very likely that the main reason for the fact that fewer of the women in the MP grades are married is that the majority leave, or at least have left in the past, when they have children, and do not return. In the study of two industrial firms, we saw that among the women managers, although over 40 per cent were married, only a very small proportion had children. Our sampling and interviewing suggest that, although it appeared to be easier to continue working in the BBC than in industry with small children, nevertheless, the numbers who managed to combine working their way up the ladder with a family were small.

People interviewed

In 1968, we interviewed 33 members of the BBC staff, 22 women and 11 men. In addition, we interviewed three former members of staff. When we returned in 1979, we found that ten women and seven men were still working for the BBC. Most of the other staff had retired.

We drew a new random sample of ten women between the ages of 35 and 44 from women in Grades MP5 and above. This gave us four television producers, one television designer, one radio producer, two from personnel, one from presentation in television and one from planning in radio. It was suggested to us by the BBC that our sample did not represent the interests of women in the BBC outside London, so we also interviewed one senior woman from local radio and one from Scotland. This gave us 12 women in our new sample.

We interviewed nine women from our former sample, giving us the views of 21 women working in the BBC. All except two of them were in jobs with grades of MP5 and above. In addition, we interviewed one of the women Governors of the BBC, a member of the BBC staff to give us information on the crèche campaign and other aspects of the problems of combining a career and bringing up a family, a member of Women in Media, and an officer of the ABS.

We interviewed nine men working for the BBC, most of whom were concerned with personnel policy. This gave us a total of 34 interviews, and it is through these interviews that we gathered most of the evidence on which the rest of this report is based. This evidence must, of course, be seen in the context of the structure and history of the BBC already described.

References
(1) Published in *ABStract*, November, 1978.
(2) Op. cit. p. 165.

CHAPTER 13

Career Opportunities

Careers in the BBC

It was noted in *Women in Top Jobs* that the striking characteristic of careers in the BBC was the difficulty in discerning any regular type of pattern on the Civil Service model: 'The very term "career pattern" is frowned upon, and it was frequently stated that there was no such thing in the BBC.'

The BBC's system of promotion is through its competitive appointments system, by which most jobs below controller level are advertised internally, and for which anyone can apply. Short-lists of candidates are drawn up and people are interviewed by a board chaired by a member of the Appointments Department. The initiative to apply for a board rests very much with the individual, and the system means that career development, in the generally recognised form, is not easy to implement; indeed, the concept of career development is thought to be incompatible with the BBC's system of promotion.

There is a continuing appraisal system of staff in which each person has an annual report written about his or her performance in the job over the year, usually by an immediate superior, which is endorsed by a more senior member of staff. The report is discussed with staff at an annual interview at which people can raise any points they wish about their own prospects and career. It is at these interviews that any career movement can be discussed, either at the initiative of the management or the member of staff.

The BBC is very much in favour of its present method of promotion, which, it says, is approved by staff and unions as well as management. However, it did tell the Annan Committee that in recent years the open system has sometimes failed to get the best man for the job from among the staff.[1] Professor Tom Burns in his evidence to the Annan Committee observed that, while open boards sanctified a success system, they also underlined a failure system and thereby bred resentment.[2] It was suggested to us by some respondents that the open system could inadvertently discriminate against women, who were said to be less willing to apply for jobs which they did not think they were certain to get. This meant that they were less likely to be seen by boards, less likely to gain experience in being boarded, and, of course, they reduced their chances of being promoted, since so few promotions, particularly at lower levels, took place without a board.

It has been said that it is very difficult to demonstrate ability to do a job without actually doing it. To try and help solve this problem, the BBC has a training attachments system, in which people are attached to a department, usually for a six months' period, while retaining the same grade and salary as in their previous job. At the end of the attachment they are expected to return to their old job, although, if they have done well in their attachment, they will usually be regarded favourably if a post for which they wish to apply comes up in the department to which they were attached. Sometimes an attachment is a stepping-stone to a new career, while, in other cases, it helps to crystallise a person's career plans within their original area. It is certainly a very useful way of assisting the lateral career movement which evidence to the Annan Committee suggested was not well enough developed in the BBC.

Over a ten-year period from 1969 to 1978, 430 attachments were arranged by the Central Attachments Officer, 42 per cent of them for women. Other attachments are arranged for television, and women do not do as well in gaining these.

Training courses of all kinds are run by the BBC. For example, Annan reports that in 1975 there were 366 non-engineering courses of 89 different types, attended by nearly 4,000 staff. It said: '. . . in general, most of us consider the BBC can be proud of its training record.'[3]

It is important to remember that the BBC is made up of all types of specialities. It is possible to have a career in engineering, computing, publishing, personnel or accounting within the Corporation, as well as the more obvious career of a radio or television producer. This makes it very difficult to have straightforward career lines leading to top management. The BBC is not a tidy organisation in this respect. There is no set entry gate through which all senior staff come, as in the Civil Service or the professions, and no laid down procedure for promotion from grade to grade as in the Civil

Service. It is against this background that we look at how people come into the BBC and how they rise in the organisation. We shall consider the evidence of how much the system has helped women to further their careers.

Recruitment – training schemes

In common with most other large organisations, the BBC is interested in attracting young graduates and other qualified people to come and work for it. Its demands are different from those of large industrial concerns, in that the main need is not so much for trainee managers as for people who can apply a trained mind to the practical problems of radio and television production. It is extremely unusual to move into BBC management without having had experience in posts exposed to the technicalities of broadcasting, which, as we have seen, may have a large managerial element without being termed managerial posts.

Over the years, the BBC has run a number of schemes intended to attract and train a variety of talented young people, with the hope that some of them will be its future top management. It is stressed, however, that the mere fact that anyone has a traineeship is no guarantee that any particular career path is mapped out for him or her.

(i) *General Trainee Scheme*

The original General Trainee Scheme ran from 1954 to 1970, with the aim of recruiting outstanding graduates from all disciplines to be the BBC's top managers and star producers of the future. The scheme was restricted to men until 1960, when it was opened to women. In the period 1954–70, 106 graduates were recruited to the scheme, of whom seven were women (6.6 per cent). Nobody could have argued that the scheme was a good way of recruiting outstanding women graduates, since so few women candidates were successful. In spite of the fact that in the late 1960s they accounted for around a third of the applicants, no woman was recruited to the scheme after 1966.

The General Trainee Scheme was discontinued in 1970, but was re-introduced in 1979 because the other training schemes described below 'seek to recruit those with particular interests, and there may be potential applicants who lack the specialist skills called for in the other four schemes but who are nonetheless strongly committed to public service broadcasting'.[4] The BBC states that it will 'look for around six people of considerable intellectual merit and with a proven record of achievement at university and elsewhere. The degree of maturity implied in the demands will probably make this scheme more appropriate for graduates with work experience after graduation; but undergraduates of outstanding ability will also be considered'.

(ii) *News Trainee Scheme*
This scheme was first introduced at the end of 1969 with the aim of training graduates to be professional journalists in broadcasting. The BBC states that if an applicant has not practised some form of journalism at or outside university, there is little point in applying for a News Traineeship. In the period 1969 to 1978, the BBC recruited 110 people for the scheme of whom 27 (25 per cent) were women. There had clearly been a shift from the recruitment policy of the General Trainee Scheme. This could have been due to the differing demands of the two schemes. The former General Trainee Scheme was thought to be looking for outstanding generalists who performed well at all stages of the selection process, while the News Trainee Scheme required more specific skills and experience which were perhaps more easily objectively measured. The shift could also have reflected a genuine desire to recruit more high-calibre women into the BBC through training schemes. It certainly appears in all the training schemes which have been set up in the 1970s that women have had a very much better chance of recruitment than they did under the old General Trainee Scheme.

One of the arguments put forward against a high recruitment of women graduates is that they are more likely to leave than the men, which means that the investment in their training is wasted to the organisation. An analysis of the 110 recruits from 1969 to 1978 shows that 33 per cent of the women had left the BBC by 1978 compared with 28 per cent of the men. The 'wastage' rates are not very different, and do not imply that women are a less reliable investment than men, at least in the short-term.

The competition for News Traineeships is intense, and Table 13.1 shows how men and women performed in the 1979 competition. The figures are broken down for internal and external applicants and show the proportion of women at each stage of the selection process. The proportion of internal applicants is also shown separately for this and the other schemes. A more detailed analysis for all the training schemes is published each year by the BBC.

Table 13.1 *News Trainee Scheme 1979*

	Internal applicants				External applicants				Total applicants				
	Men	Women	% women of total	Total	Men	Women	% women of total	Total	Men	Women	% women of total	Total	Internal as % of total
Applied	1	2	66	3	315	301	49	616	316	303	49	619	0.5
Preliminary Interview	0	2	100	2	75	62	45	137	75	64	46	139	1.4
Final Board	0	2	100	2	30	22	42	52	30	24	44	54	3.7
Selected	0	0	0	0	7	8	53	15	7	8	53	15	0

The majority of applicants for the News Trainee Scheme come from outside the BBC, and most of these are from the universities rather than polytechnics or elsewhere. The success of the women in the 1979 competition was striking, in that they took 53 per cent of the places offered, having been 49 per cent of the applicants. They did considerably better in 1979 than in the previous two years, when they had represented well over 40 per cent of the applicants but had gained only 25 per cent of the places in both years. The BBC remarks on the 1979 success of women in its review of the training schemes: 'It may be that more women are taking up journalism at university and, in becoming more aware of what is open to them, are breaking out of artificial constraints.'[5]

The BBC has always been said to have a tradition of favouring Oxford and Cambridge graduates for its training schemes. It was common in our interviews in both 1968 and 1979 for women graduates from other universities to say that their university appointments officers had told them that they had no chance of getting into the BBC General Trainee Scheme because they were women and not from Oxford and Cambridge. In the News Trainee Scheme 1979, students from Oxford and Cambridge represented 20 per cent of all the university applicants, but 40 per cent of those selected. This ratio was much more striking among the women, where Oxford and

Cambridge students represented 13 per cent of the female university applicants but 50 per cent of all the women selected. The BBC says that it had the impression that universities with a strong journalistic tradition did score well in the News Trainee Schemes.

(iii) *Research Assistant Trainee Scheme*
This scheme was introduced at the end of 1976 with the aim of providing 15 trainee researchers a year for television departments, in particular for the factual and educational areas. Like all the training schemes, it was open to both internal and external candidates. Candidates, aged between 20 and 30, were required to have an informed interest in the arts, sciences, entertainment, education or current affairs. A degree or considerable experience of television production or evidence of journalistic abilities were essential qualifications.

Table 13.2 *Research Assistant Trainee Scheme 1979*

	Internal applicants				External applicants				Total applicants				
	Men	Women	% women of total	Total	Men	Women	% women of total	Total	Men	Women	% women of total	Total	Internal as % of total
Applied	31	61	66	92	654	901	58	1555	685	962	58	1647	6
Preliminary Interview	10	15	60	25	74	68	48	142	84	83	50	167	15
Final Board	4	3	43	7	21	22	51	43	25	25	50	50	14
Selected	1	1	50	2	4	6	60	10	5	7	58	12	17

The scheme has attracted increasing numbers of applicants, although the proportion of internal applicants had dropped from 18 per cent of the total in 1977 to only 6 per cent in 1979. It was also notable that in 1977, the first year of appointments to the scheme, women accounted for 80 per cent of the internal applicants and even in 1979 for two-thirds. It has been said in evidence to the Annan Committee, as well as in the course of our investigations in 1979, that women graduates are encouraged to join the BBC as secretaries and work their way into production. The internal applications for the Research Assistant Training Scheme reflect this to a certain extent. In the first year of the scheme, four internal candidates, all women graduates, were selected. Two were Studio Managers, one an Assistant Film Editor, and one a clerk in Programme Correspondence. In 1979, the internal candidates who were selected were both graduates working as Assistant Film Editors, one male and one female. As Table 13.2 shows, women represented 58 per cent of the candidates in 1979 and 58 per cent of those selected. In 1978, the success rate was not as high, with women representing 56 per cent of the candidates but only 33 per cent of those selected.

The success rate of candidates from Oxford and Cambridge was even more marked in the Research Assistant Training Scheme than in the News Trainee Scheme. Students from Oxford and Cambridge represented 27 per cent of the applicants from universities and 90 per cent of those appointed. Again, Oxford and Cambridge women did particularly well, representing 19 per cent of the female university applicants and 84 per cent of the women appointed in the external competition.

(iv) *Studio Manager Trainee Scheme*
In our 1968 research, some BBC senior respondents suggested that the failure of women to be recruited for the then General Trainee Scheme was perhaps not as serious as it looked, since at the time the scheme was tending to become a rather specialist one for training young men in television Current Affairs. It was suggested that a better measure of women's opportunities might be the Trainee Programme Operation Assistants' Scheme, which was the training scheme for studio managers. At the time, it was the generally recognised 'second-tier' scheme for recruiting graduates and similar calibre entrants in their early twenties into the BBC.

Studio managers are responsible for the technical and artistic presentation of all studio programmes in radio. There are about 400 of them, working in both domestic radio and External Services, and the numbers recruited as trainees each year vary considerably according to the vacancies. Although experience as a studio manager is a recognised path to production, nevertheless it is not usually a very quick progression, even if it happens at all. Some of the women senior producers interviewed in both 1968 and 1979 stressed that it could be very difficult to move out of studio management.

The BBC notes that experience in amateur or professional radio is very useful for potential trainee studio managers, and it appears that, with the introduction of both the News Trainee Scheme and the Research Assistant Trainee Scheme, the Studio Manager Trainee Scheme is no longer the 'second-tier' scheme for would-be producers that it once was. There is perhaps more emphasis today on the fact that studio managers are recruited strictly for their ability to do operational work. Nevertheless, graduates wishing to join the BBC still apply in large numbers for the Studio Manager Scheme.

Table 13.3 *Studio Manager Trainee Scheme 1979*

	Internal applicants				External applicants				Total applicants				Internal as % of total
	Men	Women	% women of total	Total	Men	Women	% women of total	Total	Men	Women	% women of total	Total	
Applied	31	31	50	62	288	148	34	436	319	179	36	498	12
Preliminary Interview	31	31	50	62	233	122	34	355	264	153	37	417	15
Final Board	21	25	54	46	143	58	29	201	164	83	34	247	19
Selected	6	17	74	23	63	28	31	91	69	45	39	114	20

There are certain interesting differences between this scheme and the others. The proportion of internal applicants is usually higher, and their success rate was much higher than their application rate in both 1977 and 1979. Internal women candidates do particularly well, but external women candidates generally do less well, probably because they apply in much fewer numbers. It looks as though women university students do not usually have the same experience of radio operations as men do, and it is equally possible that they are not attracted to the idea of 'twiddling knobs' as a path to production. This is one area in which women are doing less well than in 1968 and 1969, when over 50 per cent of the trainee studio managers selected were women.

It is not only women, however, who do not apply to this scheme in large numbers. Of the university candidates, 18 per cent came from Oxford and Cambridge, and of the 80 university graduates selected in the external competition, those from Oxford and Cambridge accounted for 23 per cent, so that their success rate was only just above their application rate in this competition. Among the women graduates it was even more marked, with Oxford and Cambridge graduates accounting for 14 per cent of the female university candidates but only 4 per cent of those selected.

Another interesting factor was that in 1979 students from poly-technics and people with no further education accounted for 12 per cent of those successful in the external competition and, among the internal successful candidates, less than a third were university or polytechnic graduates.

(v) *Personnel Trainee Scheme*

This scheme was initiated in June 1977 as a departure from the traditional BBC system of recruiting personnel staff who had already had experience in other organisations. Candidates for the scheme were required to have 'a good degree, a demonstrable commitment to work in Personnel, the capacity or potential to carry out the essential administrative tasks of the job, and a balanced and mature personality as well as a positive interest in public service broadcasting'.

There were over 1,500 applications in 1977, but this number fell to 1,200 in 1978. The 1979 figures are given in Table 13.4.

Table 13.4 *Personnel Trainee Scheme 1979*

	Internal applicants				External applicants				Total applicants				
	Men	Women	% women of total	Total	Men	Women	% women of total	Total	Men	Women	% women of total	Total	Internal as % of total
Applied	2	6	75	8	340	622	65	962	342	628	65	970	0.8
Preliminary Interview	2	4	67	6	58	83	59	141	60	87	59	147	4.0
Final Board	0	0	—	0	13	10	43	23	13	10	43	23	—
Selected	0	0	—	0	3	4	57	7	3	4	57	7	—

In the first three years women applicants outnumbered men by just under 2:1. In 1977, 71 per cent of the successful candidates were women, in 1978, 56 per cent, and in 1979, 57 per cent. In the 1979 BBC review of the training schemes, it was stated that some work experience in personnel or administration after graduating was now emerging as a 'highly desirable indicator of motivation and commit-ment'. Those who were already taking an IPM course were obviously at an advantage, and graduates in one of the social sciences appeared to do better in this competition than other graduates.

It is in the Personnel Trainee competition that Oxford and Cambridge students almost disappear from the scene. They accounted for 7 per cent of both male and female candidates from the universities and none were selected.

(vi) *Women and the training schemes*
When these four training schemes are looked at together, it can be seen that 3,734 applications were made and 148 people selected in 1979. (Some people applied for more than one scheme.) Women represented 55 per cent of the applicants and 43 per cent of the successful candidates. In the two schemes designed more directly for production, the News and Research Assistant Trainee Schemes, women accounted for 56 per cent of the applicants for the two schemes together and 56 per cent of those selected.

These are very remarkable figures for an organisation which in 1968 was talking about the relatively poor quality of women graduates applying for its General Trainee Scheme. It seems very unlikely that the calibre of women graduates has altered so dramatically in eleven years. It looks as though some other factors have influenced recruitment to these schemes. First, there are more openings through more schemes, and the choices are not restricted to either being recognised as an outstanding high-flyer or being prepared to serve an apprenticeship as a studio manager. Secondly, it appears that women today are either more able to present their qualifications and personalities in their applications and in interviews at boards, or the selectors are better able to recognise those qualities. It is particularly interesting that women from Oxford and Cambridge do so well. The report on the Civil Service notes the relative success of women from Oxford and Cambridge. Perhaps women from Oxford and Cambridge are better equipped to present themselves as the kind of people that the BBC and the Civil Service wish to recruit. Their success in the BBC News and Research Assistant Trainee Schemes is quite disproportionate to their applications. It would surely be a great pity if women from other universities were discouraged from applying, as women in general were in the 1960s.

The long-term implications of this success in the training schemes are very interesting. The BBC is putting into practice what other firms say it is not in their interest to do. Industrial enterprises that are worried about recruiting more than 20 per cent women to their management training schemes argue that women leave and the training is not cost-effective. We have already seen that in the first eight years of the News Trainee Scheme, the 'wastage' rates of men and women were not very different. It will be instructive to see what happens to the women trainees taken on by the BBC in the late 1970s. If they stay, or even if some of them stay, the proportion of women in senior jobs in the BBC must surely improve considerably over the next twenty years. But the question has to be asked whether they will stay, and, if they do not, why they leave. If they stay and do not do well, it must also be asked why this has happened. The recruitment people have done their bit in removing unreasonable obstacles for women. It is now up to the women themselves and those responsible for promoting them.

Recruitment – other methods of entry

Apart from the training schemes outlined above there are certain engineering training schemes, for both graduates and those with 'A' levels. Graduates are usually required to have qualifications in electrical engineering, electronics or physics and those with 'A' levels are expected to have physics and mathematics. In 1968, none of these traineeships were open to women, but they have been for some years now, although very few women apply for the graduate traineeships.

There are also traineeships in film and make-up. Some of the film traineeships used to be restricted to men, but are now open to both men and women.

Although the BBC fills most of its jobs from internal competition, it does advertise certain posts in the press. These usually require specialist experience of some kind, and are not generally suitable for new graduates. There is no monitoring on the application and success rates for women for these other entry gates.

Women graduates are also told that they can enter the BBC to do secretarial and clerical work. The BBC states in its 1979 review of the training schemes: 'There are no guarantees of promotion in our open competitive system, but a number of staff in these categories can and do move on to other types of work here.'

There has been considerable resentment reported recently among women graduates who have understood that the opportunities to move from secretarial work into production or into training schemes were greater than they in fact are. Although movement is possible, as illustrated by the fact that some of the women in both our 1968 and 1979 samples entered as non-graduate secretaries, it is thought that this movement is diminishing with the present relative lack of opportunities compared with the 1960s. The ABS evidence to the Annan Report said: '. . . even if a woman applied for a training course which could be the prelude to a production career, she would be unlikely to succeed because her present job would probably be of low status.'[6] It must be asked whether a graduate woman is wise to think that she may be better eligible for training schemes or jobs in production having worked as a secretary for the BBC rather than having tried to increase her experience in a higher status job outside the BBC and then applied for a training scheme or another post in the BBC.

Effects of structural changes

There was some disagreement about whether any of the changes since 1968 had affected women's careers. It certainly appeared that the post-McKinsey reorganisation was seen as a reorganisation of top management which had little direct relevance for the careers of either men or women further down the scale.

There were thought to have been certain other changes in structure with implications for women's careers, particularly the expansion in the late 1960s and early 1970s after the opening of BBC 2, which had been followed by contraction in some areas and a standstill in others. Several of the new sample of women pointed out that they had moved very quickly 'on the boom', but that people recruited after them had not had the same opportunities for quick promotion. It was thought that this relative lack of opportunity had meant that the recent openings had gone to men rather than women, since women were not so 'pushy'. One senior producer, who had come into the BBC as a studio manager, thought that it was much more difficult for a studio manager to move into production now than a few years ago.

Other women thought that it was more difficult than it had been to move from radio to television or between departments, and this reinforced the Annan Report, which commented on the views of staff of the 'insufficient opportunities for lateral career movement' in general in the BBC, not only in the production departments.[7] It is difficult to say to what extent this is new in the last ten years, but it has certainly been exacerbated by the fact that the expansion following BBC 2 has meant that there are now what Annan calls a 'large number of staff who are under 40 with expectations which cannot be satisfied'.[8]

A number of respondents thought that the introduction of local radio had made a difference to the prospects for women, although there was some doubt about whether women had actually prospered in it as much as they might have done. Local radio was considered to be easier for women to do well in, partly because it tended to recruit locally and partly because it was said to be rather more flexible in its deployment of staff, so that anyone showing promise or initiative would be given a chance not available in the more structured central departments. In addition, because of its small size, local radio was said to give a better all-round training and experience in radio techniques than was available centrally, where there were specialists for different jobs. It was also thought that local radio presented more opportunities for freelance or part-time work by women with family responsibilities who wished to keep their hand in without taking a full-time job.

In general, it was felt that, although some women might have been swept along with the tide of expansion of the early part of the 1970s, it had probably become more difficult for women later in the decade, as job opportunities had decreased and there were more producers chasing promotion. Although the number of jobs in the BBC had increased quite considerably overall in the eleven years, nevertheless some people said that women did not have the expertise to compete in the specialist and technical areas where jobs had expanded most.

Policy changes and management attitudes

There was a surprising lack of knowledge of any policy changes within the BBC as far as women's careers were concerned. A number of men said that the Corporation had always had an equal opportunities policy for both men and women, and that there had been no changes in the eleven years because they were not necessary. Women were not so sanguine, and the majority of both the old and new samples thought that there had been no change in the BBC's policy towards women in spite of the fact that women were in such a minority in senior posts. Little mention was made of the various statements by management over the years, referred to in the chapter on developments between 1968 and 1979, and most respondents gave the strong impression that they knew nothing about them. Some of the women thought there had been more interest in women's careers from the top management after the Sex Discrimination Act was passed, but others considered that any changes that had been made were 'cosmetic' or that the BBC was paying 'lip-service' to the requirements of the legislation.

Some respondents thought that women Governors had made the top management pay more attention to women in recent years, but it was only one or two very senior women respondents who said that there had been a definite movement towards trying to encourage women to apply for more senior jobs. This view was endorsed by some of the men, who, as we have noted, were usually concerned with personnel policy. However, even among them, not everyone was convinced that the statements of intent and policy made by the BBC over the past few years had made any fundamental difference to the position of women in the organisation.

One senior executive was concerned that women's progress had been so limited over the last few years, and wondered whether it might not be necessary to introduce some system of 'reverse discrimination' to help women. But this solution was quite unacceptable to other men, and was certainly thought to be at odds with the competitive appointments system. However, some women expressed the view that women were rarely if ever 'positively counselled', while, the competitive appointments system notwithstanding, men were encouraged to apply for posts. One woman said: 'They say they have no careers structure, but that's not true. If they want people to move up, they do.'

Among the women themselves, some commented that they had been blocked for a time because of the personality of a head of department, but had moved very quickly when the person holding the job had changed. One senior producer said that the whole atmosphere in her department had changed when the head of department changed, with the result that a department with very few women in it had within a few years greatly expanded its numbers of female production staff. The power and influence of the individual head of department in implementing policy has been noted several times in our research on women's careers, and it certainly appeared to be as true in the BBC as elsewhere. It was striking how many of the new sample of women interviewed said that they owed their promotion to encouragement or pushing from their head of department or immediate superior.

However, the majority of respondents thought that opportunities for women to rise to senior posts in the BBC had remained about the same since 1968, mainly because most people said that the opportunities had always been there. Although the majority of respondents approved of the present system of open competition, some thought that it might act against the interests of women, who were said to be more diffident, less likely to apply if they did not think they were certain to get the job, and, in general, less prepared to take a long-term view which might include being turned down. One senior woman said:

> Women are less sure about the first steps to take . . . You're going to find young men dancing about in front of Appointments Boards. They're prepared to spend two years in the provinces if it might mean the chance of a good job back here. Men like the intriguing bit. They spend hours planning things.

It was possible that women did not apply for jobs because of their fear of failure. Some respondents thought that women might not apply because they were happy where they were, and several senior men expressed fears that too much emphasis on promotion and movement tended to 'stir the compost too much'. There had been criticism of personnel staff raising false hopes, by encouraging people to apply for jobs which they were very unlikely to get. And one senior man thought that some people felt worried if their superiors brought jobs to their notice: 'Do you go around saying, "Have you seen this job?" They might think, "Do you want to get rid of me? What's wrong?" And then if you dwell on it, they feel, "Why does he go on saying it?"'

We did not find the same reaction in the BBC towards positive management policies for women as we found in industry, where such policies were often interpreted as positive discrimination for women and treated as quite unacceptable by men and women alike. The problem in the BBC was seen to go hand in hand with the ethos of the open competitive system, that everyone was treated alike and either did not need positive encouragement or should not have it because it was unfair.

Some of the men said that the situation had improved over the past eleven years because there was more recognition of the fact that women did not do as well as men under the open competition system and might need more encouragement. It was said that personnel staff were asked to point out opportunities for women, and that heads of department were asked not to overlook women for management courses or promotion opportunities. There were more women in the Appointments Department at senior levels and it was no longer unusual to have a woman on an Appointments Board or even chairing it.

There was some fear that too much encouragement for certain people, whether men or women, could be construed as 'career development', and this was seen to be in conflict with the system of open competition. It was said that the unions and staff wished the open competition system to continue, and that 'talent-spotting' was not the BBC's way of doing things. However, one senior executive thought that the present system led to some difficulty in 'correcting built-in trends', which only some system of career management would help.

Although it was said that personnel staff were asked to encourage people to apply for promotion, there were several comments from women of all ages and grades that they had received very little advice or help on career planning from personnel staff. The system of annual appraisal, which is one of the cornerstones of the BBC's structure, also came in for some criticism as an efficient method of furthering individual careers, particularly when staff reached a higher level:

> My annual interview is with my head of department, but I see him constantly, every day, and the interview tends to turn into an ordinary conversation . . . I think there are a reasonable number of people at my level in the BBC. There could be a point where careers like mine are reviewed, but the BBC says that it doesn't provide careers structures for its staff. Unless you alter that, you can get stuck. I think access to the higher echelons is not as good as it might be, so that you could discuss career possibilities.

Several women were worried that experience in one department for too long would not be recognised in other areas, and they pointed out that people who reached top management had usually had careers which had covered several departments. It was thought to be difficult to move out of a department to gain experience elsewhere in the BBC. Some of the problems encountered by women in this respect were clearly common to most staff. The Annan Report referred to the evidence they received many times during their visits to Television Centre that 'departments were fortresses', and that this tended to reinforce problems of communication as well as staff movement.

Appointments and promotion were seen to be very much in the hands of heads of department or above. Certainly, at this level, the personnel officers responsible for staff were generally not thought to have sufficient information or influence to be able to give enough helpful career advice.

As we have seen, the BBC lays some importance on its system of attachments to other departments as a way of giving people experience in other areas, as well as the possibility of more permanent jobs. Some women thought that not enough emphasis was given to the importance of attachments, and that personnel officers as well as heads of department gave little encouragement or information about the possibilities.

The same was felt to be true of the many training courses that the BBC runs. Some women said that they had had to ask to be sent on a course, whereas they felt that they should have been sent. Much of this is due to the emphasis in the BBC on individual initiative, and senior men thought that people who wanted to go on courses should make this clear to their heads of department.

In 1968, we found that there were certain areas of the BBC which were virtually closed to women in any capacity, let alone in the more senior posts. At the same time, we found that the women in senior posts tended to be found in certain departments and areas. We have seen that since 1973 no job in the BBC has been closed to either men or women, and the 1975 Sex Discrimination Act has made it illegal to discriminate on the grounds of sex. Nevertheless, engineering in the BBC remains an area in which there are very few women, mainly, it is said, because so few women in the country as a whole have engineering qualifications. What were the views of the staff on whether women did better in some parts of the BBC than others, and to what extent did they think that the situation had changed since 1968?

The respondents were almost unanimous that women still did better in some parts of the Corporation than others. Although half of them thought that the situation had improved since 1968, over a third thought that it was about the same as in 1968, in spite of the legislation.

Women were thought to do better in production jobs than in other areas, and within production jobs they were thought to do better in departments which had a tradition of employing women – in children's and women's programmes and in education. Among those who said that the situation had improved, reference was made to the increasing numbers of women in current affairs, both in radio and television, and this was seen as a definite change since 1968. However, in spite of the presence of women newsreaders and reporters, it was thought that there had been little, if any, change in the proportion of senior women in the newsroom production staff. One woman thought that this was important, because it meant that the actual selection and balance of news were still determined by men: 'I don't think that having women as newsreaders was an important milestone in terms of the real entrenched positions. Nothing really important is run by women.'

Although women were said to be doing better in documentaries and features, arts and music, and, to a certain extent, in drama than they had done in 1968, the reservation was expressed that a few outstanding women did not actually mean that the situation was really any better, and some women thought that the presence of one or two women in senior or prominent positions might hide the fact that women in general were possibly doing less well in these areas than ten years before. In production areas, it was thought that women were still not doing well in sport and outside broadcasts, and that light entertainment, in spite of one or two very talented women, was still very much a male enclave. The reasons put forward for this were still much the same as those found in 1968, and the argument appeared to be circular – that women did not apply so that they were not appointed, and that the reason that women did not apply was that they thought they were unlikely to get a job in an area which was so male-dominated.

Apart from production areas, there was thought to have been an improvement in the representation of women in the planning area, where there had been a tradition of women holding responsible jobs, and in the presentation departments. They were also thought to have done much better in personnel, and it was pointed out that there were now some very senior women in personnel, which had certainly not been the case in 1968. It must be questioned whether this lack of women in 1968 had something to do with the BBC's traditional policy of recruiting retired men from the armed or overseas services to staff their personnel departments, and whether, in fact, they were only now catching up with other firms where women had more traditionally been employed in personnel posts.

However, the big gap remained engineering and all the technical jobs which, although not strictly requiring higher engineering qualifications, were traditionally male preserves. Movement towards more representation of women within these areas was thought to be dependent on movement within society itself. Some respondents, however, thought that the BBC, as a public corporation, had a duty to lead the way, and there had been discussion both within the management and with the unions, on whether more could be done to encourage women to enter the BBC in engineering or technical functions.

Women's own attitudes

Most people thought that the position of women in the most senior jobs was about the same as it had been in 1968 or worse, although there was some optimism that, further down the line, the improvement at MP5 level might mean that there would be more women in senior jobs in the future. Many people remained sceptical, however, and held that, although the number of women at producer or senior producer level might increase, other factors would combine to ensure that they did not get any higher in any great numbers.

Several reasons were put forward for the decline, or at least, static performance of women in the top management jobs. One was said to be historical – that the women in senior posts in 1968 had 'come to prominence in the war years, and the second generation has simply not come along'. One of the respondents in External Broadcasting noted that there had always been a tradition of at least one senior woman there, but this tradition appeared to have come to an end in recent years. Many of the respondents said that when the women holding senior posts a few years ago had retired they had not been replaced by other women, but several pointed out that there had been no natural female successors for these or, for that matter, any of the other senior posts. One or two people thought this might be due to fewer women in that post-war generation with qualifications or higher education than today, although it did seem odd that an older generation with even fewer qualified women had thrown up some high-flyers in the years before.

Some women thought that it was part of the 'years of benign neglect' pattern, and that the BBC had not done anything positive to help women get on:

> I think that in the early stages of their careers women need more fostering. They're not as pushy as men. I don't think that many women set out to make careers. They find themselves on the road because someone has given them a push – as happened to me in the initial stages. Then they will start going places.

Several women agreed with this view of women and their careers. It was said that women were less single-minded and ambitious than men, particularly at the beginning of their careers. The evidence to Annan pointed out that women tended to start their careers at a lower level than the men and then to take longer to get going if they stayed. Several women thought that some of this was due to women themselves, as this senior woman producer confirmed:

> Having got a good job satisfies women as a thing in itself, rather than being a top person. I have been prepared to settle for where I was as long as people told me I was good at it. Only negative reasons have forced me along. I was the first one through the net for a whole generation of girls behind me, and I felt responsible . . . If *I* didn't apply for boards, they were using me as an excuse for not promoting women.

There was little doubt that many women considered production jobs a lot more interesting than management jobs, which were regarded as involving too many administrative duties and taking people away from 'doing things'. In *Women in Top Jobs*, it was made clear that many women preferred to stay close to the camera or the microphone, and we found the same thing in 1979. One of the women interviewed in 1968, who had remained a senior producer, travelling all over the world making films, was not sure whether she would have wanted to move up in the management structure as one of her female colleagues had: 'She said to me, " I *do* envy you . . .".' I'm not sure that I envy her. The more desirable and interesting jobs are technically lower down, but they're much more fun.'

There were women who had moved into management, but had done so reluctantly. Some, like the woman quoted above, had accepted promotion because they felt a sense of responsibility to women coming after them. There were doubts expressed about whether this was a 'fair burden', and there can be little doubt that women at the more senior levels were under considerably more scrutiny than those at lower levels. Some women were sceptical about whether moving into management would actually help other women: 'Having got the token women, it's *more* difficult for the next one along. They won't want another.'

One senior woman thought that the structure of the BBC made it unlikely that women would want to get to the top: 'Women don't want to leave the creative jobs, and the only way to the top is through administration . . . I think we've somehow got to change the nature of who's at the top. Why should it be the administration?' But one woman thought that the really top jobs at the BBC were held by the talented producers: 'The people who really matter are those who've made outstanding programmes'. And from a prestige point of view, as well as for personal satisfaction, it was generally thought to be much more satisfying to be responsible for pro-grammes watched by millions than to have a title and to be 'driving a desk', as one woman put it.

Several of the administrators agreed that it was women them-selves who did not want to go further, and pointed out that women were relatively less likely to apply for jobs, especially of MP5 and above, than men were. Under the competitive appointments system of the BBC, if people do not apply, they do not get the job. But was it really so simple, that women do not reach senior positions in the BBC because they do not apply for senior jobs, and they do not apply for these jobs because they want to remain producers? Many of the respondents, both men and women, did not agree.

There can be little doubt that in 1979, there were far fewer examples given of blatant prejudices affecting women's progress.

Attitudes had changed, and women recognised them to have changed, but nevertheless, there were still thought to be 'intangible' factors operating against the promotion of women. In 1968, there were references to the 'male club'. There were still shadows of it in 1979: 'A lot of men are simply more comfortable having other men around. When I went to [a male-dominated department] it was very strange. They were so unused to women that they behaved in an almost courtly manner.'

Experience in women's, children's and even educational programmes was thought to have less prestige in the BBC pecking order than current affairs, news, light entertainment or sport, where women have traditionally been less conspicuous. One woman from one of these departments thought this counted against women: 'We believe we're very influential in terms of the audience, but we're not regarded so in terms of BBC internal politics. When I go abroad, I'm feted as being from my department in the BBC – but not here.'

It certainly looked as though women did start moving up the ladder later in their careers than the men, and this was held to be one of the reasons why there were so few women in line for senior management now. When they were starting their careers, there were said to be very few heads of department who would give them a chance at the beginning: 'Women are in the number two or three position now and they're too old to be considered for the top job.'

It was generally agreed that it was easier for women to move out of certain departments than it had been, although, as we have seen, people thought that this movement was becoming more difficult. Certainly the women who had entered the BBC as secretaries had had a longer haul up than those who had come in as producers or into another specialist function. This later start was also thought to be complicated by the fact that many women, particularly in the past, had not come into the BBC intending to make it a lifelong career. It was the same initial short-term view of careers that we observed among the women in industry:

Women do not have a long-term view of their careers at first. They don't have a ten-year plan like men have. Having got themselves launched after the first five years or so of dithering about, I think some women run out of puff . . . Some of the MP5 or MP6 women have attained that position after such long years of service. They've got to their early forties, say, and they feel really quite whacked. They say, 'It's all such an effort. I'll take my money and I'll do my job . . .' I think they run out of ambition.

But this may well be true of men too, as one senior male executive pointed out: 'Both men and women fall into two categories – the diffident and the unambitious, and the ambitious and pushy. I would maintain that the BBC is as wide open for an ambitious and pushy woman as for a man.' Many people would disagree with him, since the women are patently not in senior jobs, and it could hardly be argued that all men in senior jobs in the BBC are ambitious and pushy, while there are no ambitious and pushy women further down the line.

The crux of the matter to some of the senior men was that women had babies: 'I personally think that the reason there are so few women at the top in the BBC is due to the fact that men don't actually acknowledge women's need to work and the difficulty that having a baby has on her career.' Perhaps the problems were summarised by another senior man who said:

> I see no reasons why women can't do the top jobs. *But* you can't expect a young woman to be able to join an organisation and say, 'I want a career which will give me a chance to be Director-General *and* will give me a chance to have one baby or more and expect to come back and continue like a man . . .' It would be grossly unfair to the organisation and to males.

And it is this problem which is the theme of the next chapter.

References
(1) Op. cit., p. 439, para. 28.17.
(2) Op. cit., p. 106, para. 9.26.
(3) Op. cit., p. 437, para. 28.11.
(4) BBC Appointments Department, *BBC 1979 Training Schemes (non-engineering)*, 1979.
(5) Ibid.
(6) Op. cit., p. 440, para. 28.21.
(7) Op. cit., p. 439, para. 28.19.
(8) Op. cit., p. 439, para. 28.30.

CHAPTER 14

Women and Children

In the past, most women gave up work, at least temporarily, when they had children. Since most women have children, the proportion of women left in work was considerably smaller than that of men, and, although the BBC does not keep figures on whether or not their employees have children, it was clear that very few of the women in MP5 jobs and above had children.

It was obviously regarded as very unusual, as well as very difficult, for women with children to reach positions of any seniority in the BBC, in spite of the fact that it had always been generous with its maternity provisions. Although many respondents noted that it was a very flexible employer to all its staff and that there was a tradition of sympathetic help to anyone in temporary difficulties, the difficulties observed elsewhere of combining a career and family were thought to militate against women's progress in the BBC as much as anywhere else.

Was there anything that an enlightened employer like the BBC could do to help women stay at work while they had small children, while, at the same time, giving itself a larger pool of women to consider for middle and higher management jobs? We have looked at some of the pressure which has been brought to bear on the BBC as far as women in general are concerned. What about pressure for women with children?

Over the past ten years, there have been various attempts to establish crèche facilities, starting in 1973, when, after some years of pressure by the ABS for a crèche in London, the BBC agreed to open a day nursery for members of staff in Pebble Mill in Birmingham. It was set up on the initiative of the local management and was considered by many members of staff to be an experiment to see whether such a scheme was viable, although in 1979 we were told by BBC management that it was established on a specific understanding that it was not a pilot scheme and that there was no indication that any day care would be provided elsewhere in the

Corporation. Birmingham had good available premises which could be converted to nursery use and a committee was set up to establish the scheme, which was designed for twenty children under school age. It was agreed that it would run as an experiment for two years, but would have to be self-supporting. The Pebble Mill nursery opened in October 1974, with places for fourteen children. Only five children attended to begin with, three of them part-time, and after six months there were still only eight children, half of whom did not have parents who were members of BBC staff and half of whom were part-time. A decision was taken to close the nursery in May 1975, and it closed in August, after ten months of existence. The Pebble Mill saga has passed into BBC folklore, and there are arguments on both sides about what happened and whether the demand was ever properly assessed before the nursery was opened, whether it was prematurely closed, whether it should have been given longer to establish itself, and whether the BBC has used the Pebble Mill experience as a reason not to try again.

After Pebble Mill, the question of nurseries subsided as a topic of pressing concern, although the ABS regularly brought it up with management. The Annan Report commented: 'Day care facilities should be provided wherever possible; we were disturbed to hear that it was found necessary to close the crèche at Pebble Mill because it had become too expensive.'[1]

In November 1977, the BBC decided to do a survey of all the women in the BBC having babies in the year April 1978–March 1979, who had been working for the Corporation for at least a year. This survey was carried out by the Assistant Corporation Welfare Officer, who found that 177 women working in the BBC had had babies in the year in question. Their average age was 29.1 years when they had their babies, and they had worked for the BBC for an average of 6.6 years. She found that women in the management, production and operational grades had had babies at an even later age – an average of 33 years – having put in many years' service with the BBC. As a result, there was a strong feeling among those who had had babies that money used for training new staff would be better spent providing nursery facilities; that their high level of commitment to the BBC should be recognised in practical terms; that a forward-thinking employer with positive policies for the welfare of its staff would be able to see the increasing need for nursery provision and act on that need; and that the problems of recruitment in certain areas, e.g. secretaries and personal assistants, could be lessened by the provision of a nursery and by the introduction of more flexible working hours and increased part-time posts.

The figures are given in Table 14.1. Overall, just over 30 per cent of the women in the survey took maternity leave and returned to the BBC, while nearly 70 per cent resigned, some after having intended to return. It is here that the most striking difference occurred between management, production and operational grades and the others. Whereas nearly two-thirds of the management and production and half the operational grades took maternity leave and came back, the average was considerably lower for the other grades, with none of the Administrative Support staff returning and only 17 per cent of the secretarial and clerical staff. Those who returned to work after maternity leave in all grades tended to have longer service and to be rather older than those who resigned.

This evidence suggests some interesting possibilities, although of course, the numbers are fairly small. A recent PSI study by W. W. Daniel[2] on the effects of the maternity provisions of the Employment Protection Act has indicated that women in management or professional jobs and women in unskilled jobs are the most likely to return to work after having a baby, with the latter more likely to return to part-time working. The BBC figures are in line with this finding, and it appears that women who have high job satisfaction combined with enough money to pay for substitute child care are more likely to return than others. In the BBC this also goes along with the possibility that women who had worked for as long as these women had before having a baby might feel more committed to their work and might be less prepared to give up either the job or the money than younger women with less commitment and experience. There is also the question of the extent to which skills are transferable, and it is probable that it is easier for a secretary to find alternative work near her home or part-time, either immediately or later, than for a BBC producer or studio manager. There is another factor which may be relevant to the fact that none of the women in Administrative Support returned to work. There is often a certain flexibility in both job content and arrangement of working hours in the MP and OP grades. This may be less likely to occur in administrative support jobs.

Table 14.1 *Women in the BBC who had babies, April 1978–March 1979*

Grade	Nos.	%	Average age (years)	Average length of service (years)	Maternity leave Nos.	Maternity leave %	Maternity leave Average age (years)	Maternity leave Average length of service (years)	Resigned Nos.	Resigned %	Resigned Average age (years)	Resigned Average length of service (years)	Maternity leave/resigned Nos.	Maternity leave/resigned %	Maternity leave/resigned Average age (years)	Maternity leave/resigned Average length of service (years)
All grades	177	100	29.1	6.6	55	31	31.6	7.7	111	63	28.1	6.2	11	6	26.3	5.9
MP (Management, Professional and Editorial)	34	19	33.1	7.5	21	62	34.0	8.7	12	35	32.0	6.0	1	3	26.0	2.0
OP (Operational)	30	17	33.5	10.0	15	50	34.0	9.8	14	47	33.3	10.8	1	3	29.0	11.0
AS (Administrative Support)	14	8	27.1	7.0	—	—	—	—	12	86	27.7	7.5	2	14	23.5	4.0
Musicians	5	3	28.6	4.0	2	40	26.5	4.5	3	60	30.0	3.6	—	—	—	—
SC (Secretarial and Clerical)	77	44	26.8	5.5	13	17	27.0	5.1	59	77	26.6	5.5	5	7	24.0	6.0
CO (Clerical Operator)	14	8	27.2	4.2	4	29	28.2	4.7	9	64	27.1	3.8	1	6	29.0	5.0
CC (Catering Craft)	2	1	20.0	2.5	—	—	—	—	1	50	19.0	2.5	1	50	21.0	4.0
GS (General Service)	1	<1	19.0	3.0	—	—	—	—	1	100	19.0	3.0	—	—	—	—

The Assistant Corporation Welfare Officer conducted interviews with samples of those who took maternity leave and those who resigned. She found that enjoyment of their work was the main reason for wishing to return, although the money was a very important factor as well, and she pointed out that women were certainly not now working for 'pin money'. There was a considerable demand among both those who had returned and those who had left for more part-time work or job-sharing, and there was considerable anxiety expressed about the nature of the child-care facilities which those returning to work had been able to arrange. Although only a tiny proportion of returning women had been able to find nursery facilities, over half of these returners who were interviewed felt that a nursery was an ideal environment for their children, at least after the first one or two years. Most of the women thought they would use a nursery if one were available, and more than half of them said they would prefer it to be near their work, with the important reason given that they would expect a BBC-run nursery to be of a high standard. Among the women who had resigned, there was a sizeable minority who said that they would have returned to work if there had been an established nursery at the BBC.

In 1978 a group of women working in television began to press for crèche facilities, calling themselves the 'Crèche Campaign'. They conducted their own survey, which was specifically designed to try and assess the 'immediate and potential need for crèche or child-care facilities in the West London area', where most of the BBC television staff are based. They pressed management to provide crèche facilities and proposed a working party to be set up to look at the practical issues involved in establishing nursery facilities. At the time of writing, a joint sub-committee has been set up by the BBC management and the recognised unions to examine the costs involved in setting up nursery facilities and the likely take-up, and to assess the extent to which the provision, or assistance towards the provision, of nursery facilities would prove to be effective in reducing the costs of recruitment and training of new staff.

But what were the views of the people we interviewed on whether the BBC could do more to help women return to work after maternity leave and remain working, or whether it could do more to help women to return to work after a period of time away to look after small children?

Help for women to remain

Both male and female respondents were almost unanimous that the BBC could do more to help women who wished to remain working while their children were small. Far more of the women in the BBC thought that their employer ought to do more to help, and that it was a practical proposition, than the women in industry. Partly this was due to the fact that the women in the BBC did not recognise with the same clarity as those in industry that their organisation was unlikely to do anything which was not of immediate and measurable cost-effectiveness. Although both industrial companies studied had a strong and long tradition of paternalistic management policy, nevertheless they were seen to be in business to make profits, and this undoubtedly coloured the responses of the people working for them. The BBC, on the other hand, was thought by some respondents to have a public duty to be seen to be an enlightened employer, and this meant, in their view, that every help should be given to women who wished to continue working while they had small children.

The campaign for crèche facilities had made some impact, although very few of the women we interviewed were directly affected since so few had small children. Rather more than half the women thought that the BBC ought to offer crèche facilities, but it was interesting to note that the younger women were more in favour of crèches than the older sample, apart from some of the women in the 1968 sample who had worked while they had small children. It was not generally thought to be an ideal solution, and most women with children said that they would only use it as a fall-back if other arrangements failed. Several women thought that it would be most useful for more junior staff, and cited instances of their assistants or secretaries who would have continued to work if there had been a crèche. Some of the respondents thought that any crèche ought to be open for men too, and others said that it would be unfair to offer it only in one part of London, without offering something to all the other BBC staff who might like to use child-care facilities. There were seen to be great complications if everyone in the BBC who had a baby wanted to be offered either crèche facilities or the equivalent in cash or allowances, and some people thought that the campaign might founder if the unions insisted on equal treatment for all members of staff with babies.

The male respondents were divided about the question of crèche provision, with about half of them saying that the evidence must be carefully considered to see whether the scheme could be cost-effective and whether it would, in fact, help to retain people who would otherwise have left. Some respondents thought that the provision of a crèche was not the responsibility of the employer, particularly one which was accountable to the public for the money it spent. It was pointed out that there were a number of competing groups for any money which might be spent on a crèche, and one senior man thought that the BBC ought not to be expected to offer facilities over and above those offered by employers in the rest of the country.

The women in favour of providing crèche facilities in West London, the district close to most of the television studios, thought that the take-up by staff was likely to be greatest in this area, where the most demand had been demonstrated. One of the reasons that the Pebble Mill nursery was thought to have failed was that there were not enough women prepared to put their children in a crèche which was said to be an experiment. Therefore, it was thought that any crèche should have a guaranteed life so that people would be prepared to use it. Although some people agreed that men should be able to use the facilities, it was thought that women would have the greatest need and that they ought to be given first priority on places. The question of recompensing people working outside the immediate vicinity of a crèche who could not use the facilities was one which had not occurred to most people, and was clearly one which needed careful consideration by the committee looking into the subject. Those in favour of crèches thought that women with small children represented a special case, in that if no support were offered to them at this particularly vulnerable time of their lives and careers if they wished to continue to work, there would be little likelihood of much improvement in the proportion of women in senior posts in the BBC, since the problems of combining work and a family without help with child-care facilities were too great for most people.

Very few of the respondents had considered all the arguments for and against the provision of a crèche or nursery. In general, there was a polarisation of opinion between those who thought that 'of course' the BBC ought to offer nursery facilities and those who thought that it was out of the question or unnecessary. Those who were undecided were deterred by the potential cost involved, while recognising that some women were prevented from returning to work when they wanted to because of the lack of child-care facilities. However, among this group there was the fear that the provision of a crèche might not necessarily help to retain the people who might be difficult to replace, like producers, technicians or others in whom the BBC had invested training.

It was recognised that the crèche had to prove cost-effective in an economic climate where there had to be strict control of money. The high proportion of management, production and operational staff returning to work after maternity leave suggests that there is some evidence that highly-motivated staff will find a way of making child-care arrangements if they want to return. The irony is that those in perhaps the greatest need of nursery facilities – the single-parent families or the low-paid – are those who are unlikely to satisfy the cost-effectiveness criterion, and are the least likely to be able to afford the contribution which the employees would have to make to the cost.

Among the women in industry whom we interviewed, there was a consensus of opinion that one of the reasons that so few women managers or scientists returned to work in the two companies was that the employers presented them with an 'all or nothing' alternative. If they wanted to stay at work, and certainly if they wanted to be promoted, they had to continue to work in exactly the same way as they had before they had the baby. The twin demands of work and family in a competitive atmosphere were thought to be too great for most women, who usually left when they had babies. This was not found to be as true in the BBC as in industry. The BBC was seen to be a very flexible employer, and the type of work often involved much more flexible hours than those in industry. While this meant that production and technical staff had to be prepared to work unsocial hours, it also meant that flexibility could be available when pressure was less great. Nevertheless, some respondents thought that this flexibility could be made more available to more women, since often it depended on the policy and sympathy of the head of department. The 'Crèche Campaign' reported that some people, in response to a questionnaire they had sent out about crèche facilities, expressed the view that a job in production was totally incompatible with parenthood, and they would wish to switch to something less demanding for a time. The campaign organisers said that these views were often echoed in meetings they held, where there was a constant demand for more part-time work and job-sharing. The BBC survey of women who had had a baby in 1978–79 found that over three-quarters of the women interviewed who had taken maternity leave would have preferred to have been working part-time. This was also true among women who had resigned, many of whom said that they would have stayed if they had been offered part-time work. The provision of part-time or more flexible working hours was suggested by more than half the women we interviewed for this study. One woman with two small children said: 'Almost every full-time working mother I know would prefer to do part-time work.'

Several women thought that more flexible working hours or job-sharing could be introduced into the BBC, not only for women with small children but for other staff who might want to work less than full-time. There had been examples of shared contracts in the past, and at the time of writing, there was a shared post in Schools Television, an area which was generally recognised to be sympathetic to the problems of women at work. The BBC, with its complicated work schedules for many of its staff, was thought to be capable of designing and accommodating almost any pattern of work. Some women said that this could easily happen in their own department, but was unlikely to take place because the men saw no need for it. There was some disagreement on the question of whether flexibility could or should be institutionalised. Some women thought that it worked well where there was a sympathetic head of department or senior producer, but not in other departments. There was a fear that if it were institutionalised some departments might simply not take on part-time or less than full-time women, or might refuse whatever flexibility they allowed at the moment.

Very few people pointed out that it might be more difficult to move up the promotion ladder for a woman who had had a spell of part-time work. The problem certainly looked different from that found in industry where a step sideways from line management was seen as the end of the promotion line. Nevertheless, some of the men thought that any lengthy period of part-time work would certainly not be any help in 'pushing a woman up the ladder'.

The Board of Governors has recently expressed a wish that

personnel and line managers should be encouraged to examine the possibilities of part-time work and flexible hours, especially in jobs which have proved difficult to fill on a full-time basis. Certainly, the provision of more part-time work or job-sharing or a more flexible approach to work, including working at home, may in fact attract more women to stay with the BBC than the provision of a crèche. At the moment, the vast majority of part-time jobs are for cleaners, catering staff and secretarial and clerical staff. It is, of course, in these areas that it is either most difficult to attract full-time staff or where the demand is for part-time staff.

At present, however, as with many other organisations, the success of job-sharing or part-time working or more flexible conditions of work depends to a large extent on the attitude of line management and, to a lesser extent, on the co-operation of other people in a department. Unless there is a willingness to recognise that both women and the organisation may benefit from some adaptability at certain times, nothing will change, and the BBC and other organisations will continue to lose women who might, with a little help, have remained working and risen to the top.

Help for women to return

However, not every woman wants to continue working when she has small children. Some women want to bring up their children themselves, some cannot find satisfactory substitute child-care, some cannot cope with the demands of work and children, and some are prepared to reduce their standards of living to look after their children. But increasing numbers of women who do stay at home while their children are small return to work when their children are school-age or older. The increase in the labour force over the past few years has been almost entirely made up of women returning to work, and the proportion of married women working continues to rise.

The respondents were more divided on the question of whether the BBC could do anything to help women return to work after a small-child break, than on whether it could help them after maternity leave. Nearly a third of them, both men and women, said that the BBC did enough at the moment, and should not do more.

The problems encountered by anyone who has left an organisation and wants to re-enter are familiar enough. The problems for women who have had small children and have not been working for several years are even greater. Respondents pointed out that they could have lost touch with people with whom they had worked, would probably have become out of touch with technical and other developments, and could easily have lost confidence. There was certainly a problem seen with accommodating returning women into a system which, like the companies we studied, was based on internal promotion. Some of the women interviewed were very much against the BBC going out of its way to help anyone to come back:

> If they're going to get out of the mainstream of the organisation for six years or so, I don't see why the organisation should bend over backwards to promote them over the heads of people who've been slaving away all that time.

Even among young people who were sympathetic to the idea of women wanting to return, there were grave doubts whether they could fit into the system again:

> You take your prospects in your hands if you take off more than six months. Our attitudes and technology are changing all the time. If you come back after five years, the change would be almost total. And which level would you come back at? A producer wouldn't want to be a production assistant.

A few people thought that the loss of skills envisaged by so many of the respondents was grossly exaggerated. The case of one producer who returned to television was described:

> She came back in at a lower grade. She had to be terribly careful. People said, 'Oh, you wouldn't know about that . . .' but nothing had really changed. It was like riding a bicycle. Techniques have not changed that much in the last few years. In any case, they can run refresher courses.

Several respondents commented that it must be cheaper to retrain someone who had already done a job than to train someone from scratch. Others thought that it was not difficult to get back in, although very few knew anyone who had returned. Some respondents thought that not many women wanted to return to full-time work or to work their way up. In radio there were thought to be opportunities for freelance work if people were 'good enough'. Some women were more optimistic about the opportunities for returning women than others:

> She must establish herself first before she goes off. No employer is going to turn down the right person with the right experience. The right people will find their way back, given the will and the initiative. It's a good idea to try and keep your hand in – work one day a week.

Some women would argue that this advice was not so easy to put into practice. It was said that much depended on whether colleagues or 'patrons' had moved on in the meantime, and whether anyone remembered how good a woman had been. Some people thought it ought to be the responsibility of the personnel departments to keep a register of women who might like to return, or who were available for part-time or freelance work. It was thought that the present system was based too much on chance and luck that people had not changed jobs.

The BBC has recently decided to adopt a new approach to staff who resign to have a baby or to look after elderly relatives, who want to come back to work. Until now they have had to apply for jobs as if they had never worked in the Corporation, which meant that they were only considered for posts advertised externally. They are now eligible for consideration for posts advertised internally within five years of leaving, but the onus of keeping in touch with vacancies rests with the individual. A BBC internal document has stressed the value of retraining former members of staff who could bring some previous experience to a job.

Certainly there were respondents who were worried about the lack of women in the BBC with experience of bringing up families. They thought that editorial judgement was sometimes not as sensitive as it might be to the audience in which women and children were in the majority. Some thought that returning women might bring experience which would be useful and help to solve the broadcaster's 'isolation from the audience', mentioned by Annan.[3]

Some respondents thought that the best thing for women who wished to return to work at a later date was to keep their hands in with freelance work, if they could not get part-time work or did not wish to commit themselves to a regular pattern of working while their children were small. Some women pointed out the unions' concern about the increase in freelance work, which again was noted by Annan in a section on 'Short-term contracts and freelance employment'.[4] There can be little doubt that the unions are in favour of cutting back the amount of freelance and short-term contract work, partly to protect people employed in that way from exploitation and partly to protect those permanently employed from being undercut. However, there is the danger that concentration on full-time employment as the norm will squeeze out some of the very people that the unions want to help. If some women cannot keep their hands in with freelance work while their children are small, potential top women managers may be deprived of the experience and contacts necessary to give them the credibility to return to the BBC in competition with those who have not been away.

References
(1) Op. cit. p. 442, para. 28.26.
(2) W. W. Daniel, *Maternity Rights*, Policy Studies Institute, June 1980.
(3) Op. cit. p. 442, para. 28.26.
(4) Op. cit. pp. 443–449, paras. 28.32–50.

CHAPTER 15

Effectiveness of Agencies of Change

Internal pressure groups

In view of the description of the pressures on the BBC from various quarters outlined earlier in this report, it might seem unlikely that anyone could have been unaware of the fact that the Corporation had come under pressure over the past eleven years as far as women were concerned. Nevertheless, a third of the respondents working for the BBC, both male and female, said they did not know of any pressure brought by any formal or informal pressure group.

There appeared to be a number of reasons for this. Among the women, there was a general impression that they were either too busy to interest themselves in pressure for or on behalf of other women, or they said specifically that the unions did not take up the cases of women but were more interested in other matters. Even among women who said they knew of pressure groups, several were very vague about the existence of any group and thought that Women in Media was defunct. Less than half the women mentioned the crèche campaign, which had been very active in the months before this research took place in most parts of the BBC where women were employed.

There was not the same reaction in the BBC towards pressure groups that we found in industry – that any connection with a pressure group for women was the kiss of death as far as promotion was concerned. The general reaction was rather one of lack of involvement or indifference. There were women who were committed or felt strongly about the provision of a crèche, but there was no feeling of a great need for pressure to be brought on the BBC to improve the lot of women working for it in any other way. It should be remembered that these women were all in senior posts, and in this respect there was a similar reaction to that found in industry – that they had got there on their own merits, and that it had sometimes been a bit of a struggle in what was still a man's world. Some of the women felt strongly about women secretaries who could not move out into production, or graduate producers' assistants who, they felt, had been recruited with false expectations of a career in production. One or two thought that the problem of whether there were any women in top jobs was irrelevant, and that more concern ought to be expressed about the majority of women, who were in low-paid jobs. But, in general, the women interviewed had little knowledge of any formal or informal pressure group acting on behalf of women within the BBC.

The men were hardly more knowledgeable, in spite of their greater involvement in administrative or personnel work. Reference was made to pressure for crèches, and some knew of pressure from the union, although this was reported to be sporadic by those not closely involved in it. One senior man thought that any pressure brought in England was nothing to what had happened in the United States, where women had used the available legislation in a much more militant manner. No reference by those not directly involved was made to the regular meetings held between the recognised unions and the management since the end of 1978 to discuss any problems of discrimination.

One of the non-members of staff interviewed said:

> For the numbers of women employed here, it is extraordinary how little pressure there is. I find it particularly surprising, because they're a very intelligent group of women. I suppose they're very busy – the people who are successful work very hard and have to run homes.

Perhaps it is this, that these women are busy, that they do not feel discriminated against, having made it to a relatively senior position, while those who have not made it do not have the numbers or the power to make much impact. Certainly, with one or two notable exceptions, there was no indication that any pressure would be brought to bear on the BBC by any of the senior women interviewed.

The Sex Discrimination Act 1975

Only one respondent thought that the Sex Discrimination Act had made a great impact in general, but most respondents thought that it had had some effect, mainly through removing barriers to applying for jobs which had hitherto been restricted to men. Some of the women thought that the legislation had made employers think twice, or even three times, before automatically appointing a man to a job, and some thought that it had helped to change attitudes towards women and work. But a few of the women were very sceptical about any real impact of the legislation: 'A few trivial battles have been fought and won.'

The men thought that it had had rather more effect in general, in that it had 'given a focus for a general debate', or that it had made employers more careful about drafting advertisements, or that it was supportive of those who wished to remove discrimination.

The majority of respondents considered that the Act had had little or no effect on the BBC itself, a view held by almost all the men, mainly because the BBC had always implemented equal opportunities in any case. It was stated several times that the Corporation was ahead of the legislation, and some women said they were sure it thought that it had never discriminated in any case. Some thought that the legislation had made people at Appointments Boards think twice before they asked any question which could be construed as potentially discriminatory, and that women were not now asked whether they thought they could look after their children as well as their jobs. One senior woman thought that it had made the BBC try harder to recruit or promote women, and that it had resulted in women being boarded for jobs more frequently than before, even if they had not been appointed. There was a fear among both men and women that it might have made the BBC more anxious to appoint a 'statutory woman', but 'having appointed one – that's enough!'

None of the women thought that the Act had had any effect on them personally. There was overwhelming agreement that the BBC was active in implementing the Act, although some women thought that 'active' was perhaps not the right word: 'They're more or less active. I believe the BBC is generally woolly-mindedly well-intentioned.' 'The BBC like to be good employers and on the whole they are in the forefront. But they are a tremendously Establishment organisation . . . a male-dominated structure.'

One of the senior men thought that legislation was not the whole answer:

If the situation is going to change, you have to bring about changes in people's attitudes about other people. I don't know that it's something that can be imposed. Institutions must create a context in which attitudes can change. They must always be careful that they are providing this context.

But other men were more satisfied with the situation: 'Our attitudes were on the side of the legislative angels.'

Although most of the women were sure that the BBC was 'a very law-abiding organisation', some were worried about 'unspoken attitudes' which still affected appointments:

> People will always say things privately – for example, that men have a wife and children to support or that they'd go to another company if they don't get the job. Men will get promoted when they're not acceptable . . . They have calculations about how to keep people happy, and keeping a man happy is still seen as more important than keeping a woman happy by most male administrators. They see no reason to 'buy' a woman. She's only too happy to be where she is.

And it was these attitudes which made women unsure about whether the Sex Discrimination Act had increased opportunities for women to rise to senior jobs in the BBC. Some thought that the opportunities had always been there and that legislation had made no difference. Others, including some of the men, thought that the Act had drawn attention to the fact that there were few women in senior jobs in the BBC, but one man underlined the central problem which has been noted before: 'How can the Sex Discrimination Act influence the line manager who's scared or unwilling to promote a woman?' It was stressed that legislation alone was not enough to change attitudes, and some women wondered whether it could have any effect as far as really senior jobs were concerned:

> The terms of the Sex Discrimination Act don't really apply at that level. The appointment of really senior members of staff is based on factors which are difficult to quantify or assess except by a small internal body, and if they have a small internal bias, no Sex Discrimination Act can do anything about it. No one can prove anything.

Most respondents thought that the BBC did not monitor the performance of women *vis-á-vis* men, although, of course, they have done so for some time, at least in the MP grades. It all depends on how the concept of 'monitoring' is interpreted. In the eyes of some respondents a regular head-count was not monitoring. They thought that monitoring implied the necessity to employ a certain quota, and this was regarded as quite unacceptable, particularly by the women. There were several references to the undesirability of treating women as a special group.

Although the performance of women is measured quantitatively, it was thought by some of the men that it would be difficult to measure the performance of groups qualitatively. The BBC's annual appraisal system was said to measure the individual's performance qualitatively, but could not measure that of groups. There was a strong disinclination to consider doing so. However, one or two senior people thought that monitoring was a good idea so that the situation was recognised and that, not only were the overall statistics available, but that these should be used to see whether women were sent on training courses in proportion to their representation in each grade, or encouraged to apply for attachments or promotion. It was argued that, unless the facts were known, no assessment could be made of whether the situation was changing or not, or whether women were being overlooked.

The majority of respondents thought that there was no way in which the Sex Discrimination Act could have been made more effective, and indeed, there was a strong feeling, particularly among the men, that it had gone as far as it could in any case. Some people were against compulsion, and a frequent comment was that attitudes could not be changed by legislation.

The Equal Opportunities Commission

The overwhelming majority of respondents thought that the Equal Opportunities Commission had had little or no effect in general or on the BBC in particular. The women were unanimous that it had had no effect on them personally. There was evidence of ignorance and lack of interest in its functions.

Several respondents confirmed the views of women in industry who thought that the EOC had had a bad press. Some women thought that it was a good thing that the EOC existed as a 'Court of Appeal', although one or two respondents considered that it had not been given enough teeth to act as a proper watchdog. The very existence of institutions like the EOC was queried by one respondent:

> I think its very existence may be counter-productive. I would rather see women's aggravations come out in other ways – in industrial tribunals for

example. I think institutions like the EOC are not 'achieving' organisations. What do they represent? What teeth do they have? They do more harm than good in raising expectations that they can achieve what they can't.

The BBC and the unions were said to have had contact with the EOC over various matters, but the general consensus among both men and women was that the EOC had little or no impact on the Corporation because the BBC's policies and practices were in line with those advocated by the Commission.

There were very few suggestions of what the EOC could do in future, and much less emphasis than we found among the women in industry who thought the EOC could increase its educative function. There were perhaps surprisingly few suggestions that the EOC could do more to help working women with small children, especially in view of the crèche campaign, but this reinforces the comment made earlier that our respondents were mainly senior women without children, and their immediate interests were not in supporting the problems of working women with children.

The women's movement

The women's movement was thought to have had far more effect than either the legislation or the Equal Opportunities Commission, although not everyone thought that the effects had been positive. Most of the women thought that the movement had made people more aware of women's rights, and echoed this respondent's views: 'It's heightened awareness and made people stop and think, and occasionally made people listen to things they don't want to. It's brought things out into the forefront. You always need people to vocalise about any inequality.'

Some of the older sample of women who had been interviewed in 1968 were rather worried about the effect of the women's movement on women who did not work, particularly in 'underplaying' the role of the housewife. Others in the older sample thought that the women's movement tended to emphasise the glamour of working, while, in reality, most women were in low-paid, unattractive jobs: 'The women's pressure groups are *of* intelligent women *for* intelligent women. They care too little for women not of their group. Intelligent women don't need pressure groups. They're always able to rise.'

There was some disagreement about the methods used by the women's movement, but, in general, the women expressed some relief that the 'shrillness' of the early days had died down. The men on the whole were less in favour of the women's movement, and the view was expressed that it had tended to overstate the case in a way which some of the men thought was unacceptable to women as well as to themselves.

The women's movement was judged to have had some effect on the BBC, if only indirectly in that it had been shown on the news or in programmes. Some women thought that this had made some of the women working for the BBC do 'a bit of thinking and reading'. Others thought that any women working for the BBC who became actively feminist would find that it militated against them. There were several comments about membership of a women's group being 'counter-productive'. There was some comment that women in the BBC, particularly those at more senior levels, did not like 'collective activity'. One woman described the importance of the women's movement as raising the consciousness of individual women by means of small-group support, which was what another woman called 'a bit of mutual encouragement'. It looked as though women aiming to rise in what was still essentially a man's world felt that membership of any such group would count against them, and it was quite clear that some felt no need for mutual encouragement.

Other external changes

The main external factor affecting women's careers was seen to be the economic climate which had led to a different attitude towards work among women, particularly married women. Some of the women said that middle-class married women, who might not have gone out to work ten years ago, now felt that they had to work because of economic necessity, and that among those were women who would want to progress rather than remain in relatively low-status jobs. There was some doubt, however, about whether these expectations could be fulfilled, and there were fears that, if the economic situation grew worse in the next few years, women would be the first to lose their jobs, and that recruitment of women would slow down. Some people expressed the fear that it was going to be made much more difficult than at present for women with children to work, since there was going to be a decrease, rather than any increase, in child-care provision. This was going to cause a great deal of anger, since women's expectations were rising at a time of diminishing funds and facilities.

The maternity provisions of the Employment Protection Act were thought to have improved the situation by some respondents, although, unless they were directly involved, people knew very little about them. The BBC was said to have always been very reasonable about maternity leave, and it was thought that the legislation had therefore affected women in the BBC far less than in most firms.

Very few respondents mentioned the increasing numbers of qualified women as having affected the prospects for women, and even fewer mentioned the effect of the pill in helping women plan when or whether they would have a family, although there was reference to the fact that women in the BBC, particularly those in management, production or operational grades, tended to have their babies later than the population as a whole.

In general, although external factors were thought to have made it more likely that women would continue to work after marriage or having a baby, there was no evidence that people thought this had made it more likely that they would reach more senior posts.

CHAPTER 16

Future Prospects

The people in the BBC did not see the future prospects for women in quite such a gloomy light as those in industry. This was partly because there were more women around, at least at the middle levels, in the BBC, and partly because more people thought that the BBC had an equal opportunities policy, even if it did not appear to result in many women at the top.

However, over two-thirds of the respondents considered that the BBC could do more than it was doing at the moment to help more women reach senior posts. Some people thought that there should be a positive lead from the top to try and overcome what some people saw as the undue influence of departmental heads on appointments. One senior man was of the opinion that if line managers thought they were being judged by the extent to which they were seen to be giving women a chance, there would be a considerable movement towards greater opportunities for women. There was general agreement that the policies at the top were good in principle, but that they were not always implemented by those further down the line – the same view we found in industry.

It was thought that if the BBC's present competitive system of promotion continued, there was a need for more positive counselling and advice for people on their careers, both by departmental heads and by personnel officers. The BBC is aware of the need for this and a recent internal document drew the attention of both line managers and personnel officers to the fact that the proportion of women in senior posts was relatively small, and stressed the importance that women with potential should receive equal consideration and encouragement to apply for senior posts and attachments.

Some people judged that the emphasis on reaching senior posts at a relatively young age acted against women, since, as we have seen in other studies, early promotion often comes at the age at which most women have babies. Certainly, there was a feeling that age-limits ought to be more flexibly employed, and this had been put into practice in the training schemes, some of which used to have an upper age-limit of 26.

In industry, we found that there were doubts about whether the position of women would alter very much in the future because of the economic climate and the possibility of redundancies and a general cut-back in any flexibility of employment which favoured women. There was generally a greater optimism in the BBC, partly because, at least at the time of interviewing, staff there appeared to be more protected from the cold winds of economic cut-backs, and partly because the women had more faith in the possibility of more women rising to senior posts. It remains to be seen whether the present climate of cuts and stringency will mean that women's chances will be affected. Certainly, the opportunities for all staff are bound to become more limited over the next few years, and this will be compounded by the fact that the staff taken on in the years following the introduction of BBC2 will be getting older and looking for promotion and management jobs. To a certain extent, the advent of the fourth television channel may alleviate the situation, although it is more likely to be looking for bright young people in their twenties than executives in their forties. The Annan Report pointed out the problems which were going to face all staff, and, in the light of recent economic developments, Annan looks optimistic:

> . . . the broadcasting organisations will need to step up lateral movement, retraining, secondment to other organisations and early retirement. The personnel departments in both the BBC and the ITV companies should grow in importance because, unless this problem is handled sympathetically, there will be widespread resentment. Positive policies will have to be worked out through which men and women can plan their careers.[1]

Although the figures appear to have improved slightly in the last year or so, the BBC still does not even have the same numbers of women in its most senior grades as it had in 1968, while the proportion has dropped. It is within this context that people's views on the future must be assessed. If they say that things are going to improve, they are judging it on the basis of today's figures. It would be a sad state of affairs if the only improvement which can be seen in ten years' time is a catching up with the situation of twenty years before.

Reference
(1) Op. cit., p. 439, para. 28.20.

D. Women in the Architectural Profession[1]

Introduction

To assess women's progress and prospects in the architectural profession requires a framework different from that of the other case studies. They deal with single large employers. About half of all architects, and rather more than half of all women architects, likewise work for large employers, mainly in the public service but also in business, or, in the case of local government, for employers with a common, nationally agreed, set of employment conditions – what we have called the 'bureaucracies'. There are interesting differences between the conditions of employment of women architects in, for example, local government and the Civil Service, but there is a family resemblance between the findings about progress towards equal opportunity for architects in all 'bureaucratic' employments. In their case the findings of the study of architects are also similar to those recorded in the other case studies.

The other half of the architectural profession, however, work for small autonomous enterprises in architectural private practice; often very small indeed, down to the scale of the individual freelance professional. This is the only sector of small-scale enterprise included in the case studies, and, as will be seen, some of the most interesting and suggestive findings refer to differences in practice as regards equal opportunity between this sector and the 'bureaucracies'.

There is also a difference between architecture and the other occupations studied as regards the point of entry. A student who is interested in a career in industry or in Civil Service administration may take a course which is likely to lead to this. But the courses in qustion may also lead in other directions and, whichever of these careers is chosen, there are various types of course which might lead to it. In architecture, on the other hand, students are committed from the start to a course of professional training which leads either into architecture itself or into immediately related employment such as town and country planning, and offers few opportunities in other directions. In the other cases studied the entry gate is the point of initial recruitment by an employer. In architecture it is entry into an architectural school.

Reference

(1) The re-study of women in architecture was undertaken, like the initial study in 1966–8, in collaboration with the Royal Institute of British Architects. Sheila Miller and Michael Koudra, of the RIBA's statistical section, carried out a statistical survey of women in the architectural profession, on a basis permitting comparisons both with material from the earlier study and with the RIBA's regular surveys of earnings in the profession. The survey excluded women with addresses overseas and the 19 per cent of others who had already been included in the 1978 sample for the RIBA's annual Employment and Earnings Survey. From the 1,052 women finally included it obtained a response of 76.2 per cent.

The Policy Studies Institute interviewed fifty-one architects in local authorities, private practice, and the Civil Service, including thirty-two women architects and two in related professions. Other material was supplied by architectural schools, the Universities Central Council for Admissions (UCCA), the National Association of Local Government Officers (NALGO), the Local Authorities Conditions of Service Advisory Board (LACSAB), and the Local Government Training Board.

PSI's report and the report of the RIBA survey were prepared in the first place as working papers. These were considered by a committee of the RIBA and then, in December 1979 and January 1980, by the RIBA Council, which gave them general approval and passed them on for action to its relevant standing committees. These working papers are available from PSI. The 1966–68 study was not published as such. Data from it were incorporated in *Sex, Career and Family*.

CHAPTER 17

The Entry Gate

In architecture as in the other occupations studied, the number and proportion of women coming in through the entry gate has in recent years been rising rapidly. In the 1960s 8–9 per cent of students entering schools of architecture were women. By 1979/80 this proportion reached 18 per cent, and the actual number of women entering doubled.

Whereas also, in the early 1960s the wastage of women during training was much higher than that of men,[1] by the end of the 1970s a large part of this difference had disappeared. Though there are differences of detail between individual schools, architectural training has in principle three stages: an undergraduate course of three years, usually leading to a degree in its own right (Part I): two years of postgraduate study (Part II): and two years of practical experience (Part III) leading to registration with the Architects' Registration Council of the UK (ARCUK). There are no up-to-date national statistics to show the progress of individual students of architecture through the schools, but a rough overall comparison shows that in 1974/5 women were 12.8 per cent of all new entrants to the schools, and in 1979/80, after the normal interval of five years, they were 13.2 per cent of all students who passed Part II. Women continue to be less likely than men to complete Part III promptly, or even at all (see Table 17.1), and this of course means that women still have a smaller chance than men of achieving registration within the normal seven years. In 1979/80 they were 9.2 per cent of all students who passed Part III, whereas they had been 12 per cent of new entrants in 1972/3. But the improvement at Parts I and II has had its effect on final achievement, for on statistics from earlier years one would have expected the proportion of women among students passing Part III in 1979/80 to be around 6 per cent.

The head of one polytechnic school commented that in his experience women architectural students tend to show rather different qualities from men and to play a distinctive part. They are,

Table 17.1 *Situation in 1978 of men and women architecture students who passed Part II in 1977*

	Men	Women
Working full-time	93	83
Member of the RIBA	25	16
Intending to take Part III		
(to complete their qualification) in:		
1978	67	46
1979	19	17
1980	3	12
Sometime	11	25
Never	1	—

Source: RIBA, *Student Employment Survey*, 1978.

for instance, less likely than men to lead discussions or to contribute original ideas, but more likely to take a level-headed, moderating role which makes for cohesion in the school and the working group. But differences like these do not, he said, put women at any disadvantage in their architectural course: or at least, as the national statistics bear out, as regards Parts I and II.

There are still some questions. Why are women still a rather small minority of entrants into schools of architecture, though a growing one, and why is there still more wastage among women than among men at Part III?

Discrimination against women who apply for entry into schools of architecture was mentioned by some informants, though usually in the past tense ('the last Principal had his own ideas'). But it does not show up in national statistics: indeed (see Table 17.2) they show the opposite. Women who have applied for architectural courses in universities in recent years have had a much better chance of acceptance than men, and a smaller risk of being diverted into other fields of study. Nor is there any clear indication that higher standards of qualification are expected of them. Women who are accepted by the schools tend to be academically better qualified than men, with a higher proportion of 'high scorers' at A level. But, on the other hand, fewer of them bring qualifications associated or combined with practical experience, such as an Ordinary or Higher National Certificate or Diploma. Figures for the 1960s – there are none more recent – also showed that men were much more likely than women to have had previous working experience, particularly in an architect's office.[2]

The question is why more women do not apply. There is still a marked bias by social class, type of secondary school, and region in the recruitment of women to architecture. In the case of all entrants into universities in 1975–8 the proportion of women who came from local authority schools were higher than that of men, 73 per cent against 68 per cent. In the case of architecture entrants, however, this relationship was reversed: 64 per cent of women from local authority schools, but 67 per cent of men. Among students in all types of architectural school (not only universities) who completed a first year of practical training in 1979, usually after passing Part I, 38 per cent of the women but only 28 per cent of the men had attended independent secondary schools.[3]

If the family background of women architects aged under 35 in 1978, who would have started their training from 1962 or 1963 onwards, is compared with that of recent (1974–8) entrants to all university courses, it appears that the proportion from managerial or administrative backgrounds is similar, but the proportion from professional backgrounds is twice as high among the women architects as among university entrants generally, and the proportion from junior white-collar and manual backgrounds only one-third as high. The high proportion from professional backgrounds is not accounted for by inheritance within the architectural and related professions, at least as measured by the father's occupation. Among fathers who were in one of the professions, only about 15 per cent were in architecture or other construction professions.

Regionally, 46 per cent of women entrants in 1977 found their way to a limited number of architectural schools in London and the South, including Bath and Bristol Universities and Oxford and Portsmouth Polytechnics, compared to 24 per cent of men. There are schools with a low recruitment of women in the South and some with relatively high recruitment in the Midlands and North. But in general it is true that even the universities, which tend to attract women more than polytechnics or colleges of art and design or higher education, have a relatively low recruitment of women for architecture if they are in Scotland, Wales, or the North of England.[4]

These biases in the recruitment of women to architecture have changed over the years, but the changes have not all been in one direction. The tendency to recruit from independent schools is far less pronounced than it was at the start of the 1960s.[5] On the other

Table 17.2 *U.K. Candidates Applying and Admitted to University Schools of Architecture, 1972–1978*
Applications and Nominations

	Men				Women			
	Applicants	Accepted for Architecture		Other subjects	Applicants	Accepted for Architecture		Other subjects
		No.	Per cent	Per cent		No.	Per cent	Per cent
1972	1,516	425	28	3	176	80	45	5
1973	1,620	489	30	4	216	107	50	2
1974	1,655	425	26	4	232	91	39	3
1975	1,650	459	28	7	234	115	49	5
1976	1,638	447	27	7	260	115	44	5
1977	1,572	429	27	6	263	108	41	5
1978	1,234	381	31	6	257	104	40	6

Source: The Universities Central Council on Admissions.

hand, the proportion of women architects with a manual or clerical family background was in 1978 only half as high among those aged under 35 as among those aged 35–54.

Another factor to which many informants referred is the length of architectural training, seven years to full registration even if no examinations are failed, and the high degree of commitment required for entry into a course not only of this length but leading to one specific employment.

There are as a matter of fact a number of reasons why this at first sight formidable prospect is actually less formidable than it appears. One is that earning is not delayed till full qualification. In 1978 women working full-time while completing their practical training after Part II, that is normally after a five-year course, were earning an average of £3,420 a year. The average in that year for first degree graduates in all subjects was £3,440, with premiums of £100–£300 for a master's degree, acquired normally after a total of four or five years' study.[6] Nor does earning necessarily have to wait till after Part II. In 1979 architecture students on their first year of practical training, usually four years into their course, earned an average of £2,950 a year, with almost identical figures for women and men.[7]

There was once a tradition that marriage should be postponed till after qualification. Of married women architects who in 1978 were aged 50 or over, 80–85 per cent qualified before marrying. But this has changed, and among women architects aged up to 39 in 1978, 52 per cent married before qualifying.

There may in future be a third saving factor. A number of schools of architecture have moved towards re-defining their Part I course as a general purpose degree which could lead to careers in other fields as well as in architecture, and so reduce the professional commitment initially required of architecture students. This, however, is still a matter of dispute in the profession.

These considerations about the length of architectural training, however, are not necessarily well known: and lack of information to potential recruits on this point has to be taken together with the finding that the message that architecture is a profession for women has, as yet, spread more widely in middle class than in working class families, in independent than in local authority schools, and in the South than in the North. It was not possible in this study to go in depth into the ways in which information reaches or fails to reach recruits. Various informants pointed, however, to what they saw as gaps in transmission both within the schools and at the level of the profession as a whole.

Several of those who stressed the deterrent effect of the length of architectural training, and suggested that it was likely to be greater in the case of women than of men, also argued that this was largely a matter of better information for teachers in schools, and so far as practicable also for parents; for the tone of the advice which they gave, on imperfect information, tended to be such as to magnify this deterrent.

Officers of a Midland local authority, which in recent years has had a generally good record for efforts to promote equal opportunities of qualifications and careers for boys and girls, made a point about information directly to potential applicants themselves. Students of high ability, likely to proceed to higher education and professional training, are a minority, and one whose needs have not the same *prima facie* urgency as those of boys or girls who will shortly be going directly from school to work. In principle the authority provides career advice equally to all pupils. In practice, pressures of time, and the need to give priority to students facing immediate career choices, might lead to some bias in the work of careers advisers towards students of medium rather than professional standards of ability. A Careers Service Officer with this authority said that he was now in a position to run for individual pupils a print-out showing the whole range of careers to which particular choices of O and A level subjects around age thirteen may lead. He added, however, that his service still has difficulty in obtaining from schools the time and opportunity to reach and influence pupils at the stage when these crucial choices have to be made.

The architectural profession's own organisations provide a wide range of information about architectural training and architecture as a career, but have obvious difficulties in reaching their whole range of potential recruits at the stage in school careers when choice is needed. The schools of architecture, for example, recruit nationally and internationally, and it is difficult for them individually to maintain more than a limited range of contacts with particular secondary schools. But the findings suggest that much more could be done to reach potential women recruits, and to widen the range of sources from which they come, if the RIBA developed in co-operation with the Careers Service and the schools a more comprehensive and coherent nation-wide recruitment plan. It has felt under no particular pressure to do so when, as in recent years, architectural work has been cut back and the number of architects already in the profession has seemed more than adequate.

The question of wastage at Part III raises issues of a different kind, but again of a kind which point to a gap in the machinery of the profession as a whole. The problem, as Table 17.1 shows, is that after completing Part II women are more likely than men to drift; to put off completion of their qualification to a later though still definite date, or to say simply, as 25 per cent of women but only 11 per cent of men did in 1978, 'sometime'. The gap here is in procedures for monitoring what is actually happening to women at this stage of their training, and for keeping in touch with them and encouraging them to continue. There is a similar gap in career guidance and support for women already engaged in an architectural career. This, and possible procedures to cover both cases, are discussed below in Chapter 19. As regards monitoring, a useful beginning has been made in recent one-off surveys by the RIBA, including the *Student Employment Survey* from which Table 17.1 is taken, and a series of new figures on women's examination performance collected by the RIBA's *Education Statistics 1980*.

References

(1) V. G. Wigfall and R. Fisher, Final Report of ARCUK, *Follow-up of Ex-Students of Architecture*, mimeo, School of Environmental Studies, University College, London, 1975: data for entrants of 1960 and 1964.

(2) Ibid., Tables II 1, 3 and 4.

(3) RIBA, *Student Survey 1979*.

(4) Data from RIBA.

(5) Wigfall and Fisher, op. cit., Table II.10. Among 1960 entrants to all schools of architecture 54 per cent of women and 31 per cent of men were from independent schools, and 17 per cent and 15 per cent from direct grant schools: leaving 29 per cent of women and 54 per cent of men from local authority schools.

(6) Architects' data from RIBA, *Student Employment Survey, 1978:* general data from N. Scott, 'Graduate Supply and Demand in 1979', *Department of Employment Gazette*, February 1979.

(7) RIBA, *Student Survey 1979*.

CHAPTER 18

Women's Careers in Architecture: Three Environments

In 1978 the rapid recent increase in the number and proportion of women entering schools of architecture had not yet had time to work its way through into a corresponding increase in the number of women in architectural practice. Women were 5.2 per cent of all registered architects in that year, only a marginal increase over the 5 per cent of 1972.

The great majority of registered women architects – 82 per cent of those who had not actually retired – were 'active' in 1978: in employment, unemployed or ill, or full-time students (see Table 18.1). Family size has fallen among women architects as in the rest of the population, and the proportion who work at some time while their children are under five has risen through successive age groups. It reached 90 per cent in the case of those who in 1978 were aged 30–34 (see Table 18.2). As a result, in no age group short of retirement was the proportion of women architects who were in employment in that year below 75 per cent. The effect of family commitments shows up nevertheless. Forty-eight per cent of married women architects with children up to age five and 35 per cent of those with children between six and ten were not in employment in 1978, and only 19 per cent and 30 per cent respectively were working full-time. Even among those with children between 11 and 16, the proportion not in employment was 15 per cent. Forty-four per cent of these were working part-time and 43 per cent full-time. Among all women architects aged 35–39, about half were in full-time employment and between 23 and 34 per cent, according to the age group, worked part-time. Four per cent of men in architecture also worked part-time, but two-thirds of these were over age 60.[1]

There are some differences between men and women architects in the type of work which they choose to do and the type of employer for whom they work. A greater proportion of women architects in full-time employment than of men, 19 per cent against 8 per cent, were employed in 1978 in teaching and research, town planning, or

Table 18.1 *Employment Status of Women Architects, By Age, 1978*

Age	Per cent of all women architects in this age group	Per cent of women architects in each group who were:				
		Employed full-time	Employed part-time	Unemployed, ill, student	At home/ children	Retired
Under 29 years	12	86½	7	1	4	1
30–34 years	20	60	15	1	24	1
35–39 years	11	45	32	2	19½	1
40–44 years	8	51½	24	1½	23	—
45–49 years	12	50½	34	3	9½	3
50–54 years	22½	55	23	4	16	2
55–59 years	6	47	29	6	6	12
60–64 years	4	25	31	6	16	22
65 years and over	4½	22	6	6	11	56
Total		55	22	3	16	5
Number	799	437	173	23	124	42

Source: *RIBA Survey*, 1978.

Table 18.2 *Married women architects with children, 1978* (%)

Age	Number of children					Per cent of married women architects who worked when children were under 5 years
	One	Two	Three	Four	Five	
Under 29 years	89	11	—	—	—	50
30–34 years	48	38	12	1	—	90
35–39 years	28	52	19	2	—	86
40–44 years	10	58½	29	—	2	86
45–49 years	7½	46	30	13	3	77
50–54 years	12	46	26½	15	1	
55–59 years	8	46	21	21	4	70
60–64 years	25	25	25	25	—	53
65 years and over	—	29	47	18	6	50
All ages	21	44½	24	9	1	73
Number	86	181	96	38	6	

Source: Ibid.

outside architectural work altogether. This difference was particularly marked in the case of single women, of whom 25 per cent were in these fields. The distribution of women architects in full-time employment between the main types of employing organisation – 44 per cent each in private practice and in local and central government, including nationalised industries and the National Health Service, and 12 per cent in education and 'other', including private industry and commerce – was much the same as that of men. The distribution of those working part-time, however, was very different. More than 80 per cent of women architects working part-time were in private practice: 41 per cent as principals, 18½ per cent in freelance work, and 21 per cent as salaried employees, leaving only 10½ per cent for local and central government and 8½ per cent for education and 'other'.

Though architects often move between these major types of employing organisations, there is no common code of employment conditions, nor are women's prospects under the different types of employer the same. It is best therefore to look separately at the three main environments in which they work: in order of the amount of employment provided, private practice, local government, and the Civil Service and other branches of central government.

Private practice

Private professional practice in architecture is carried on in small independent firms. Ninety-three per cent of principals, whether single-handed or partners, worked in 1978 in offices employing fewer than thirty architectural and technical staff. These small firms have many of the characteristics of small business generally. They operate in highly competitive markets. Their terms of employment are more flexible than those of the public sector. A number are family enterprises. More than half of all married women architects in employment in 1978 – 52 per cent of those working full-time and 62 per cent of those working part-time – were married to other architects, and 37 per cent of these were working in the same firm as their husbands. The enquiry turned up cases where this family partnership continued even after divorce.

In architecture, this type of environment has proved from the point of view of women's prospects to have three characteristics.

First, it is favourable, in fact by far the most favourable of any of the employment environments covered in these studies, from the point of view of a woman who wants simply to work in her profession at a moderately responsible level, combined with easy opportunities to vary her work load to allow for family responsibilities. Among the women in full-time salaried work in private practice in 1978, 62 per cent were at levels such as that of an assistant architect responsible for large jobs or a group leader or associate partner. Overall, the corresponding figures for central and local government are higher, but a main reason for this is a difference in age distribution. In that year 45 per cent of women architects working full-time in central government, and 55½ per cent of those in local government, were under age 40, but 72 per cent of those in private practice. Part-time salaried work is more often at routine levels, and often insecure: as some informants put it, the 'extra pair of hands' to meet temporary surges in demand. On the other hand, it is relatively freely available, and so is freelance work.

For those who want the fuller responsibility of a principal it is not very difficult to build up at least a modest practice, either part- or full-time. In 1978, 53 per cent of the women architects working in private practice were principals – including, not surprisingly, two-thirds of those working in the same practice as their husbands – compared to 60 per cent in the case of men. Two out of five of these women principals were part-time, and of those working full-time only 18 per cent, compared to 41 per cent of male principals, were in offices employing (including themselves) more than five architectural and technical staff.

Secondly, however, the chances of women reaching the top level of private architectural practice, as principals in substantial practices, with earnings at or above the median for all principals, are much smaller than those of men. A number do so, and women have contributed a number of well-known names to the profession since Elizabeth Scott made the first major break-through by winning the competition for the Shakespeare Memorial Theatre at Stratford on Avon in 1928. But overall statistics show that the top, as defined in this way, is still mainly for men. The median earnings for full-time women principals in 1978 were 63 per cent of those of men. In 1971 they had been 71 per cent, so that the gap had actually widened. The median earnings of full-time principals in 1978 were £8,941, and those of principals between age 40 and retirement were £9–10,000. Over half of all male principals had earnings at or above these levels, but only 24 per cent of all full-time women principals. Men were more likely to be partners in large practices, and principals' earnings correlate strongly with office size. The median earnings of all principals ranged in 1978 from £6,643 in offices with only one or two architectural staff to over £18,000 in those with over fifty staff. But full-time women principals' earnings in offices of each size tended also to be well below the median for that size. And, of course, this comparison of full-time earnings ignores the fact that two out of five women principals were not full-time.

Both men and women architects may move during their careers between the public sector and private practice, and the proportions of each who at any time are working in private practice are similar; somewhat lower in the case of women, if only full-time workers are counted, but somewhat higher when part-time and freelance workers are included. A useful test, therefore, is to ask what proportion of the whole population of experienced architects were 'high earning' principals in 1978, with earnings of £9,000 or more. In that year the number of high earning male principals was equivalent to about 20 per cent of the number of male architects aged 35 or over, but the number of high earning women principals to only 3.3 per cent of the corresponding age group of women.

One main reason for the shortage of 'high earning' women principals – though not, as will be seen, the only one – is that, though private practice offers good opportunities to women who wish to adjust their working timetable for the care of children, it does not provide good opportunities for accelerating back into a high level career once a break or slow-down has occurred.

One category which is relatively well placed in this respect is architects' wives working in the same practice as their husbands. Their advantage is not simply that family influence makes it easier to be formally classified as a principal. Conditions in a family practice also make it particularly easy to combine career progress with responsibility for children. A wife in this position can if she wishes reduce the contribution which she makes to the partnership while she has young children, yet also remain fully in touch with the practice and maintain not only her architectural skills but, what in the case of a principal is even more important, her network of clients and contacts. She can then ease back into full participation in the practice at her own pace. How husbands and wives divide their work varies, and PEP's study in the 1960s noted that one pattern was for the husband to act as the front man of the practice, while the wife worked more in the background. But it was clear both then and at the end of the 1970s that neither this division of labour, where it occurs, nor the process of partial withdrawal and return need mean that the wife in this type of practice is less than an equal force within the partnership.[2]

For other married women architects the chances of moving on to a partnership in a substantial practice after a period when work commitment is reduced because of the care of young children are much less good. Practices tend to seek partners who are young, in their early or at the most late thirties, and to look for them either from internal recruitment or from an informal network of contacts arising out of the practice's current work. A prospective partner needs to have not only a demonstrated record in the design and construction of buildings but a network of contacts and an established position in the profession such as is likely to ensure that she (or he) will bring in business to the practice. A young married woman who reduces her work load, as most do, because she is starting to raise a family is likely to have less of a track record to show than a man of equal ability, and much less in the way of a network of contacts. At an age when existing partners are looking (as one of them said) for a young new colleague with the energy and dynamism which they may feel to be fading in their own case, a married woman with children, even if working full-time, may not be able – or may be thought to be unable – to make the all-out commitment to work in her first years as a partner which this would imply.

The effects of these differences between the prospects of substantial success as a principal for married women who are or are not working in a family practice show up in the statistics of earnings in 1978. Wives working full-time in partnership with their husbands did not necessarily have higher earnings than other married women principals. But they tended to make a clearer choice between limiting their earnings to under £4,500 a year and going for high earnings, with fewer 'weak' earners in between. And whereas in the case of other married women architects the number earning £9,000 or over was equivalent to around 2 per cent of the number aged 35 and over, in that of wives sharing a practice with their husbands it was 8 per cent.

Considerations about family responsibilities do not apply with the same force to single women who, as the 1978 data show, work with practically the same continuity as men. These data also, however, point to a third characteristic of architectural private practice. Of all the fields of work covered in these studies, this is the one where, in spite of the clear commitment to the principle of equal opportunity found both in the RIBA and (unanimously) among individual respondents, the *prima facie* evidence of discrimination against women as such is strongest.

It is strongest of all when single women's chances of achieving high earnings in salaried work, for which all but a few of the opportunities are outside private practice,[3] are compared with their chances of becoming high earning private practice principals. The general finding from the other studies in this book is that it is women without family responsibilities who have the best chance of reaching the top. The experience of single women architects in salaried work is in line with this. In 1978 single women were 19½ per cent of all women architects aged 35 and over, but filled nine of the 19 salaried posts paid at or above £9,000 a year which the RIBA's sample recorded as held by women. Five of the remainder were held by women who were widowed or divorced, leaving only five for those experienced women architects, the large majority, who are married or re-married.

As regards their chances of becoming high earning private practice principals, however, single women in 1978 did only marginally better than married women. The number of single women principals who earned £9,000 a year or more was equivalent to 4 per cent of the number of single women architects aged 35 and over; better than the 2 per cent of the corresponding population of married women not working in a family practice, but far behind the corresponding 20 per cent for men. Only a handful of single women principals turned up in the 1978 sample. The distribution of earnings among those who did suggests that if single women become principals during their peak age of activity, they are likely to do so on the same footing as men and to earn at similar rates. But very few do, and in their case this cannot be explained by career breaks and delays.

There is further evidence of discrimination against women in the

Table 18.3 *Median earnings*[a] *of full-time salaried architects by age and employment field: all architects and single women architects* (£)

Age	Private practice			Local government		Central government and National Boards		All women architects excluding private practice
	All architects	All women architects	Single women architects	All architects	Single women architects	All architects	Single women architects	
Under 29 years	4,817	4,950	4,700	5,161	5,499	5,100	5,500	5,550
30–34 years	5,550	5,000	5,600	5,769	6,333	6,115	6,000	6,600
35–39 years	6,276	5,200	5,750	6,439	6,625	6,800	7,000	7,000
40–44 years	6,583			6,527		7,318		
45–49 years	6,800	5,800	6,000	6,966	6,750	7,975	7,750	7,650
50–54 years	6,900			7,396		7,563		
55–59 years	6,100			6,956		7,900		
60–64 years	5,625	5,300	5,749	6,692	n.a.[b]	7,500	n.a.[b]	7,350
65 years and over	4,500			7,000		n.a.		
All ages	5,664	5,062	5,220	6,388	6,599	7,189	7,000	6,850

[a] The earnings figures for all architects are for June 1978 and for single women architects for October 1978.

[b] There was only one single woman in the sample of each of these categories.

Source: *RIBA Earnings Survey 1978* and *Survey 1978*.

statistics of salaries in private practice, again by contrast with what is found in the 'bureaucracies'. In central and local government the median salaries of women architects in 1978 were in line with the medians for all architects, and this comparison also holds age by age (see Table 18.3). A difference between the medians for men and women in local government which still existed in 1973 had disappeared by 1978. In private practice, however, the median for women in October 1978 was 89 per cent of that for all architects in June, and when allowance is made for salary increases between these dates this comparison becomes still less favourable to women. The gap has apparently closed somewhat since 1973, when the median for women was 77 per cent of that for all architects, but this improvement is smaller than it seems when allowance is made for the difference between the two 1978 survey dates.

Even without an adjustment for this discrepancy in dates, the RIBA surveys show that in 1978 women's salaries for full-time work in private practice, age for age, ran well behind the medians for all architects at all points beyond age 30. Between ages 35 and 54 the gap was upwards of £1,000 a year. Single women did better than married women, but even they lagged behind 'all' architects from age 25 till their early fifties. The data do not make it possible to distinguish how far these differences reflect discrimination in pay, job for job – pay structures in this sector are often very informal – and how far discrimination in job assignments.

There is also some evidence of regional bias, though it is not easy to interpret. Compared to the distribution of all architectural posts in the United Kingdom (see Table 18.4), relatively few women architects find posts outside London and the South-East, and relatively more of those who do so can find only part-time work, or work in the same practice as their husbands. The proportion who become full-time principals is far smaller. If women in the Midlands and North become full-time principals, they have as good a chance as those in the South of also becoming high earners. There were several comments from informants outside London and the South-East to the effect, to quote from one region, that 'architecture in the Midlands is first and foremost a business', in which a principal, woman or man, is expected to be able to earn good money and actually to earn it. But it was particularly informants from outside London who pointed out that building a personal network and the contacts which bring in business to a practice, and may lead to a substantial partnership, often arise out of informal relationships in clubs, sport, and so on from which women may be excluded.

Table 18.4 *Regional location of architects, 1978*

	Located in:	
	London and SE England	Rest of UK
All full-time architects	44	56
Women architects:		
All	57	43
Full-time	59	41
Part-time	51	49
Architects' wives:		
All	53	47
In same firm as husband	48	52
Full-time principals:		
All	61	39
Earning £8,000 p.a. and over	50	50

Row percentages

Source: *RIBA Survey*, 1978.

Though these findings about women's salaries and promotion prospects in private practice provide *prima facie* evidence of discrimination against women as such, there are reservations about interpreting them solely in terms of this. Since, however, these reservations refer to considerations about women's own motivation and skills in career management which arise in all branches of architecture, they are discussed separately below in relation to all three main sectors together.

Senior women architects, as well as men, insisted during the study that a woman architect who is determined to make a career in private practice, and stays with it in spite of family commitments, will find the necessary opportunities open to her. In the sense that some women can and do make their way to the highest levels of the private practice side of the profession, this is true. In the sense, however, that women, as a matter of statistical probability, have the same chance as men of reaching the top, or even of equal earnings at lower levels, it clearly is not. And behind this lies not only the same difficulty as has been found throughout this series of studies in reconciling family responsibilities with a career leading to the top – perhaps even aggravated by the temptation, in this sector, of easy opportunities to settle for a lower level of achievement – but also a larger question than arises in any other case studied about discrimination directly on grounds of sex, as distinct from marital and family status.

Myths about the degree of equal opportunity available in private practice are not surprising in view of the lack over the years of systematic effort to establish what the facts of the situation are. There has been discussion in the RIBA's Council and its committees on the careers of women architects, and RIBA's statistics section uses the opportunity of its Earnings Surveys to obtain a modest amount of data on them from time to time. But up to the date of this study there was no provision, whether by the RIBA or otherwise, for systematically monitoring women's progress in private practice or taking action to promote it.

Local government

In moving from private practice to the public sectors of architecture one returns to situations more directly comparable to those considered in the other case studies. There are standard conditions of employment, a firm commitment to the principle of equal opportunity and to the practice as well as the principle of equal pay, but also a number of the same problems as are brought out in the other case studies, particularly over reconciling career continuity and progress with family responsibilities.

In 1978 local government employed 22 per cent of all women architects, including 27 per cent of those working full-time and 7 per cent of those working part-time. As seen through the eyes of both women and men informants, it is a good area for a woman to start her architectural career. Full responsibility may not come quickly; it could be six or seven years, as one woman said, before you could show built work of your own. But it might actually be easier, another said, to make you own contribution to a design in a large local government office than in a private practice where the general design work on a project is strictly a matter for the principals. Women informants saw local government and general conditions of service as good, and earnings statistics bear this out. In 1978 salaries, age for age, were markedly higher in local government than in private practice for both men and women. Local government is fully committed to equal pay, and in 1978 men's and women's median earnings were similar. As noted above, the difference in actual earnings which existed in 1963 had disappeared five years later.

There might also, however, be reasons for moving on after a time to some other branch of architecture. These might be ordinary career reasons such as looking for wider experience. As one woman architect asked: what are my prospects in the profession if I have built nothing but CLASP schools? But there were also considerations of two other kinds.

One refers to the limited practical possibilities in local government for reconciling responsibilities for young children with a career. Local government is committed as strongly to the principle of equal opportunity as to that of equal pay. An officer of the Greater London Council illustrated this from his authority's most recent competition for promotion to Grade C of its architectural service, job architect with full job responsibility. Forty-six candidates applied for seven posts. There were five women among them, and three of these were promoted. He also noted that women themselves, if passed over, are now much readier than in the past to stand up and protest. As a group of GLC women architects themselves said: 'People expect us to behave like ladies . . . It took a long time to realise that in the GLC you have to agitate.'

Equal consideration by promotion boards, however, though it helps women who work through continuously and with a full-time commitment, does not solve the problem of those who have young children and therefore wish to reduce their work commitment to part-time, or to take a break longer than the standard period of maternity leave and then be reinstated. Opportunities of this kind are much less freely available in local government than in private architectural practice. Even where they are available, a break or slow-down at this point in a career may permanently damage the chances of women who might otherwise hope to go on to the highest posts, for in local government as in private practice assumptions tend to be made about the ages at which the careers of high flyers need to take off. A comment from the LACSAB, local government's central organisation for manpower and industrial relations, is that a local government officer who hopes to reach the highest levels needs to have made his or her mark by the age of 30 or 35, just when many women feel it necessary at least temporarily to slow down.

At the date of the survey in 1978, opportunities for temporarily reducing work commitments and for reinstatement after a break had been exceptionally curtailed as a reaction to the severe squeeze on public expenditure from the middle of the 1970s. Local authorities became reluctant to make special arrangements for part-time or for extra maternity leave. In 1973, still a time of high demand for architects' services, 24 per cent of women architects working part-time were in local government. By 1978 this became 7 per cent. For men as well as women the tendency by the end of the 1970s was to insist that those who wanted special conditions beyond those laid down in the standard local government conditions of service, or who wished to take a career break, should depart and not return: or, if they wished to return, should apply on an equal footing with new applicants. Exceptions might still be made if this suited the convenience of a local authority, or in a special case like that of staff seconded to developing countries. But in general, as one informant put it, at a time when the volume of architectural work is falling and establishments are being ruthlessly pruned, the departure of anyone for any reason is greeted with a sigh of relief.

Reluctance over part-time work or reinstatement after a break is not, however, purely a product of the recent pressure on public expenditure. Even in more prosperous days, part-time work for experienced architects was not encouraged in local government, nor, often, by local government architects themselves. Women architects as well as men said during the study that, since so much in local government depends on continuing contact with a network of officers, councillors, and outside interests, part-time work by professionals with full responsibility for projects is a nuisance to be resorted to only when full-time staff are not available. A group of GLC women architects argued for their own part that there should be a right to reinstatement up to one or two years after a birth, but recognised the resistance which this was likely to meet from senior men. 'Attitudes still tend to be that women are liable to go off and have babies at any time': though the actual record was 'about two babies among the architects in seven years'.

Local government does not have a fully considered policy for reconciling family responsibilities with continuity in careers, and the local government unions, as well as management, have moved rather cautiously in this area. NALGO, which except in the Greater

London Council is the union relevant for architects, is fully committed to the principle of equal opportunity, and has a number of relevant policy aims. It supports the right of a woman to return to her previous job up to one year after a birth, and at the end of the 1970s promoted a campaign for nursery facilities in local government offices, and published a do-it-yourself guide for local negotiations on this. It also calls for six weeks paid paternity leave, and for paid time-off for fathers as well as mothers to attend ante-natal or child welfare clinics or to look after a sick child at home.

NALGO has, however, no policy for promoting part-time work, and has been cautious over extending the time for reinstatement beyond a year. In 1978 a resolution in favour of the right to return to the same grade up to five years after a birth was passed only with a National Executive Committee amendment that this provision could be suspended if it were likely to be severely detrimental either to the service or to the careers of other members of staff. On nursery facilities, the high cost of the facilities actually planned by one or two local authorities has given the union and its members grounds for hesitation, particularly at a time when pressures on local government expenditure mean that improvements in one direction are likely to be offset by cuts in another. The London Borough of Camden estimated the gross cost per child of a staff nursery at the end of the 1970s at £48–£49 a week. The cost in its public day nurseries averaged at the time £50 a week, or £36 net of parents' contributions. Another relevant union, the GLC Staff Association, gave only what informants called 'sporadic' support to a campaign over several years for staff nurseries, in which GLC women architects took a prominent part. The campaign was unsuccessful.

A further consideration for experienced women architects who aim for the top level of local government is that there are some questions – let us underline *questions,* because the answers are not clear – about the effectiveness of local government procedures in ensuring equal consideration for men and women by boards and committees when it comes to promotions to the most senior posts: as distinct from posts at middle and junior professional levels such as those to which the comment quoted above from a GLC officer refers. It is a fact that there are very few women at the top levels of local government, either in architecture or generally. A survey by NALGO in 1972 found no woman officer above the junior level of the Principal Officer grade (PO 1), well short of the top level in even moderate-sized districts. Some exceptions slipped through NALGO's net, notably for example, in town planning. In 1979 there were two women Chief Planning Officers in large local authorities, and one woman Chief Planning Officer and Architect in a New Town Development Corporation. There was, however, no woman Chief Architect as such.

Several factors probably lie behind this. One, evidently, is that just mentioned, the limited opportunities in local government for women with family responsibilities to slow down their careers and then resume them, with the prospect of equal consideration for later promotion even if they have passed conventional promotion ages. Another is mobility, since promotion in local government often involves moving to an authority in a different area. A third is certainly the reluctance of some women themselves to take on work of the kind and with the level of time commitment required by top local government jobs. One of the few really senior women in local government graphically illustrated this point from her own experience, and it is discussed further below as an issue which also arises from women in other branches of architecture.

Several informants from different parts of the country argued, however, that in promotions to senior local government posts there is also still an element of discrimination by officers, councillors, or both. In one or two cases chapter and verse were quoted. It was not always or necessarily due to a bias against women as professionals or managers, though there were suggestions that this might be the case in some authorities in the Midlands and North. It might be more a case of bias towards the man as the breadwinner with a mortgage and dependent children, or the older man who was thought to need a final step to improve his pension.

One factor opening the way to this element of discrimination might be, some informants' comments suggested, a degree of informality in local government promotion procedures. These procedures are formal compared to those in architectural private practice, but still depend much more than, notably, those of the Civil Service on informal relationships ('office uncles' was one woman architect's phrase) and on applicants' own efforts to put themselves forward. This is true even within individual authorities, let alone where it is a case of seeking promotion by applying for a post elsewhere. As senior officers in two large authorities explained, a system of appraisal and of sifting the field of potential candidates – even from within their existing staff – as comprehensive as that of the Civil Service would entail too much administrative time and cost. One added that the results would not necessarily be acceptable to potential candidates themselves. His authority had initiated a more elaborate system for discovering which members of staff might be available for promotion. The staff reaction had been that this suggested, not impartiality, but the use of the Old Pals Act.

The data from this study provide no clear basis for deciding whether a significant element of discrimination does or does not occur in more senior architectural appointments in local government. We can only record informants' views that it sometimes does. There is at least one case where the statistical evidence also gives reason for thought. The GLC architects' service is large enough to provide a continuous career for either men or women, so that the problem of mobility does not arise to the same extent as elsewhere in local government. It has also a significant number of experienced women architects who are certainly not averse to promotion. Nevertheless, the most senior GLC woman architect is at the fifth level from the top, and the percentage of women in each grade tapers strongly from the bottom (see Table 18.5). It may be that, if there has been discrimination in senior architectural appointments in the GLC, it is a thing of the past. Informants quoted examples of how attitudes have changed in recent years. But current figures like those of Table 18.5 still raise a question.

Though it is a principle of local government that careers should depend on merit alone, it is also true that in applying this principle to women local government has tended to rest on its traditional oars. The comment of one Establishment Officer is that the Sex Discrimination Act of 1975 made practically no difference to his authority's practice, except for more careful scrutiny of the wording of advertisements. The significance of the sections of the Act which deal with indirect discrimination – maintenance of conditions of employment which, while equally applicable to all, put women or men at a disadvantage because of sex or marital status – seems to have been little appreciated. At the level of individual local authorities, as just said, procedures for appraisal and for sifting the field of candidates are less comprehensive than those of the Civil Service. General local

Table 18.5 *Men and women architects, Greater London Council, December 1978*

Grade	Number of women in grade				Total staff in grade	Per cent of women
	Housing	Education	Thamesmead and general	Total		
Principal architect	—	—	—	—	3	—
Divisional architect	—	—	—	—	10	—
Deputy Divisional architect	—	—	—	—	11	—
Assistant Divisional architect	—	—	—	—	4	—
Architect Grade I – section leader	1	1	—	2 } 3	43 } 91	} 3
Deputy section leader	1	—	—	1	48	
Job architect	9	5	—	14	124	11
Assistant job architect	17	2	1	20	146	14
Grade A and Technician [a]	5	—	6	11	67	16
Total	33	8	7	48	456	10

[a] Not qualified as an architect.

Women architects working in Housing Branch: 21 are married; 12 have children
Education: 5 ",   4 ",   "
Thamesmead and general: 8 ",   1 ",   "

Source: Greater London Council

government manpower statistics do not distinguish between men and women, and no regular national statistics are available for monitoring women's progress in local government service. NALGO and the Local Government Training Board were both at the time of the study undertaking surveys to remedy this. But an official of LACSAB expressed some doubt whether his organisation's mandate would extend to monitoring discrimination. In the case of another organisation, the Association of Official Architects, it was clear that little thought had been given to this question.

The Civil Service

The Civil Service, which in this case means in particular the Property Services Agency and the Department of the Environment, together with State organisations such as the National Health Service and the nationalised industries, employed in 1978 18 per cent of women architects who work full-time and 3 per cent of those working part-time.

The Civil Service itself is a particularly interesting case because of the formality, and up to a point the strength, of its procedures for ensuring equal opportunity. Civil Service promotion procedures are highly formalised, and designed more effectively than those in local government to ensure that men and women architects do in fact receive equal consideration for promotion. In the Property Services Agency, for example, all potential candidates for normal promotion are sifted on the basis of reports from an annual job appraisal. The resulting short-list is published and can be challenged, and final decisions are then made by a separate board. Candidates do not need to put themselves forward, though it may be an advantage to them to have attended voluntary biennial career development reviews.

In general, these procedures appear to work acceptably and effectively so far as women architects are concerned, and to minimise any difficulties which might arise from reluctance on women's own part to put themselves forward or – as an industrial manager said in the 1968 study – to 'package' themselves for promotion. As one woman who is herself a member of a militant women architects' group commented, 'The Civil Service does watch its percentages and look for women to promote'. Or, as another senior woman Civil

Service architect put it, 'The machine is strong enough to beat discrimination'.

The results of this show in statistics of earnings and levels of responsibility. In 1978 the median earnings of women architects in the central government sector were above those of women in both local government and private practice, and, even after allowing for the difference between the two 1978 survey dates, were at least in line with those of 'all' central government architects. The proportion of women at the more senior levels of work, at group leader or similar level or in posts with general management responsibility for architectural work, was well above that in local government: 34 per cent compared to 15 per cent. Statistics of women in architectural posts in the Civil Service do not show the same tapering in the proportion of women from junior to more senior grades as in local government (see Table 18.6). At one point where tapering apparently occurred in 1975–8, between the grades of Professional and Technology Officer I and Principal P & TO, detailed examination of the statistics shows that this can be explained by differences between the age and length of service of men and women in grade P & TO I. The women were on the average between four and five years younger – 40 against 45 – and had served in the Civil Service only half as long.

Table 18.6 *Women architects in the Civil Service, 1978*

	Civil Service [a]		Property Services Agency [b]	
	Number	Per cent of all employees in this grade	Number	Per cent of all employees in this grade
Directing grades	1	4½	—	—
Superintending grade	3	4	2	5
Principal P & T Officer	6	2	2	1½
P & T Officer I	29	7	14	5
P & T Officer II	8	14	5	12
Total	47	4	23	4

[a] Professional and Technological grades – Architecture discipline.
[b] These figures are included in the first two columns.

Source: Civil Service Department and Property Services Agency.

There is a difference in age distribution between women architects in local government and in the central government sector. The proportion of full-time women architects aged 40 or over was 55 per cent in central government in 1978, but only 44½ per cent in local government. Civil Service practice is in some ways specially favourable to the recruitment of older women. The Department of the Environment, because of the nature of its work, recruits fully experienced architects in their thirties. The Property Services Agency can and does recruit up to age 35–40 in the P & TO I grade. But the difference in age distribution does not account for the earnings advantage of women architects in the central government sector over those in local government, for in the case of experienced architects aged 35 and over this advantage also holds age for age.

There are some practical difficulties which even the best promotion procedures cannot overcome. One is mobility. The Property Services Agency has to move its staff between regions, and commented on the difficulty which this could cause in the case of married women, though it also pointed out that reluctance to accept inter-regional mobility has recently increased among men as well.

There are also stereotypes about ages for promotion, or for the recruitment of experienced staff, which may work to the disadvantage of women whose earlier careers are delayed. The Department of the Environment, in recruiting women architects in their thirties, looks for those who by that age have already made their mark and reached, if not a partnership in private practice, at least a senior salaried position in which they have fully proved their competence. A senior Property Services Agency officer commented (though he hastily corrected himself on realising what he had said), that candidates for higher posts are 'hopelessly too old at forty'.

Where the Civil Service does compare badly with private architectural practice, and even with local government, is in its lack of opportunities for part-time work during the period when women's family responsibilities are heaviest. This is not specially a point about architects in the Civil Service. The Professional and Technological group of civil servants, as a whole, with its related grades, employed 41,747 staff in 1978, including 252 women, and at the beginning of 1979 had only 22 part-time staff of either sex. The position as regards Civil Service administrators was discussed in case study A.

In architecture, as a matter of fact, the position over part time was by Civil Service standards relatively favourable. Senior architects saw the same objections to part-time work as senior administrators, though it might have to be accepted from time to time as a practical necessity. In 1978 the Property Services Agency had two women architects with family responsibilities working part-time, but in the early 1970s it, like local government, had been 'in the business of employing mums'. But the PSA had in fact had a rather favourable experience with part-time work for architects, and might in future welcome more of it. There could be a case in PSA's own interest, one senior officer (a man) said, for having a certain number of men as well as women architects working part-time, and probably using the balance of their time to develop their own private practices: though a senior woman informant from another department commented that precisely this possibility of divided loyalties was one of the chief objections to part time. Meantime, however, opportunities for part-time work were in 1978 few and *ad hoc* for Civil Service architects, as for other Civil Servants, and at the date of the survey the Civil Service Department was advertising only for full-time posts.

Lack of opportunities for part-time work may not lead to women architects with family responsibilities leaving, but certainly adds to their difficulties in reconciling family and career. An informant (a man) in the PSA suggested that the lack of opportunities of this kind may in one way be more of a hardship to women in professional grades than to those in clerical or similar grades where part time is at present much more freely available. In the areas where they live, he said, and given the degree of geographical dispersal of middle class extended families, they are less likely to have an easily available network of relatives and neighbours to help in child care: notably by comparison with staff from ethnic minorities. In the case of local government a GLC officer made a similar comment. The same PSA informant added that the problems associated with child care may in a sense come as more of a surprise and strain to women in professional work, because they are more likely to have taken it for granted that they will return to work after a birth.

The study of architects gives the same general impression as that of Civil Service administrators of Civil Service policy on reconciling career progress with family responsibilities. For a woman who is prepared to work through irrespective of her family responsibilities, there is genuine equality of opportunity, more so even than in local government, and much more so than in private practice. Assistance in reconciling family and career at the time when family responsibilities are at their peak, however, is *ad hoc*, a matter of local arrangement and departments' convenience, and not systematically developed or monitored. It was, for example, suggested during this study of women architects that it would be useful to re-analyse the excellent personnel records kept in the Civil Service, to trace differences in the career profiles of both men and women architects, and so to identify ways in which women's difficulties in reconciling family and career could be minimised. The PSA was willing for the research team to approach members of their staff directly for an analysis of this kind – time and resources, in the end, prevented this – but the Civil Service had made no such analysis itself.

References

(1) RIBA, *Earnings Survey 1978*.

(2) See e.g. the discussion in R. Rapoport and R. Rapoport, *Dual Career Families*, Penguin, 1971.

(3) Only one woman in salaried private practice was recorded in the RIBA's 1978 sample as earning £9,000 or more. See also the RIBA's general *Earnings Surveys* and Table 18.3 for the generally low level of salaries in private practice, particularly in older age groups where success means promotion to higher salaried work in the public service, but normally to a partnership in private practice.

CHAPTER 19

The Three Environments – Some Common Issues

In architecture as in other professions there was a time when it was questioned whether women had the capacity to undertake the whole range of work done by men, for example in designing large buildings and complexes or in managing work on site. By the time of the earlier study in the 1960s negative views of this kind had been overtaken by experience, and at the end of the 1970s they did not appear at all. Some informants did, however, make a more positive point. As one senior woman architect in effect put it: if the whole population of women architects is compared to the whole population of men, the women will be seen to add something distinctive to the profession.

In a general statistical sense, it was said, women are more likely than men to be aware of the detailed realities of how people (and especially women) use buildings, of the importance of size, weight, and location of objects within them, and of shapes, colours, and fabrics. They might be somewhat more motivated to work for the client rather than to 'make a splash' or to gain promotion. The male head of one local authority department said that there was value in having a mixed team of men and women, for one thing because the women tended to communicate more effectively without regard to rank. Other informants similarly suggested that women tend to be better at listening and communicating when dealing with clients, with other professionals such as surveyors, or on site; the comment by the head of a polytechnic department of architecture, quoted in the first chapter of this study, on the role of women students in his department is worth recalling here. In other respects also women were no more likely than men to be at a disadvantage in controlling work on site. Even the Irish, as one woman architect said, tend not to swear at a woman. Several woman informants said somewhat unflatteringly that their male colleagues tend to be more bound than women by theories and customary practice, whereas women have more earthy common sense and capacity for identifying nonsense and breaking out of routines.

Considerations like these about the broad average differences between populations of men and women architects are relevant to the recruitment of women to the profession, and may have some relevance to the make-up of a large architectural team. No informant suggested, however, that they had any relevance to assessment of the capacity of particular architects, men or women, in individual cases of appointment or promotion. Differences in capacity and performance, it was universally agreed, are related essentially to differences in individuals' abilities and interests rather than to sex.

Certain other general issues, however, arise out of experience in all three of architects' main work environments. These are about women's own career objectives and skills in achieving them: about the reconciliation of family and career, including the assumptions made in the profession about appropriate ages for promotion: and about the pressures and machinery for equal opportunity.

Women's motivations and career skills

Many, particularly younger, women informants had a very clear idea of how far they intended to go in their profession and how they intended to get there. Older informants, however, women as well as men, queried whether these younger women would find in the middle stages of their career, particularly when they came up against the problems of family and career, that their motivation would remain the same or that their skill in career planning was as great as they thought. Women as well as men saw women architects as less likely than men to have the drive and motivation to go after posts at the top, and more likely to need encouragement and guidance to reach levels of work corresponding to their own capacities and interests or to the best practicable accommodation between their family and career. From this follows a question about the adequacy of the architectural profession's career guidance and promotion procedures.

For one thing, many informants saw a tendency for women architects to be more reluctant than men to seek promotion into posts where the responsibility is 'administrative', in the sense of managerial, rather than professional. This needed rather careful interpretation. Management responsibility may be an acquired taste, but it is one which women as well as men can and do acquire. 'Reluctance' may mean a dislike of certain types of work when they have actually been experienced, but may also mean initial lack of interest which would disappear with experience, or hesitation about applying for a job which would vanish if the job were actually offered. Public service informants who suggested that women architects may be reluctant to apply for senior posts with management responsibility tended, when asked for an example of a woman who had been offered such a post and refused it, to find that their memory failed. What informants had in mind appeared, when analysed, to amount to three things.

First, women are less likely than men to press for a managerial post unless it is actually offered to them. They may in fact be the best candidates for the job, and likely to be personally satisfied once they are in it: but they are less likely to push strongly for it. As one woman architect in private practice commented, it was only when she reached a position where she could influence policies and get things done that she realised how satisfying this situation could be.

Secondly, many middle or even senior management posts are on the face of them more administrative than creative, by contrast both with professional work and with top management, and women were seen as less likely than men to look for promotion into these, and away from 'creative' work, as a stepping stone to the top: whatever, once again, these same women might feel about such a job, and the further prospects beyond it, if they actually had it. As a woman architect in the GLC said during the previous enquiry: she would not mind exchanging the drawing board for the top job in the department, but not for anything in between.

Thirdly, a number of informants emphasised the sheer energy required to combine raising a family with the responsibilities which go with senior architectural posts, and in managerial posts there may be the additional factor of rigid and sometimes 'unsocial' hours. A Chief Officer's post in local government, as one of the few women who have attained one pointed out, involves not only a full day's work but substantial evening commitments for committee work and public relations, and a general commitment to development and maintaining a wide network of contacts at the social as well as the strictly official level. It may also require a political commitment in the sense, obviously not of party politics, but of the manoeuvrings necessary to obtain attention for a department's needs and its proposals for action.

Informants also pointed to a difference between the attitudes of men and women to maximising their income. They were not implying that money is unimportant to women architects. One of the points made about family and career was, precisely, that to decide to give up a substantial professional salary through dropping out of work is no small matter. One of the features of the campaign for nursery facilities in the GLC was stronger support from among higher paid professionals, who have most to lose in money as well as in career interest, than from clerical and other junior grades. To drive on to maximise income, however, once a satisfactory salary has been obtained, is another matter. Given that the main breadwinner role still tends to fall to the man, many informants saw the pressure of mortgages and other family responsibilities as driving men in architecture as in other fields to maximise their income with a force not equally felt by women. As one woman architect said, 'Men will do anything for money and power'.

In PEP's studies of *Sex Career and Family* and *Women in Top Jobs*[1] in the 1960s respondents often questioned whether women, whatever their job preferences might be, were likely to be as clear-headed and determined as men with similar qualifications in pursuing those jobs which they did prefer. In this respect there was a change by the end of the 1970s, in the case of women architects as of others. The comments quoted above on promotion procedures and women's attitude to them in the GLC are a case in point. There were still, however, many comments to the effect that women tend to be more hesitant than men in going forward for posts where the initiative for being considered lies with the applicant, and that men continue to be more likely than women to make themselves visible by active participation in professional meetings or by taking on professional or union office. Some women do come forward, and on the RIBA Council itself women have for many years been represented more or less in proportion to their numbers in the profession. But at lower levels of professional participation the consensus of informants was that women still fall short on professional visibility.

Women architects who responded to a survey in the Midlands by Phyllis Degens[2] brought out another point: uncertainty over how best to handle the reconciliation of family and career, and the lack of clear models for women to follow. Respondents to the present study returned to this.

The most common view was that it was best to work through without a break, though dropping if necessary to part time. 'There is obviously great demand from women for part-time work', as the Midlands survey concluded, and the present study confirms this. There were also, however, other views. A woman architect in private practice, who has an active record in practical action to enable women to maintain continuity in their professional work while they have young children, nevertheless argued that there should be more chance to leave the profession, perhaps for several years, and then return. Working through with a divided mind and divided responsibilities was not necessarily the best course from the point of view either of professional performance or of personal development. She herself had felt a difficulty here, and saw the same difficulty in the experience of others. Similar arguments appear in the Midlands survey. Some women architects felt that 'having produced a child, their artistic creativity diminished and took many years to reappear'. But there was the counter-argument that neither a mother's responsibility nor the 'divided mind' end when children leave their nursery stage. Some women architects who had worked continuously said that they saw a tendency to loss of creativity and receptivity among colleagues who had in fact dropped out for a long spell as housewives at home.

If the decision is to work through, there is the question whether, from where, and how far understanding and support while caring for young children can be relied on, given the unsystematic and often uncertain nature of the adjustments available within the profession, the varying attitudes of department and practice heads, the uneven availability of support from husbands, extended families and the community, and differences in women's own preferences. Some women architects are prepared to spend most of their net earnings on full-time child care at home. Others will use child-care facilities – family, community, or employer-based – if they can find them, and may (as in the GLC) campaign for them. But the statistics quoted at the beginning of the previous chapter show how many women architects remain reluctant to leave their child's care to anyone else during its first years, whatever arrangements they may make themselves.

There is in any case a prior question about the time for starting a family and the size of family at which to aim. Is it best to have children early, and move back into an accelerating curve of work while still young enough to fit into a junior job without difficulty: or to postpone children till a solid record of architectural performance has been built up? Many informants would argue for the latter policy, but also recognised that it means that the heaviest period of family commitment will come just at the time when the opportunities for progress and promotion are greatest and most likely to be missed. And the Midlands survey, again, brought out the difficulty which its respondents saw in deciding on their number of children: the geometric ratio in which the difficulties of combining family care with a career in architecture increase as the number of children rises from one to three.

Many informants, notably some women who have themselves reached the top in architecture, underlined that it is up to women themselves to decide what goals to pursue, whether in terms of level and type of work, of earnings, or of the reconciliation of family and career, and to learn how to pursue them and act accordingly. So indeed women architects do, to the best of their ability. They are doing it, however, in a context where there are many objective reasons for uncertainty which arise much less strongly for men – particularly other ways of reconciling family and career – and where it is a fact that clear models for finding a way through these uncertainties are lacking. Nor are the models as clear for women as for men when it comes, for example, to choosing between remaining in obviously 'creative' work and accepting, or pressing for, a higher paid and higher status managerial job.

It may well be that the career paths and the balance between career and family responsibilities chosen by women in architecture would differ from those chosen by men even if many of the present practical difficulties and uncertainties over reconciling family and career were cleared away, and there was a better general understanding of the commitments involved in different types of work within the profession, of the opportunities which they offer, and of ways of obtaining them. Only experience could show this. But what does seem clear from the study is that the present situation is one in which better guidance and encouragement could help to clarify women architects' choices and to bring more of them on in the profession, to their own and the profession's advantage.

This points to a gap in the profession's procedures similar to that indicated in Chapter 17 in connection with the greater wastage of women than of men during Part III of architectural training. Employers have of course a first responsibility for career guidance and encouragement for members of their own staffs, but in a profession like architecture, which spreads across several different employment sectors, with literally hundreds of employers and a high degree of mobility between employers and sectors, it would be unreasonable to leave this responsibility to employers alone. It would, for example, be quite unreasonable to expect individual district councils to 'trawl' the whole field of potential candidates for their architectural posts with the thoroughness applied by the Civil Service in its internal promotion procedures: and this is still more true when it comes to appointments in small individual practices. There is a case here for action by the profession as a whole.

The number of women architects in the key age groups for promotion and mobility, from age 30 to 50, was in 1978 around seven hundred. It would not be a very large task for the RIBA to monitor these women's careers, and to make the resulting data the basis for a twofold approach.

One approach would be directed to employers: towards making it the custom and practice of the profession for employers, including private practices, to consult the resulting files when considering middle level and senior appointments. Failure to do so might eventually be taken, in line with the use made of codes of practice in other fields, as *prima facie* evidence of discrimination in the case of proceedings under the Sex Discrimination Act.

The other approach would be directly to individual women architects, to ensure that advice and support are available at key points in their career or on re-entering after a break, and to assist the existing trend for women to press their claims more effectively on their own. In this case there could be a role not only for the RIBA but for groups of women architects themselves, using data collected by the RIBA as a basis for direct contact with their colleagues. We return to this question of the role of women's movements within the profession in a more general context below.

Family and career

In architecture as in the other professions studied, difficulties over reconciling family and career are still a major obstacle to women's progress towards the top. Most of the top salaried jobs held by women go, as has been seen, to those who are either unmarried or under special pressure, because they are divorced or widowed, to put full-time earning first. In private practice it is only those married women architects who work in family practices whose chance of becoming high-earning principals is in any way comparable to that of men. Architecture has in the case of architects' wives working as principals in a family practice a working model of how a temporary reduction in work commitment can be reconciled with continuing contact with the profession at a responsible level, and with opportunities for returning progressively towards full-time work and high earnings. But for other married women architects in all three main sectors the possibilities of making a similar adjustment are much more limited.

In the public sector opportunities for part-time work are, as has been seen, relatively scarce, and in both the public and the private sectors opportunities for part-time salaried work are most often at routine levels and unprogressive. In 1978 three out of ten women architects working full-time were assistants working under supervision, and these were mainly the youngest and least experienced. By contrast, nearly three out of five women working part-time were at this low level, and this ratio held for experienced architects in their forties as well as for their juniors. Working part-time as a principal offers more responsibility, but, except in the case of wives in family practices, is unlikely to lead on to full responsibility in a major practice. Opportunities for part-time work are in any case unsystematic and, particularly in the public sector, cannot be relied on in planning a career.

For a woman who takes a career break longer than the ordinary period of maternity leave there is no guarantee of reinstatement in local government or in private practice, and the rather half-hearted position in the Civil Service was discussed in case study A. And women who either break or slow down their careers are likely in all three sectors to find, if and when they do return to full-time commitment, that they have passed the ages at which promotions leading to the top are customarily made.

In discussing what might be done to change these conditions, many respondents were cautious. They were not anxious to rush into measures which might cause extra costs or administrative problems in practices and offices. That, however, many of their further comments indicated, need not be a barrier to change if the options available are systematically explored.

Respondents recognised that extra administrative effort is needed to organise part-time work, and sometimes there might be other direct costs. As one woman principal said during the 1968 study, in a central London office the space for an extra drawing board carries an appreciable rent. It was also, they pointed out, obviously harder to introduce part time in jobs carrying full professional responsibility, and involving a wide and continuing range of contacts with colleagues and clients, than at more routine levels, and this was an obstacle to making part-time work progressive. But some respondents said that in their experience the direct costs of part-time work were often offset by greater productivity per pound of salary paid. A number argued that, if the effort were made, it would prove possible to go much further than at present in carving out posts with substantial responsibility which could nevertheless be filled part-time, and in putting opportunities for part-time work on a more systematic basis.

Several women respondents quoted as a useful parallel the scheme established by the Department of Health and Social Security for women doctors returning to the National Health Service, with possibilities for training and for progress in levels of work and range of experience, and with separate finance and a specific establishment. This would be directly relevant to the public sector, but could also be extended, perhaps with the help of tax or direct cash inducements, to suitable private practices.

Another possibility has arisen out of discussion in the architectural profession in recent years of the case for organising architectural work more on co-operative and less on hierarchical lines. At the time of the present study this was being considered by the RIBA in the context of a wide-ranging report on the future structure of the profession. The proposition is that architectural work, whether in private practices or in public offices, should be organised less than at present through a pyramid of authority and more through teams in which members have different capacities and responsibilities, but all have the chance to contribute their ideas and practical skills at any level at which they can, and the division of responsibilities is flexible enough to allow each member of the team to develop and advance at his or her own pace.

The argument for moving in this direction has arisen from general considerations about the nature of architectural work. It is a question of balance, for there is evidence that hierarchical and co-operative organisation can both be appropriate, depending on the type of architectural practice.[3] If, however, the balance is in future shifted towards the co-operative side, a number of informants pointed out that this would incidentally provide a more favourable environment for women who wished to reduce their work commitment and then re-expand it as family circumstances required, and also for those who took a career break and then needed to work their way back over a period into full professional responsibility.

There has also been discussion in the profession of an approach which would start from the idea of agency work. A small number of architects, men as well as women, already work through commercial employment agencies. These are commercial organisations concerned with finding spare hands for routine work, and therefore unsatisfactory as a means of enabling women (or men) to continue the progressive development of their careers. Nevertheless, there is in them the germ of an idea. One informant commented on the French practice of organising architectural work around a bureau which provides technical support and handles business details, leaving to architects themselves the concept and design of buildings. A bureau, he points out, could act as a centre for a network of part-time as well as full-time architects, providing support services and a permanent point of contact with clients, and passing on work to each participant architect as her or his circumstances allow.

This idea has in fact been tried for the benefit of women interested in part-time but responsible work, and, though the initial experiment faded in the end, it proceeded far enough to show both what the problems are and how they might be overcome. In the early 1970s a woman architect in private practice, Mrs Santa Raymond, noted the difficulties experienced by many women with families in coping with an architectural practice – often a one-woman practice – and with their family responsibilities at the same time. She saw a case for establishing a central agency around which their work could be focused. The agency would provide office and technical facilities, a library, and a point of contact for clients. It would act as a partnership, passing on work to individuals or project groups. This idea attracted a good deal of publicity. A Company of Women in

Architecture was started, attracted some projects, and led to the launching of at least one successful partnership. It was less successful on the side of its central business organisation, for example over sorting out problems of professional liability and insurance, or effectively organising the flow of work from clients to architects. But its experience indicated that defects in this respect were essentially a matter of planning and staffing, not of any inherent deficiencies in the concept itself.

For architects who are not accepted as partners in a substantial existing practice, to quote one comment based on the experience of the Company, the essential problem is access to clients. A co-operative organisation with its office run under suitable professional management – not necessarily by an architect – channelling projects to a network of architects, but also building its own collective reputation, and so ensuring continuity in the flow of work and of clients' interest, could clearly have very considerable interest for the three out of five women architects in part-time employment who are either sole principals or freelance, and possibly for a number of others who would like to follow their example. It need not, of course, be confined to part-time workers or to women, and – as in the case of co-operative organisation in the profession generally – that could be one of its main attractions.

Informants made other comments on the possibility of extended maternity leave and of reinstatement after a more prolonged career break. There was support for an extended right of return, but with caution as to how long this extension should be. Even the group of GLC women architects who argued strongly for extension did not want the right to return to run beyond one or two years. Too much, they said, changed in three years in an organisation such as the GLC. NALGO, as has been said, supports a right to return up to one year, but hesitates over extending this to five. A number of respondents pointed to the obvious difficulties which an extended right of return could create for small offices.

Our previous study explored the practical problems of reinstatement properly so called, that is of returning to the profession after a prolonged career break. It noted in particular the outcome of a major drive by the Architectural Association in 1964 to attract housewives back into the profession. The Association organised a course with strong stress on re-acquiring professional skills. That, however, turned out not to be a main problem: basic technical skills, even if rusty, are quickly restored by practice. It was more important that women long out of the profession had lost the network of contacts needed both in their professional work and to make themselves known and obtain new jobs, and often also their own confidence. From these points of view, co-operative organisation in offices and the maintenance of contacts through a co-operative group such as the Company of Women in Architecture could clearly have a great deal to offer.

The issue of stereotyped promotion ages is best presented as a question. Career breaks and temporary reductions in work commitment, however well they are organised, necessarily mean that women with family responsibilities are likely to build up the experience and contacts needed for promotion to the most senior posts at a later age than men. Is there in that case objective justification for the idea that candidates for these posts are 'hopelessly too old at forty', so that, for example, to appoint a new partner after that age is to take a real risk?

For architects in general – men or women – the best test is probably the earnings of principals in full-time private practice, which reflect combined performance on both the business and the professional side in a highly competitive market. The RIBA's Earnings Surveys show that in the 1970s principals' highest average earnings were consistently between ages 45 and 55, with a varying pattern thereafter. In 1977 and 1978 (see Table 19.1) there was an irregular plateau from around age 40 to at least age 60, with some downward tilt in the fifties but a new peak after age 60.

Table 19.1 *Median earnings for all full-time private practice principals by age, June 1978*

Age	£ per annum
25–29 years	n.a.
30–34 years	5,333
35–39 years	7,833
40–44 years	9,400
45–49 years	9,568
50–54 years	9,286
55–59 years	9,125
60–64 years	9,750
65 years and over	6,250
All ages	8,941

Source: *RIBA Earnings Survey*, 1978.

There is not much justification in these figures for the idea that a practice which takes on a new partner at, say, 40 rather than age 30 or 35 is taking a significant risk. The impression is that age is likely to be a rather marginal consideration, to be strongly outweighed by differences in individual merit. The figures, in any case, refer to a population overwhelmingly of men, for whom the pressure towards productivity tends to be strongest when there is a growing family to support and a mortgage to pay off. In the case of women with families, it is precisely at the point where family commitments ease off that work commitment recovers.

Finally, however, the main finding of the present study about family and career in the architectural profession is that in none of the profession's three main environments have possible adjustments to existing practice to assist the reconciliation of careers with family responsibilities been systematically examined by the profession and its major employers, with a commitment to action.

It is reasonable to be cautious about adding unnecessarily to the costs and personnel problems of architectural offices. This study does, however, show at least *prima facie* evidence that more could economically be done to ensure to other women architects opportunities of reconciling family and career such as are available to architect wives in family practices. These practices, after all, are themselves economically viable. There are also costs and benefits to consider other than those which most directly affect individual offices. The profession as a whole would gain in quality if women of high ability who at present face obstacles over family and career were promoted according to their abilities. Public expenditure considerations are becoming more important as the proportion of women in the schools of architecture rises. Removal of obstacles to the reconciliation of family and career will in any case improve the return on their training costs which, as elsewhere in higher education, fall mainly on public budgets. They might also reduce training costs themselves if fuller use of women architects' services made it possible to reduce the number of men and women trained. The direct effect of some of the measures needed to reconcile family and career would be to reduce the time spent in employment by some women – or some men, if proposals like NALGO's for paternity leave were adopted – at some time in their lives. But it is possible that the final effect might be to increase the average time spent in employment by women architects over the whole of their lives. That is not certain: but the possibility deserves to be examined.

Neither local government nor the Civil Service, however, has a comprehensive and considered policy in this area, and in the private sector and the profession as a whole discussion has been sporadic and ineffective. The initiative of the Company of Women in Architecture has not been followed up, and co-operative organisation was up to the time of the study a matter for debate rather than action. Systematic monitoring of women architects' career patterns such as was suggested above, and comparison of these patterns with those of men, would provide an essential data base for policy on family and career, but, as the example of the PSA quoted in the previous chapter showed, not even the Civil Service has undertaken this.

One factor which is likely in future to cause greater attention to be given to issues of family and career is the changing composition of the architectural profession. Family and career is still seen in the profession primarily as a 'women's question', and so by implication as one affecting a small and not very influential section of its members. It is still women architects rather than their husbands who are expected to adjust their careers to family responsibilities, though one of the most interesting individual cases to come to light was that of a man who is head of a large local authority architect's department and had himself been a lone parent with a daughter to bring up from the age of four. It is not surprising that the comments of junior staff in his office showed that it is one where understanding of the problems of women's careers in architecture is unusually good.

If social custom changed, and men as well as women were expected to share in the career adjustments required by the care of children, there is every reason to think that the difficulties at present seen by architects' employers in the way of such things as systematic opportunities for part-time work with career progression, or extended leave after a birth, would appear in a different light. Even in a time of severe pressure on public expenditure, as one local authority officer pointed out, career breaks with a guarantee of reinstatement are accepted more easily in cases such as secondment overseas, which may come the way of men as well as women, than similar arrangements in the case of maternity. In a case like that of the co-operative organisation of architectural work it could well be on the basis of men's interests that changes of special value to women will be brought in.

But in any case women in the coming years, though still a minority of the profession, will be an increasing one: the 18 per cent of women among new entrants to the schools in 1979/80 will in due course find their way into architectural practice. There is no doubt about the importance which many women informants attached to developing more comprehensive, coherent, and reliable policies to help them reconcile their genuine commitment to their profession with their family responsibilities. Phyllis Degens' Midlands survey brings out the sense of unfairness among many of her respondents at being forced into unnecessary (as many of them saw it) all-or-nothing choices between family and career, involving the loss either of professional prospects or, sometimes, of the family itself: 'a situation has now arisen in which some women are choosing not to have children'. Just how strong this combination of a sense of urgency with rising numbers will be as a force for changing the organisation of architectural work will of course depend, not least, on how effectively the demands for action on family and career are pressed by women architects themselves; and this leads to a last general issue.

The pressures and machinery for action

In architecture, as in the other occupations studied, pressures for action by employers or employers' organisations, such as those in local government, have been weak. The general climate of opinion in favour of equal opportunity which developed during the 1970s did certainly have some practical effects in architecture. These showed, for example, in the greater readiness of women architects themselves at the end of the 1970s, compared to what was found in our earlier study, to plan definitely for their careers – but with the reservations which have been mentioned – and to challenge discrimination in promotion. Another example is NALGO's moves to monitor equal opportunity in local government or to promote employer-based child-care facilities. The attitude of the RIBA itself changed. In the 1960s it co-operated willingly in PEP's enquiry, but very much as it might have done in the case of any other academic study. At the end of the 1970s a special committee was set up to report to the RIBA Council on the initial working papers of the present project, and the

Council referred these to its relevant standing committees for further consideration and action.

Nevertheless, it is clear that the impact of this change in the general climate of opinion was limited, and the position as regards practical equality of opportunity for women architects was not very different at the end of the 1970s from what it had been in the 1960s. One reason was the state of the market. In the 1960s and early 1970s, when the demand for architects' services was relatively strong, there was a strong incentive to seek out unemployed or under-employed women architects and to bring them into fuller employment. This was the period when the Property Services Agency was 'in the business of employing mums', and the Architectural Association made its drive to bring back architect housewives into employment. By the end of the 1970s the fall in the volume of architectural work and the demand for architects' services put an end to pressure of this kind.

Nor was there effective pressure from any other source, from outside the profession or from inside it.

Nothing in this study suggests that employment practices in architecture were substantially changed through any direct effect of the sex discrimination legislation of the 1970s, nor was anything heard of any direct intervention or impact by the Equal Opportunities Commission. In the public sectors the principles of equal pay and opportunity were already established before the legislation of the 1970s came in, and the Sex Discrimination Act led at most to the tidying up of some procedures, as illustrated by the comment of a local government establishment officer on advertisements which was quoted in the previous chapter. In private practice, as has been seen, there are grounds for questioning how well even the most obvious requirements of the Equal Pay and Sex Discrimination Acts have been observed. What more might be done through intervention by the law and the EOC has been discussed in Part I in the light of findings from the other case studies as well as from architecture.

In the case of local and central government, equal opportunity for women architects is part of the wider problem of equal opportunity for women public servants in general. The low tone and lack of pressure for further action in this area in the Civil Service was examined more fully in case study A. In local government some pressure developed through women activists in unions such as

NALGO, but one question which might well be asked is why there was not more organised pressure from the side of women councillors.

Wherever architects may be employed, however, the RIBA, as the profession's central organisation, has a general responsibility for watching over their conditions and opportunities of employment, and a more direct responsibility, along with the schools of architecture, for initial recruitment. It has not ignored the problems of women within the profession, but did not at the time of this study have any standing machinery for monitoring women's progress or promoting equal opportunity; and such discussions as there had been on these problems had had few visible results.

Extending a suggestion made above, a reasonable target for the RIBA might be to establish a general code of practice on equal opportunity in architecture, to be applied partly by the profession itself – through educational and voluntary action or where necessary through professional sanctions – and partly through being taken into account, on the model of other existing codes, in proceedings before tribunals and courts. In this as in other professions the implementation of equal opportunity is likely to be long drawn out and to require a sustained effort. What would be required, therefore, would be the creation of a strong standing committee on equal opportunity, with the necessary research and administrative support. Its terms of reference would cover the architectural profession as a whole, but would need to place a special emphasis on private practice, where conditions of employment are most directly the responsibility of architects themselves.

Increased administrative and research support would be important, for more effective action by the RIBA in this area would require more staff than has been available up to now, and more co-operation with other agencies inside and outside the profession. The RIBA's small statistical section played a major part in the present enquiry, and has added item by item to the information which it collects about women in the profession. For an adequate and regular programme of monitoring and studies, however, its staff would need to be increased, and co-operation developed with the schools of architecture and individual staff members interested in research in this area, and with the central employers' agencies and large individual departments and authorities in the public sector. It is not suggested that all the statistical or other studies required should be carried out by the RIBA or financed by the profession, but the RIBA's statistical section is the natural focal point round which a comprehensive statistical and study programme could be organised.

One of the surprises of this study was the lack of organised effort by women architects themselves to promote more effective implementation of equal opportunity. Many women were taking action as individuals: some as activists within the profession's official machinery, some in pressing their own claims, some, after reaching senior levels in the profession, by giving a personal helping hand to other women architects who were still making their way. But women informants were in general reluctant to consider more organised and systematic action by groups of women within the profession.

This was not necessarily out of fear that militancy would be ill regarded or would have repercussions on individual participants or on women generally. Architecture has a tradition of dissenting and militant groups. Lord Holford, for example, one of the most distinguished figures in the profession in his generation, mentioned with pride in an interview for our 1968/9 study how he had begun his career by leading a students' strike at his architectural school. Many of the women interviewed in the present study would certainly not have hesitated to join a women's pressure group if they had seen a point in doing so. They did not, however, and for this there were several reasons.

For a number both of older women who had reached high levels in the profession and of younger women who were starting their careers with a strong professional commitment and clear ideas on how they intended to go about it – but were not yet themselves fully involved in the problems of family and career – the point was that women's progress in architecture could and must depend principally on the effects and performance of individual women themselves. Many informants were not in any case particularly impressed by the achievements of such women's groups as had existed or, in the case of the New Architecture Movement, were active at the time of the study. The NAM was widely criticised by informants as too much concerned with general and abstract issues: too much, as one woman architect said, about 'the spatial dimension of our repression'.

That might be taken simply as a criticism of that particular movement, but can also be linked with what has just been said about the lack of a central agency in the profession to promote equal opportunity and of back-up machinery for it. A particular women's group can be criticised for failing by its own choice to be sufficiently specific and down to earth. But it would also be much more likely for it to be specific and down to earth if it were responding to, pressuring, and stimulating an official agency in the profession which was itself attacking the problems of equal opportunity in a considered and practical way.

Another important reason for lack of support for women's pressure groups, however, was something which can be deduced from the general tone of interviews. Women architects shared with men a tendency to under-estimate, or more accurately to be unaware of, the time and effort likely still to be needed in this profession to equalise opportunities. With this there naturally went a tendency to under-estimate the contribution which women's groups and movements might make to this effort.

In the light of the findings of this study, areas where their contribution could be effective – particularly if the number of women in the profession increased – could include the well-researched presentation within the profession of problems such as family and career, or of discrimination in the appointment of private practice principals, and of considered solutions to them: practical experiments such as the Company of Women in Architecture: advice and support for women architects themselves: and propaganda and pressure in the profession generally and at the level of individual practices and offices.

At local and individual office level there could be a particularly important part for women's groups in the case of private practice. In central and local government it is natural to think especially of action through central machinery, whose effects will then be transmitted downwards. In the case of private practice there is no central controlling machinery. Central action, through the RIBA, can still be useful: for example the suggestion above of a central file on women architects' careers and a code of practice requiring private as well as public offices to consult it when making senior appointments, or a campaign to promote better understanding among heads of practices of the dangers of stereotyped promotion ages. But private practice is an area where there is a special part to be played by local action through groups familiar with the cases and personalities involved and able to reach individual heads of practices, and individual women, directly. This is one of the areas where regional and local groups of women architects could make their greatest impact.

Conclusion

Architecture has, for better or for worse, its own special features as a field of employment for women, especially in private practice. But, when it comes to the point of choosing areas for action, the points which emerge are essentially the same as in the other case studies:—

1. Further widening of the range of recruitment to schools of architecture, for which suggestions were made in Chapter 17.
2. Better career guidance and support for women architects, by employers and the profession, from Part III onwards, based on systematic monitoring of their careers.
3. Systematic exploration by employers, unions, and the profession of ways of reconciling family responsibilities with progress in architectural careers.
4. Stronger and more systematic pressure on employers and practices: from outside the profession – as discussed in general terms in Part I of this book – and through the unions, new standing machinery in the RIBA, and an increase in organised action by women architects themselves.

References
(1) M. P. Fogarty and R. and R. Rapoport, *Sex Career and Family*, George Allen and Unwin, 1971; M. P. Fogarty (ed.), Isobel Allen, A. J. Allen and Patricia Walters, *Women in Top Jobs – Four Studies in Achievement*, George Allen and Unwin, 1971.
(2) Phyllis Degens, *Architecture as a Career for Women*, mimeo, Birmingham School of Architecture, 1978.
(3) RIBA, *The Architect and his Office*, 1962.

Index